Nowt!
A Ministry of Nothing?

All good wishes,

Nowt!
A Ministry of Nothing?

– Trevor Vaughan –

Dedication

For my wife Ann who, with our children,
has always been my source of inspiration and encouragement.

Contents

Acknowledgements

Dr Roger Kendall for reading the proofs; Barnoldswick Historical Society, Mr Bryan Hughes for information on the Laycock organ; Mrs Daphne Ripley.

Also the following who have helped with photographs and illustrations: the Churchwardens of St Michael, Markington, Mrs Gillian Garforth, Mr Brian Hick, Mrs Carol Pye, Mr John Symonds, Mr Matthew Symonds, Mrs Pat Warner, Mrs Judith Weatherall, Mrs Sylvia Whittington and my son Philip Vaughan who created the book's cover.

CHAPTER ONE

A ministry of 'nowt'

I am not sure who the Reverend J H Briggs is. Or was. What *is* known is a certain tale about him. When he was a young boy his relatives and other well-meaning adults would ask him:

"And what do you want to be when you grow up?"

Fifty or sixty years ago that was a legitimate question. Providing you did not reply with some outrageously far-fetched ambition, there was more than an evens chance that you could fulfil the dream. Remember the photograph of the boy Harold Wilson, with his dad, outside Number Ten Downing Street? There were clearly defined channels for the accomplishment of your ambition: 'O' and 'A' levels, College or University for the professions. Secondary schools and technical colleges supplied a sound route for the more practical types of work, courses locked into excellent apprenticeship schemes. In those days there existed a security not available today. A job for life would be the norm. So, with study and diligence, there was little to prevent you from becoming a teacher or technician, engineer or electrician. I wanted to be a circus clown when I grew up. More of that anon.

By contrast the employment situation at the beginning of the 21st century is precarious. Even the most highly-qualified are liable to lose their jobs. The speed by which new techniques, new developments, inventions and learning mean that almost no one is immune from possible redundancy and the need to re-train. Not so in my adolescence.

Nor in that of young Briggs. "What are you going to be when you grow up?" he was regularly quizzed. And (so he says) he always replied "Nowt!" In other words, nothing. By his riposte I suppose he meant either 'nothing worth mentioning', 'nothing to write home about' or, as is more likely from the lad's viewpoint, 'I'm not going to do any work at all'. Nowt! Why work? many a boy would ask, since being idle is a far more attractive idea.

When, however, the young Mr Briggs grew up and became an ordained minister in the Church, his father, remembering his son's customary riposte, remarked "Well, lad, tha's got thi' wish!" by which Briggs senior either inferred that his son's chosen work of Christian ministry was useless rubbish or that its whole message was not worth the parchment it was written on. St Paul, conversely, writes about *everything else* being rubbish and garbage compared to the Gospel message. Elsewhere in the New Testament he describes the wisdom of God as being utter foolishness to the so-called wise of this world. "Nowt" succinctly sums up the world's view of our calling.

'Nowt', sadly, reflected the attitude of my family. I had not considered this matter too seriously before writing this account in my retirement. Any thoughts on the subject, any hurt felt, were very casual and cursory. Nevertheless, it's true. Not one single member of my relations, other than my wife Ann and our children, of course, has ever voluntary attended an act of worship at which I 'performed' or led. Naturally, I have preached at family funerals, officiated at the marriages of both a brother and a cousin. But in all these situations they were there because they *had to be*. As my father said of me on a few occasions "Since we've got one in the family you might as well say grace." Speaking of such, not once has anyone shown some grace – and initiative – to come and "hear the lad preach." I have always tried to encourage my relations in their workday ventures. I have patronised them and their businesses when and where it was possible. They have no excuse. The Church is no secret society. It is very much public. Anyone can go. Everyone is welcome. My relations' total absence leads me to the inevitable conclusion that for almost forty years I have exercised a ministry of 'nowt'. In their eyes, a worthless waste of work.

By this late realisation I am more amazed than angry. This book is certainly not intended to be a tirade against kith and kin. But if the wider family is meant to be supportive and encouraging of its members, which I believe is most definitely its role, then I have sailed the ship of Christian ministry without their favourable winds. The family crew jumped ship and left me, like Noah and his brood, to navigate the unpredictable flood waters. I would hasten to add that on this voyage I came across other mighty trade winds of Christian folk who blew and chased us with such supportive strength. The softer breezes, too, of gentle Christians who offered comfort, calm and a welcoming haven, steering us safely through the stormy seas.

But blood is thicker than water and as I look back on my work of forty years I am haunted by their discouragement. A ministry of nothing? Of zilch and zero? Nihil and nowt? Was the Wisdom I embraced simply folly? Have I strutted and fretted my hour, like Shakespeare's poor player, and told a tale signifying nothing?

To this question an equally serious element has appeared. Almost without warning, certainly unanticipated. As I was writing the final pages of this story, the General Synod of the Church of England met in York. The focus of the gathering was the debate on the ordination of women to the episcopacy. Not many Traditionalists, of which I am one, doubted that this would proceed as planned. Indeed, we have said that the Church cannot have women priests and *not* women bishops. The real question, for the likes of me, was the absolute necessity of retaining the safeguards which protected our stance and afforded us the 'comfort' that there would always be a 'line' of male-only bishops, priests and deacons. The Church of England had actually promised us categorically, definitely, uncompromisingly, that there would always be that. World without end.

Before the York debate swung into action, however, there was the small item of 'loyalty'. The Bishop of Winchester, rather naively I suppose, proposed that the seemingly innocuous 'loyalty question' could be ratified. At the 1998 Lambeth Conference the assembled Bishops had agreed that both sides of the argument on women priests and bishops were 'loyal Anglicans'.

The General Synod thus opened the batting with a consideration of this harmless motion. A vote was taken. A massive agreement to its ratification would probably pave the way for a well-mannered and charitable debate on the bigger issues. However, to the utter disappointment of some and the sheer delight of others the Synod voted by huge majorities that we Traditionalists were no longer 'loyal Anglicans'. Take the House of Bishops, for example. Out of the 45 Fathers-in-God eligible to vote 31 decided that those who in all conscience could not recognise women's orders were now personae non gratae. (It's worth pointing out that three quarters of Christendom, or over 1.75 billion Roman Catholic and Orthodox Christians don't recognise them too).

So, there it is: I am not a loyal Anglican.

Now, the opposite of 'loyal' is '*dis*loyal'. There is no such word as '*un*loyal'. Neither does '*non*-loyal' nor '*mis*-loyal' exist. *Disloyal* sounds harsh, does it not? But if one is not loyal, then it is semantically very clear that the person is disloyal.

Loyal has its roots in a C14th French word, itself deriving from the Latin 'legalis', to do with the law. [In Middle English it was definitely to do with the Mosaic Law.] To be loyal, therefore, is to be bound, or fixed, rather like the law. And a person thus loyal describes someone who shows firm and constant allegiance, whether to another person or institution.

The upshot of this is quite simple: two-thirds of the bishops of the C of E have declared that I, with a sizeable minority within that Church, are disloyal Anglicans. We plainly do not show firm and constant allegiance to Anglicanism, that is, to the tenets of its belief and doctrine.

It is no good arguing that one can be loyal and disloyal at the same time. Unlike the curate's egg, one cannot be loyal in parts. The world of 007 with his double-agents and counter-espionage does not apply here. You are either a virgin or not. Similarly, loyal or disloyal.

But here is the rub. As I trust these pages will testify, I have served as a faithful Anglican priest.

I believe – and have always believed – in God who as a loving Father created and sustains his world. I believe – and have always believed – in Jesus Christ, the Son of God the Father, whose love for the world prompted him to enter human history and become man. Fully God, fully man. And I believe – and have always believed – in God the Holy Spirit, who inspires and guides us, as he did the prophets and saints before us. I believe – and have always believed – in the Virgin Birth and in the bodily resurrection of Jesus Christ. All these things have I taught with confidence throughout my years of ministry. Amongst the pain and pleasure, the frustration, fear and fun of that ministry I have faithfully administered the Holy Sacraments of Baptism and the Eucharist. I have absolved, blessed and consecrated, in the understanding that my orders were valid and true within the canvas of the One, Holy, Catholic and Apostolic Church.

Yet because in all conscience I do not believe that women can become priests or bishops – *and for this reason only* –I am labelled 'disloyal'. The French word for 'disloyal' is 'infidèle'. Infidel. Which lumps me firmly with the "Jews, Turks and Hereticks" of the old Good Friday Collect. Enough said.

By contrast, a survey conducted by Christian Research, a leading organisation in this field, in 2002, revealed some astonishing facts. Amongst the Church of England clergy (both male and female) just over half believed in the Virgin Birth; only three quarters that Jesus died to take away the sins of the world and two-thirds fully accepted that Jesus physically rose from the dead. The conclusion is shatteringly obvious. The clergy can believe or not believe in a whole permutation of things which were once requisite for belief – and certainly for the ordained ministry – but *not* to accept or believe in women's ordination is taboo.

Since this General Synod decision I have taken my 'disloyalty' to heart. It is now difficult to go to church and impossible to celebrate the Eucharist there. For if I have carried out that task with a misguided and flawed authority, since I am deemed disloyal by the very Church in whose name I have performed the ministry, then I am left with the devastating deduction that I have performed a 'ministry of nothing'.

To rub salt in our wounds, the Synod also threw out the 'safeguards' promises of previous years. A brilliant and decisive attack from the liberals which has left us reeling. More than reeling: there is a feeling among many that our time is up and we must go. Though where to go is not easily resolved.

Has it, then, all been 'Nowt!' and for nothing, as both my relations and my ecclesiastical family would infer? My story charts the progress of God's call, rooted in the context of my home and family and town. Solid down-to-earth stuff. 'Incarnational', as we in the trade would call it. But has it all been a massive delusion? There are several and different conversions on the way as I meet the challenge of College and parish life. Life in our vicarages and rectories was never dull and being a priest among my parishioners produced a plethora of plights, predicaments, pantomime and pleasure. Priesthood and parish, parsonage and pastoralia: all a ministry of nothing?

* * * * *

A former elderly churchwarden had his own response to my vestry prayer. Just as I was about to leave the sacristy to celebrate the Eucharist, he would hiss: "Come on, Vaughan, let's get on with it!" Amen to that.

CHAPTER TWO

Early Signs

Beginnings

Barnoldswick was, and still is, a unique sort of town. In so many ways. During my infancy, childhood and adolescence it had well over ten thousand inhabitants. People are always surprised to learn that this is not far behind Skipton's population, which was always 'understood' to be a much more important place. The town's population at the very beginning of the C19th was 769. Exactly a century later it had increased almost eight fold. My grandfather Vaughan was Chairman of the Barnoldswick Urban District Council and its Year Book for 1926-7, under his leadership, shows that the population continued to multiply and reach 13,000. 'Barlick' as we locals called Barnoldswick, was on no main road. You wouldn't go through it to get to somewhere else. A variation on the Irish joke: "if you're going to Dublin I wouldn't start from here!" All the major roads by-passed it. The Preston to York A59 intersected West and East Marton and Gisburn. From Blackburn and Burnley to Bradford and Leeds traffic crept through Colne and crawled up Earby's Whisick Hill. The West Riding's route of exodus in the first part of last century to Morecambe (known as Bradford-on-Sea) and the Lake District, dissected Long Preston and Hellifield so keenly that villagers took their life in their hands in attempting to cross the road to the village shop. But Barlick carried on unaffected by the volume of frenzied vehicles. Even the Luftwaffe could not find its Rover aero-engine plant during the War!

Not that the town was some sleepy backwater. Far from it. Whilst King Cotton was fast diminishing in the early 1950s, Rolls Royce had bought out the Rover site and its aero-engine factory had expanded to three separate sites. Silentnight's bedding factory, the largest of its kind in Europe, loomed ever large. Rolls Royce in particular spawned several light engineering firms, supplying their lord and master with small but vital parts for the jet engines. By the mid 1950s the town was thriving once again after the War. It had always possessed a welter of private shops. Apart from the Co-op, there were no big departmental stores: no Boots, Debenhams or Woolworths. There never has been. Instead, more than the average collection of individually-owned businesses. Good grocers and greengrocers, at least two splendid ironmongers, two toyshops laden with excitement, a furniture store, a long-established chemist, Elmers, which successfully precluded the likes of Boots from setting up shop here. There was a plethora of butchers and bakers, including our own family firm, established by my father's parents in 1904, many with their own speciality. The town might have been off the beaten track but it was not for nothing that it was nicknamed "Little America". There was plenty of money around.

Geography was part of its uniqueness, too. It was a Yorkshire town with a Lancashire industry. Pendle Hill, a few miles away to the west, rises 1800 ft and is responsible for bringing down over 40 inches of rain per year, thus producing the damp climate which aids and abets the weaving of cotton rather than that of wool. Consequently its mill owners travelled to Manchester, not Bradford, for their trade. Local and national government, education and health compelled Barnoldswick to turn its head eastwards to Craven and Yorkshire but Lancashire was the magnetic west for the town's historic commerce – and much of its sporting interests. This 'business' with things on both sides of the border, strangely polarised the indigenous population into Yorkshire Tykes or Lancashire Lankies. The resentment felt by the former on County boundary reorganisation in 1974 was very real. It encapsulated the very deep and hidden tensions caused by this dichotomy. It left a bitter taste. In addition, this cocktail of county affiliations gave Barnoldswick folk a unique accent and dialect: the flat West Riding vowels and the accentuated rhotic 'r's of East Lancashire were both conspicuous by their absence. So Barlickers even had their very own speech!

Up to the early 1960s there were at least thirteen churches in Barnoldswick and true to northern religious tradition, each turned out in resplendent force for their Whitsunday Procession of Witness, the "Whit Walks". They still continue these to this day, I'm glad to report, though in a tamer, more ecumenical sort of way. For decades, I would imagine, the Whit Walks were huge affairs. They certainly are in my memory. As a measure of their importance we boys always had new suits and my cousins new dresses for the Whitsunday Procession. At one time all the various churches processed around parts of the town on the same day – Whit Sunday, the Feast of the coming of the Holy Spirit. It was this biblical event two thousand years ago which kick-started the Church, brought it into being. So the day, Whit Sunday, or Pentecost, was regarded as the Church's birthday. There was tremendous rivalry amongst the organisers of each denomination – a rivalry bordering on the unchristian. Gradually – I don't know exactly when – a pattern evolved which programmed the Non-conformists to process on one Sunday and the Established Church on the following Sunday. I can't remember which lot were allocated the Festival itself. Perhaps they took it in turns. I think the Roman Catholics avoided the dilemma by walking in the morning.

Religion was taken very seriously in our town. And no less seriously in our family. Whether for it or against it, religion was still a solemn matter. For the first seven years of my life we followed the Bradley tradition. My paternal grandmother's family were staunch members of the Bethesda Baptist Church, which was situated almost directly across from its rival North Street Baptist chapel, at the bottom of Manchester Road. Then something happened. Something serious. Aunty Mary, my father's sister, had joined the Girl Guides and become one of the Company's leaders. The town's Guides were attached to the local Church of England. Every fourth Sunday was Parade Sunday and the troop marched from HQ (the Church School) down to St James'. Aunty Mary began to get accustomed to the Anglican way of worship. More than that: she *enjoyed* it and wanted to go there regularly instead of attending the chapel service. Grandma Vaughan, especially, was rather concerned at this dissenting from the Dissenters and tried to forbid her. Aunty Mary refused and said that when she got married – which was imminent – she would become a member of St James'. She kept her word and was confirmed in Skipton Parish Church. When her daughter, my cousin Barbara, was born she too was taken to church. These moves were not popular with the Bradleys but she held firm. Apparently, Edward and I wanted to go to the church. We went to the Church School and our friends attended both establishments. There followed some great family discussions, the result of which was that the Vaughans – though not the Bradleys – suddenly left the Church of their forefathers and joined the Church of England. I reckon this episode took place in mid-1949 because I have a small Prayer Book-cum-hymnal which my godparents, Aunty Mary and Uncle Frank, bought me "on the occasion of [my] christening, October 4th 1949." This little book was evidence, perhaps, of some kind of religious knee-jerk reaction, coming hard upon the unpleasant split with their Baptist friends. For it wasn't until November 4th the *following year* that a trinity of boys, Edward, our new brother Stephen and I were baptised in the name of the Holy Trinity at St Mary-le-Ghyll, the official parish church, a mile out of town. Whilst Aunty Mary went the whole way and got confirmed. Dad didn't quite make that commitment but proceeded to take Edward and me every Sunday evening to Evensong at St James', the chapel-of-ease in Church Street. It was a short step from that to our becoming members of the St James' choir. And what fun did we have!

Because we were Baptists none of us had undergone Infant baptism. The Baptist Church practises 'believer's baptism', whereby the person desiring to be a full member of that church has to be of a discerning age and declares his or her own allegiance to Christ. Godparents are redundant here! The baptism is by total immersion and certainly the Bethesda chapel had its own pool, revealed by easily removing the floor of the chapel. Since we were now attending church rather than chapel, it was felt that we boys ought to be baptised there and then, following the custom of the Established Church (and all the other churches as well!).

I was nine years old at my Baptism and can remember it. Technically I ought not to have been 'done', as they called it, at that age; but rather wait a couple of years until my Confirmation. The Vicar, however, was a canny man and he saw an opportunity and decided to cash in on the 'transfer' of a branch of a most staunch Non-conformist family. And so we were baptised, Stephen in the Vicar's arms, Edward and I standing, head bowed, at the edge of the font. Canon Colin Campbell MacKay was the Vicar, whom Dad and Grandad Vaughan knew as a fellow-Free Mason. He was a good priest, a typical Low Church Scot, very pastorally orientated and a fine preacher, whose sermons always included a fair dose of poetry. Some fifteen years later, as I embarked on my theological training, Ann and I were invited to his Vicarage in West Marton, where we shared an evening meal with him and Mrs MacKay. He gave me a number of theology books. Later still – 41 years after my Baptism – I was a successor to him as incumbent of that same parish.

My Primary School cap bore a badge with a very simple device: the letters C E C in gold on a dark blue background. They stood for "Church of England Controlled," which meant that our school was partly governed by representatives of the local C of E church. Contrary to what seems obvious, a 'controlled' church school had less control than an 'Aided' church school. Canon MacKay's involvement with the school children (he would spend much more time and energy in the work of the Governors) was a weekly foray into the top class of the Juniors, J4. Non-Conformist children were 'withdrawn' and did other things. Meanwhile this special Religious Instruction lesson comprised of reading out aloud, in turn, large portions of scripture. Perhaps we explored other religious topics but I can only recall reading these lengths of bible passages. What is vivid in my mind is the moment when I decided what I wanted to be when I grew up. I distinctly remember saying to myself 'I want to be a vicar'. I was nine years old. And I believe that I can still recall that moment so clearly because it was the first genuine stirring of GOD. The first sign, if you like, in my journey to the priesthood.

I became more involved in Church life as time went on. As a member of the Church and a pupil at the Church School, a ready-made social group existed. Most of my friends went to the Church Sunday School, held in the afternoon at the school. It was home from home or rather school from school. Familiar surroundings, familiar scholars and familiar adults whom we respected and who did their best with us. *Our* class – all boys, since we were (wisely) segregated – met on the stairs of my first-year week-day classroom. Mr Blackie was our teacher and Sunday School was fun. Seated two by two on the stairs was not particularly conducive to assimilating religious facts, though Mr Blackie was valiant in his efforts with us boys. We *always* did receive some religious teaching but invariably the topic got round to Burnley's match the previous day, what were the chances of winning next week, and so on. So much good teaching is to do with the person doing the teaching. Mr Blackie was a *good* man: we knew it and therefore honoured both him and the GOD about whom he spoke.

The Church of England Controlled School was situated between York Street and Wellington Street. It was constructed, I imagine, in the 1840s out of that local millstone grit, grim and grey. The land on which it was built had a steep downward west-east slope. The entrance for us junior children was on the lower part. Large iron gates opened up onto an asphalted playground. In my early school days this was cobbled. The addition of tarmac made a wonderful winter ski run, when we would run and slide on the ice. And it did facilitate the playing of football and cricket for us boys, though the 'pitch' was still bedevilled by another slope, this time north to south. By the chalked goal-posts were the boys' outside toilets. The girls throughout the school occupied the Infants' playground on the Wellington Street side. It was felt that the infants were too much at risk being amongst the boys – and, besides, junior girls could practise their mothercraft on them. At the other end of the boys' yard hung a large, heavy wooden door which led to the cloakroom and wash basins and J2 classroom, occupied by Mr Bracewell. [It was the siting of this classroom which gave me the idea, years later, for an Ascension Day sermon: 'going up' wasn't necessarily literal. We went *up* from J1 to J2 by going *down* the stairs.] The rest of the junior pupils had to climb twenty treacherous stone steps of varying heights to reach the school hall. No one will forget Rita Ayrton falling all the way down and breaking her arm very badly. The hall, from the top of these stairs, was a space large enough to create the top two forms, J4, then J3, the lairs of Mr Barker and Mr Marsden respectively. These form rooms had been created by means of exceedingly tall sliding partitions, with much glass. In the other direction from the top of the stairs you entered the Infant department to the right. Mr Edmondson, the Headmaster, had his office, together with an inadequate Staff Room, to the left. It was to this room on February 6th 1952 that I had been sent by Mr Barker on some insignificant errand. I returned to my class and to Mr Barker with the heaviest of news. "And Trevor," said the headmaster, "please inform Mr Barker that the King has died." Beyond the head's room lay a flight of stairs to J1, the classroom of Miss Hey, a young teacher with whom I was deeply in love throughout my Junior School days.

As we did at day-school, so each September we moved up a class at Sunday School. I and my friends spent our last couple of years under the leadership of two incredible characters, Harold Jones and Tommy Clarkson. Harold and Tommy were both postmen, lived together, holidayed together and taught together the boys of the 'top class' at the Church Sunday School. They were tireless workers. They planned their Sunday lessons – with lots of religious quizzes – organised outings and were responsible for the pantomimes and musical shows which the Sunday School produced. I recall being in two productions: a minor role in *Hansel and Gretel* and the White Bird in some show, whose title escapes me. My mother made the extravagant bird costume, covered in hundreds of white feather-shaped pieces of crepe paper, each one individually sewn into place! I was something of a favourite with Harold: he had known my mother since she was a girl. They were near neighbours and worked together at the same mill.

Sunday Schools in the 1950s were generally booming. Ours had well over a hundred children every Sunday: perhaps two hundred. Every summer the teachers would organise the Sunday School trip to the seaside. Usually Blackpool or Southport. The numbers making the trip were so great that we chartered a special train. It's hard to imagine now but we were so many that we could confidently hire our very own train to take us to the coast. The town had its own railway station – a simple branch line that went down to Earby, where it joined bigger tracks to Skipton or Blackburn. We had some brilliant times, especially in our early teens, when we were given a bit of freedom to do our own thing in the resort – provided we reported back at the departing railways station in good time!

The Choir

Meanwhile, Tuesday nights were Choir Practice nights at St James'. The church was erected in the middle part of the 19th century to serve the town's large population. The parish church, however, was St Mary-le-Ghyll, situated a mile out of town at the end of a remote lane on the road to Skipton. Because of St Mary's inaccessibility a building in and amongst the townsfolk was needed: hence St James. It was a chapel-of ease, in which the round of regular divine service could take place. It was not, however, licensed for Weddings and those couples requiring a Marriage Service according to the rites of the Church of England had to make their way to Ghyll. Similarly, St James' had no traditional churchyard. Whilst funeral services could take place there, the subsequent burials involved yet another excursion to the parish church. All these aspects of four-wheeler religion (wedding cars, funeral hearse and limousines) were, of course, good news for the local taxi firm, Fred Windle and Sons, whose gleaming black Humber Pullmans and Super Snipes were responsible for starting many Christian souls on their heavenward journey. And brides and bridegrooms on their *heavenly* journey!

The church building of St James' was very ordinary. In the early part of the C19th there *was* a Sunday School, a mile out of town, down a very muddy lane, at Ghyll. The present vicar, Mr Milner, knew that a venue in the centre of the town was vital for the teaching of the Church children. A gentleman from Rochdale, Mr Royd, generously gave some money for the building of a School-cum-Sunday School in the town centre. This was finally completed in 1838 and built, presciently, in the style of a church. Within four years it had become a church; the chapel-of-ease of St James, in what was subsequently to be called Church Street. The building was consecrated by the Lord Bishop of Ripon (Bradford Diocese not existing at that stage) in 1842. Its long rectangular nave had no central aisle but two side aisles. It faced eastwards with its altar close up to the wall (no westward-facing positions for the priest in those days) set within a very tight sanctuary. Above the altar was a stained-glass east window. Down either side were windows of opaque green glass. On the south side, squeezed in, almost apologetically, between altar rail and choir stalls, was the organ. Below this stood the lectern, the word of GOD proclaimed. On the opposite side, parallel to the lectern stood the pulpit, the word of GOD explained. Fixed to the west, north and south walls was a gallery, running the entire length of the walls. It probably doubled the accommodation afforded by the pews in the nave below. At the centre of the west wall was a door which led into a small clergy vestry – if weddings could have taken place in the church the vestry could not have accommodated more than bride, groom, best man and vicar. On the Church Street side of this vestry another entrance had been created, on to which a wooden extension had been added. This housed the cassocks, surplices, hymn-books and anthems of the choir. An incongruous but purpose-built choir vestry. Each member had his own hook for his robes and a space for his books.

Eight o'clock Holy Communion, Mattins two hours later and Evensong at 6.30pm made up the pattern of Sunday worship. When my brother Edward and I first joined the choir it was male-only. There were eight or so boys around my age, a handful of older boys (or younger men) and half a dozen older men, who had been stalwarts of the choir for years. Our organist was Mr Arnold Crabtree, who was a devoted servant both to the Church and to music. We lads gave him hell. On Tuesday nights we literally ran riot – all over the church. Mr Crabtree was silly enough to give us chase, which made things only worse. I recall once hiding down my jacket sleeve a wooden hooter, which I would blow to disrupt the practice. The men joined us after half an hour and order was miraculously restored. On our way home after choir practice a number of us called in at my uncle Bob's chip shop in Park Road. He had opened a café at the back of the shop – what would normally have been the dining room when the house was still a terraced dwelling. Six or seven of us would sit down to fish, chips and mushy peas. Every week without fail. Singing was hungry work.

It was on the way home, after one such post-practice feast that my friend Alan announced that he would not get married. I bet him five shillings he'd be married before he was twenty-five. Well over a decade later I was at his wedding – five days *after* his twenty-fifth birthday. In his speech at the reception he informed his audience of our choirboys' wager all those years ago. Undoubtedly he hoped to put me on the spot. But I, too, had remembered the bet and produced, there and then, his five shillings – one hundred and twenty ha'pennies in a blue Martins

Bank coin bag! Apparently he took the heavy load on his honeymoon and still has it to this day!

Among the choir were a number of boys, of whom I was one, who had reached the age when they could embark on training for Confirmation. Fourteen or fifteen was then deemed the 'right' age for full membership of the Church of England. Is there such a thing as a 'right' age? Do we know it all then? No. We *never* know it all: we are always learning about the faith, right up to our death. The Church has, however, to make some arbitrary decision about when to confirm. So, in late spring of 1955 Canon MacKay came round to see my parents and suggested I attend classes. I went to the first but lapsed immediately after. I have no idea why. But Thursdays came and went and I never attended another Confirmation Class. I have mentioned before that our Vicar was a canny creature. About a week before the Confirmation date he again visited my parents about the said subject. He was obviously not going to let me slip through his hands. Mum and Dad agreed that I ought to be confirmed. Consequently I spent half an hour in the kitchen whilst the Vicar gave me an intense crash-course on Christianity. I duly turned up at St James' on Sunday afternoon, October 9th to receive the laying on of (very elderly) hands by Bishop Brown, a retired cleric who assisted the Bishop of Bradford in this way. My godparents were always most thoughtful at marking important dates like this and I received from them a very thin, beautifully leather-bound King James' version of the Bible, protected by a very sturdy zip which ran along its three edges. The present came in a box and I opened it in the presence of both my father and grandmother. "You must look after it," she advised, "keep it in good condition by putting it back in its box when you finished reading it." My father, typically – but correctly – counter-advised: "Throw the box away. The book's got to be used regularly – like the Highway Code, it's no good being wrapped up. You need to get it worn and dirty with use."

I still possess my Confirmation Bible. It sits on my study shelf with my two other Bibles I received as gifts: a New Testament upon my Ordination to the diaconate and the whole Bible on my Priesting, both signed by Cuthbert, Bishop of Coventry. What my fellow-confirmands thought about my Confirmation 'through the back door', I do not know. A situation similar to the Gospel story of the labourers who received the same pay for one hour's work in the vineyard as those who had toiled in the heat all day. I reckon the Vicar knew what he was doing – and the Lord certainly did.

The choir eventually opened its doors to girls: I don't know why, because the choir was far from diminishing in numbers. Perhaps it was simply to introduce a sobering element into the situation. There were some six or seven sopranos (as opposed to us trebles) and undoubtedly these gave the choir not only a more stable base but a potential to increase its repertoire. The introduction of females, however, meant the end of the wild and crazy Tuesdays. Also the fish and chips. Ann and I were already going out together and uncle Bob's took second place to ten minutes outside the Palace cinema. It was incredible how many of the boys of the choir starting going out with the girls of the choir!

Despite the earlier shenanigans and the later courting opportunities, we learnt a lot from St James' Choir, our organist Mr Crabtree and the older choirmen. We boys became used to reading the lessons from the lectern and extinguishing the altar candles during Evensong – which, sadly, was the nearest we got to being altar-servers. With the other choirboys I was taught how to sing Anglican chant to the psalms; I came to know most of the tunes of the settings to the Canticles; and the order and music of Evensong is indelibly scored in my heart and mind and voice. They have lasted a lifetime. For these experiences, too, were part and parcel of my progression to the priesthood

Quite unconsciously, Church life began to play an ever increasing part of my life. There was the choir, though of this my membership dwindled and finally ceased as my voice broke. Trying to read the top line of the bottom line – the tenor's part – proved somewhat difficult. I was, however, still engaged in Sunday School. There was an unwritten rule that 'graduates' from Sunday School became assistants, who became fully-fledged teachers in due course. This certainly happened to me and every Sunday afternoon, after our dinner (as *we* called the midday meal), I raced off down Wellington Street to spread the Gospel to my small charges. I still attended Evensong, where I would meet up with Ann. I was present when Ann was confirmed at Christ Church, Skipton, the following year. I was surprised, but not displeased, to see my History Master, Mr Hardacre, there in some official capacity. He was the churchwarden. With both of us now confirmed, the early morning Holy Communion offered us yet another (valid and worthy) opportunity to meet each other. To go to church meant a mile walk for Ann and a three hundred yard sprint for me. On too many occasions, however, I would awake to the sound of small stones hitting my bedroom window. I had overslept. Yet again. Ann, having been to the service, called to see if I were still alive. In my defence I can only point to the example of St Augustine, who, but for the prayers of a good woman, would also not have lasted the course. But it's no excuse, really.

All Things New

There were no significant moments during my Skipton Grammar School education which particularly, consciously, pushed me in the direction of ministry in the Church. Not that I identified with those boys for whom religion was nonsense or for the weak. There were a number of lads in my form, right way up the school, who were attached to church and for whom Christianity played a part in their lives. I remember that seven or eight of us choir members were given the afternoon off school to sing at the funeral of one of our church organists at St Michael's Bracewell. In my first two years at Ermysted's I was a member of the school choir, led by the music master, Mr Sievewright, who was also the organist at Skipton's parish church and who later became organist at Carlisle cathedral. In those two years I was introduced to a repertoire of church music. I enjoyed my R.E. lessons – though the masters' comments on my school reports did not suggest that theology would play any role in my future.

Having said that, however, I did possess some sort of Christian ethic uncommon among my peers. For example, our first-form General Science teacher, Mr Naylor, would dole out his version of 'the hundred lines' to the negligent and delinquent of our class by demanding they write out one of the Old Testament psalms. A bad mark in the weekly 'slip test' might cost you the 73 verses of Psalm 78. The penalty for disobedience or disruption in class entailed a few hours' burning of the midnight oil, as the miscreant would have to struggle with the 176 verses of the hundred and nineteenth psalm. Somewhat appropriately the last verse of that psalm includes the phrase "I have gone astray like a sheep that is lost…" I remember my 'righteous indignation' at this form of punishment: this unfair encounter with sacred scripture, taking place in a punitive context, would hardly endear any boy to the Word of the Lord and could have – would have, I reckoned – produced an adverse effect. If Mr Naylor were an atheist it was a cunning way, of course, of damning religion. If he were (by some incredible stretch of the imagination) an evangelical Christian it was a very misguided attempt at promoting it. The strange thing was that none of my friends found this matter anything to get worked up about. And I was too timid a twelve year old to tackle the teacher himself! But yes: there were these markers which surfaced from time to time on the journey of my vocation.

During these formative years the Church authorities once again turned to the issue of a new parish church for the town. A purpose-built church for the needs of the congregation and community at large. A building of sufficient size – and, most importantly – licensed for the conducting of Holy Matrimony. A site behind the present chapel-of-ease, at the top of Skipton Road as it joins Church Street, had long been earmarked for the new church. It was simply a matter of waiting for the various bodies, both civil and ecclesiastical, to give the go-ahead.

I would suggest that the Church of England in Barnoldswick in the mid 1950s was in very good heart. The churchmanship of the parish was quite Low but it had never been anything else. Evensong, therefore, was still the best attended Sunday service and St James was appreciably full downstairs – and with a good smattering of young people in the gallery. There was also a large reservoir of people who would class themselves as 'Church' and supported the Establishment in a variety of ways, including financial, even if they rarely worshipped in the buildings. Canon Mackay had resigned and gone three miles down the Skipton road to serve his final few years of ministry at East and West Marton.

His successor was a much younger man who had served a curacy in Keighley and a first living in Everton in the Diocese of Liverpool. The Reverend Philip Harry Green had trained at the London College of Divinity but had previously worked in mining engineering. He was just the sort of chap the parish needed at that particular time: he was young (parishioners always want a *young* vicar!) but not without pastoral and parish experience. But most of all – if his former occupation was anything to go by – he would be a *practical* man. One who could kick-start the long-awaited new church building project. And one who would have the nous to oversee the construction work. The fact that he had three churches and ten thousand souls to care for and a curate to train really did not enter into the average layman's equation.

'Phil Harry', as everyone irreverently but endearingly called him, was inducted into the living on a cold winter's evening in 1957 at St Mary-le-Ghyll. I was there, so was Ann, and the rest of the choir, seated higgledy-piggledy in the strange box pews, which are only one of the several features which make unique our ancient parish church.

The new vicar was certainly the catalyst. Within a year of Mr Green's induction the Bishop of Bradford, Dr Coggan, came to lay the foundation stone. On Saturday afternoon, May 10th 1958, a great gathering sang "The Church's one's foundation" and, later, the unknown but highly appropriate "O Lord of hosts," which speaks of our laying a foundation stone and asking GOD's grace on all who shall work with their heads and hands on the future building. After the ceremonies, prayers and address by the Bishop, a collection was taken whilst we all sang "Now thank we all our God". The relevant Collect for Trinity Sunday and the Bishop's Blessing concluded the service and everyone repaired to the Majestic Cinema building in Albert Road for well-earned refreshments.

The Church Council was eager to use not only local materials for their new building but local craftsmen, too. Builders, carpenters, plumbers, painters, designers and even architect – all from Barnoldswick and its surroundings. Bright local Yorkshire stone on the outside was complemented by West Marton oak pews inside. A double-decker lectern pulpit was fashioned from the same timber. Vibrant mosaic work – splendidly, daringly modern for its time – adorned both altar and hexagonal font, with a triangular design, which revealed the dedication of the building: Holy Trinity. Whether it was wise to use *every* thing local became open to question. The splendid design incorporated a tower, whose stone quickly absorbed rainwater and defaced the inner decoration. Was the architect to blame? The builders? After repeated attempts to rectify the flaw, the tower was ultimately pulled down and a much smaller, insignificant spire replaced it.

However, long before the first sod was cut and the Foundation stone laid, church folk, young and old, had been engaged in diverse activities to raise money for the new church. Every conceivable, legitimate ruse was used to wrest money from the people. A giant Turkish Bazaar ran for three days in the Church School, stones were bought, pews even. And every Saturday night from September to May two fixtures were indelibly marked on everyone's calendar. The Whist and Domino Drive for the adults – in the *Infants* department of the school; and, in the extended school hall a Social for us young ones. Proceeds *always* for the new church.

Both events were always well supported. The grown-ups set about their chosen games whilst we barn-danced and Military Two-stepped up and down the hall. There was always a magnificent meat and potato pie supper, followed by apple pie or trifle. Every week a number of designated church families supplied the fare: the savoury part appearing in large enamel washing-up bowls, covered with a pastry crust and kept warm in waiting ovens until the half-time call came from the Whist Drive's Master of Ceremonies.

These Church Socials were wonderful for us teenagers. My friend Alan and I somehow found ourselves running them. We organised the music, which simply meant remembering to bring the various LP records and ensure the record-player worked. We also introduced some light-hearted 'games'. Scores of young folk attended. A proper programme was planned to which we adhered. The evenings were trouble-free and never boring. The girls taught us boys how to do the basic dances. The 'Progressive' version of the barn dance meant we got the opportunity to dance with other girls. And the twirly, waltzing bits in the Veleta gave us our first introduction to ballroom dancing. Ann was a marvellous dancer. She still is: light on her feet, rhythmic and gay. She enjoys dancing as much as anything in the world. Regrettably, by contrast, I have feet of clay and little musicality. She taught me the quickstep all those years ago but the waltz and foxtrot proved impossible for me. Nevertheless it was there, at those church socials, that I learned to mix with others and to grow up. Church life was having more than its share of forming and nurturing me.

The building of Holy Trinity progressed at a pleasant pace and on a cold Saturday afternoon in March 1960 Dr Donald Coggan returned to the town to consecrate and dedicate the new parish church of Barnoldswick with Bracewell. It was the first time that the Grand National was televised live. Ann's father had been asked to rig up the amplification system, in the church, which he did with his usual methodical care and expertise. Dr Coggan told him afterwards, by way of a compliment, that he would commend him to do a similar job in any church in his diocese.

Between these two events I had begun my 'A' level course at Ermysted's. History, German and French. I had managed to pass six out of my seven 'O' levels, failing English Literature with some style. I couldn't stand the 'Literature' part: *how* can we be sure that the author felt this or that? The trouble was that foreign language 'A' levels were also all about 'Literature'. The complaint I had about Eng.Lit. was just as relevant in my French and German subjects. For the life in me, I cannot see how healthy, robust, adolescent male sixth-formers could get academically excited – and therefore interested – in some soppy German love poetry or a boring tale about a tailor. Admittedly Maupassant's stories about Paris prostitutes made the French classes rather more tempting! That's my excuse for failing German and scraping a pass in French. I passed in History as well. Once again the thoughts of the Church's ministry surfaced in my mind. I casually but deliberately mentioned it to my mother and father as we were watching television. "You can forget that!" warned my Dad.

To make the passing of my 'A' levels even more hazardous, I had also embarked on two science 'O' levels. Because I was so unsure as to a future career, my father 'encouraged' me to choose dentistry. It was a daft idea. My German master, Dick Dulling, said as much. I should have put my foot down and insisted on that crazy notion of the priesthood. But I was too much of a coward to want to raise more battles. To read for a degree in Dental Surgery really required 'A' levels in Physics, Chemistry and Biology. Yes: these were on offer at school but my progression up the school pointed most definitely to the Arts not the Sciences. From the fourth form onwards we pupils were channelled in one of these two directions. For almost everyone it meant abandoning one or the other. There was no other answer but for me to try and add Physics and Chemistry 'O' levels to my baggage. It was a two-year course and my busy 'A' level timetable became overcrowded as I attempted to take on board the stuff of fulcrums and levers, atoms and molecules. During our termly post-mortems on my School Report, my father usually told me that Edward would one day catch me up scholastically. His words had now come to fruition! There we were in the same laboratory, studying the same subjects for the same exams. And he two years younger.

I was able, happily, to add two extra subjects to my six 'O' levels but, of course, my 'A's suffered. Not entirely because of these two science subjects. I found the two language courses – better described as *literature* courses – boring and uninspiring. Conversely the History syllabus was fascinating. To study the political rivalry between the Liberal Mr Gladstone and the Tory Benjamin Disraeli, was riveting. One cannot help but take sides in History. I couldn't. And being a keen Conservative in my teens I was very much an admirer of Disraeli, sharing in his ridicule of Mr Gladstone's Irish adventure. Later on, in my reading of English Church History my High Churchmanship swung me round to favour the Grand Old Man, whose devout Anglo-Catholicism, I came to understand, was his springboard for all his attempts to find a solution to the eternal problem of Ireland.

Towards the end of my ministry the Bishop of Blackburn 'invited' me and a handful of other priests to Hawarden Library, a Christian study centre, for a week's reading and research. Hawarden lies on the Welsh-Cheshire border and the Library adjoins the Castle, which was the home of the four-times Prime Minister. We priests on the course were privileged to be shown round part of the ground floor of the castle, where Mr Gladstone worked. His study was a vast room, basically divided into two areas by large desks. Around and upon one desk were his theological papers, his religious writings and books on the Faith. The second area was where he wrote his Parliamentary papers and speeches. Above this desk was an alabaster sculpture: a bust of none other than Benjamin Disraeli! Our guide explained that Mr Gladstone wanted to keep his arch-enemy for ever in his sights when preparing his orations for the Commons. In imitation of this practice, I had pinned up in my study a newspaper photograph of a be-sandaled, unkempt woman priest, leading two homosexual men down the path of the church, from where she had just 'married' them.

In retrospect, my sixth form days hardly propelled me towards Christian ministry. The fact that I supported 'Dizzy' says it all.

Two mere 'A' level passes were not sufficient to gain admission to any University Faculty of Dental Surgery. I therefore returned for a Third Year Sixth – and the daunting, disappointing task of having to learn about yet more French and German literati. Four weeks into the term, however, I received a letter from the Dental Department of Leeds University, offering me a place forthwith. My acceptance was sent by return of post and a week later I was an undergraduate. I was awarded a small grant from my school's Hartley Macintosh Scholarship Fund and dad paid the rest of the fees.

My stay at Leeds lasted one academic year. Looking back, the whole episode was traumatic: a waste of time for me and a waste of money for dad. Not that I did not try. I grappled long and laboriously with an Introductory Year of Physics, Chemistry, Zoology and Botany. The whole experience was utterly foreign to me. Two days a week were spent in the Chemistry lab. amongst centrifuges. Organic Chemistry was another mystery. I had never used a scalpel before, nor been anywhere near a dissected frog, dogfish or rat. Likewise, microscopic work was to me an unknown world – in every respect.

Because of my late arrival at the University, I was given a place in one of its Halls of Residence, Devonshire Hall. A splendid, large edifice in Cumberland Road off the Headingley Road. Its warden was a retired naval Commander, who ran the Hall on naval lines, with quirky rules and arcane rituals. My 'rooms' were a larger cellar in the basement. A huge roll-top desk was placed up to the wall in which there was a window, barred on the outside. Not that you could see much of the outside! Next door was the boiler room-cum-laundry. Consequently there was always a lot of heat and noise. The floor of my cellar was chiefly carpeted by a number of odd rugs and remnants; it had a good gas fire and a reasonably comfortable single bed.

The sum total of this package was pretty depressing. The cocktail of struggling bewilderingly during the day and the troglodyte-isolation during the evenings and night hardly conjured up a picture of exciting University life. It was a good thing that Ann was only one hour's train journey away: little wonder I came home most week-ends. The whole situation was very silly but I did not go under. Nor was I depressed. On a positive note, it was precisely because of this situation that I began to read my Bible and say my prayers methodically and earnestly. The Gospel according to St Luke was my starting-point and the daily explanatory 'tracts' from the Bible Reading Fellowship accompanied the study.

From my vocation point of view, the year at Leeds was far from wasteful. I met a small number of fellow students who were Christian and not ashamed to show it. It was here that I met John Newman who had also embarked on the same Introductory course in Dental Surgery. John was from Caerphilly, a faithful, staunch member of its Baptist chapel, along with the rest of his parents, grandparents, uncles, aunts and cousins. But he was full of fun and we became good friends from the beginning. He, like me, had a girlfriend – Pauline – who was to train as a teacher. We had much in common and on a few occasions we four would meet up for a week-end break. After my departure from Leeds, John and I kept in touch. He went on to qualify and took a practice in his own native town: occupying a brand new building which his family of builders had designed and constructed for him. As a mark of his Christian faith John sold the business and joined a community health team in Llantwit Major, where, he felt, his vocation could serve a wider canvas of people. His faith also inspired him to make me a monthly grant of money to help me and Ann 'survive' during my training at Lincoln. He always said it was part of his "missionary giving". GOD bless him for that!

Back Home

I was back in Barnoldswick: a complete failure. I was ashamed of myself. In retrospect I ought to have moved faculties within the University. Perhaps I could have read History. Or theology. But would I have been able to obtain a grant? Besides, the natural corollary to failure is to rush into something else with such speed that the pain is anaesthetised and forgotten. And that's what I did. Banking was a good career, advised my father. It has security, status and an early retirement. "Any duck-egg can be a bank manager," he cajoled. Again, I was too unsure as to what I really wanted to do with my life. To articulate my deepest, innermost wish of being a minister of religion would have been tantamount to initiating World War Three. I kept quiet. Cowardly quiet. I convinced myself that banking was the way forward and applied to Martins Bank to be a duck-egg.

I started in September 1960, based in the bank's Skipton branch, an imposing building in the centre of the High Street. Ann started her three years' teacher training course at St Mary's, Cheltenham in the same month and thus began a long, patient wilderness period, where waiting for letters and phone calls took predominance.

The period, however, was an opportunity to resume my church commitments. I returned to teaching at Sunday School and set about forming a discussion group for the young folk who attended our new church. The Holy Trinity Young People's Discussion Group evolved and had a dozen or so members. We met in the choir vestry every Sunday after Evensong. The vicar trusted us sufficiently to lock up the church at the end, one of the members posting the key through the Vicarage letter-box on his way home. The Group was a tremendous success. Guest speakers, usually local clergymen, were invited on a regular basis and on other evenings we set our own agenda, normally a very formal debate with members advocating or opposing some particular 'hot topic'. We had a small committee of four to oversee affairs. I chose to be secretary and therefore responsible for the programme and for arranging dates for future speakers.

Over the months the Group showed no signs of fatigue and it was agreed that we should invite some of our peers from the local Methodist church, St Andrew's on Rainhall Road. Their church had formerly been the Wesleyans and, I suppose, the main stem of the local Methodists. But there was also another active Methodist church – the Independents – 'famous' locally for their musical shows and pantomimes. They had a good representation of young folk, too. So both churches were invited. And they came. Numbers swelled to over thirty every Sunday evening. The vestry at Holy Trinity became totally inadequate and, whilst we did the rounds for a while, it was obvious that the architecture of the chapels offered far more than we Anglicans could. Within a short space of time young Baptist men and women joined us. Bethesda and North Street chapels possessed a healthy number and by now membership was approaching fifty. A handful of Congregationalists meant that we topped the half century. Some eager, enthusiastic, evangelistic folk from the Gospel Hall came for a taster but we rather disappointed them and they returned to their own Sunday night devices. The Group – still organised on those original lines – was a splendid, living example of how the various denominations could meet and work and worship together. The only regret I personally had was that there was no Roman Catholic representation. In the early 1960s Catholics were still an enigma to every other denomination. Protestants held a palpable sense of fear and suspicion towards them. I'm not too sure that some of our non-Conformist members could have easily settled in their company. Such a pity.

We obviously needed a new name to express our unity in diversity. We chose 'Barnoldswick Young Christians'. It wasn't a unanimous decision: many felt that we were unworthy of such a presumptuous title. Better would be 'Barnoldswick Young Trying-To-Be-Christians'. It would have been quite a mouthful, however – and the name would have been a tight squeeze on the cheque book! Yes, we *did* have a chequebook and a healthy bank balance, from which we paid our speakers and financed a few special projects.

Some of the various ministers – the ordained ones – were not entirely happy about it all, however. We were such an enthusiastic bunch that we decided to visit each other's churches for the evening service. There was consternation at Evensong in Holy Trinity one particular Sunday. Our ecumenical venture had taken all us Anglicans to St Andrew's Methodist church for Evening Worship. Our absence left considerable gaps in the Evensong congregation. "Where are all our young people?" a concerned lady asked the Vicar. "They've gone to the Methodists," he replied, whereupon she ranted and raved both about *our* lack of loyalty and the Church of England's lack of care for its youth. She obviously understood that we had gone to the Methodists *for good!* Viewing the situation forty five years on, and now from the side of the ordained ministry, I can sympathise with the Vicar. The Diocese bids him record with all honesty the number of those attending the various services of the day. A regular drop of fifteen or twenty could be serious. For on these figures hang future Parish Shares – and availability of curates!

Within the Young Christians was a core of thoughtful protesters. Protestants of their time, I suppose. Strangely these 'protestants' were almost all Anglican and we exhibited something of the 'angry young men' syndrome of the Sixties. It was the time of much sleaze in politics and a few of us, under the aegis of the Young Christians, set about writing scripts for a satirical review. A young person's version of television's "That Was The Week That Was" which either delighted or irritated Saturday night viewers. There were ten of us 'actors', complemented by several other members who operated lights and sound, who worked back stage or took tickets front of it. The revue was entitled "Cocktail" and, throwing superstition to the wind, was performed on Friday the 13th September and the following evening in 1963. We were given permission to use the excellent stage facilities of the 'New Ship', as the Independent Methodists were known. "Cocktail," true to its name, was a heady mixture of jibes and japes against politics and religion. The vast majority was harmless fun – comic advertisements for the various churches ("A Mass a day helps you work, rest and play..."), a sketch on immigration and so on. The show included two items of singing by Jean Hayhurst, a soprano of exceptional quality, who was a friend. Jean, of course, was the only real 'star' quality in the whole performance, though some of our scripts were not all that amateurish. It was the time of the Christine Keeler affair and naturally we could not let that pass by without a contribution. I cannot recall the gist of the sketch, except that one of the lines was about "a bed-time Tory."

In the following Friday's Barnoldswick and Earby Times the local journalist Gary Mattock gave "Cocktail" a rave review. Clever, witty, etc, etc... Then the good people of the New Ship, the Trustees of the Independent Methodist Church, heard one or two comments about the material in the show. Not necessarily criticism: just the contents. In the twinkling of an eye I received letters expressing their disgust at such a tasteless show. How dare we disparage the good name of the Independent Methodists, who, it was made clear, dissociated itself from the whole affair.

Mr Mattock who had given us such warm praise in his columns the previous week heard of this latest turn-about. His next weekly article tore us to shreds. "The only ray of light" he penned, was the solo performances of soprano Jean Hayhurst in what was obviously – now – for him – a very dark and dismal show. Mr Mattock was a good friend and form-mate of my brother Edward. His treachery and hypocrisy that week made Ann and me determined that his newspaper would be denied any photograph and details of our wedding the following summer. He actually telephoned my future in-laws a few days before the wedding and was told that no information would be given him or his paper. He did write a short column, headed 'A Lovely Wedding at Holy Trinity'. He wrote it 'in absentia'. He had had to rely, as he did before, on comments from a set of church ladies.

Par for the course, naturally, I had to deal with my father's anger. Whilst my friends' parents and Phil Harry the Vicar smiled quietly and knowingly at our half-baked amateur theatricals, I had to endure yet another tirade from Dad. Why? Had "Cocktail" affected the bakery business? My father reasoned that, over the years, he ought to have given me a more moral lead. That his lack in this department had led me to go off the rails. The result of which was a depravity for all to see. "Cocktail" was as tacky and tatty as the Sunday tabloids. As a response to my moral derailment my father immediately cancelled the family's two Sunday newspapers, 'The Empire News' and 'The News of the World'. We got the 'Sunday Times' instead.

The three years between leaving University and the locally infamous revue were a defining period in my vocational progress. It coincided with Ann's teacher training at Cheltenham. Whilst she was away my week consisted of work in the bank, letter-writing and preparing both Sunday School and Young Christians' activities for the Sunday. With a few games of Subbuteo table football with my brother Stephen thrown in.

Work was initially in the Skipton branch of Martins Bank. I began, as everybody does, doing the menial tasks, which included stamping and recording outgoing mail, answering the telephone or being despatched upstairs to look for some item, stored in one of a myriad of cardboard boxes. This basic but effective filing system held all sorts of banking documents for up to six years. These errands into the attics of the bank building were usually to seek previously cleared cheques which had become the focus of some customer check or complaint. Each morning was the 'local clearing' in which the junior staff met at one of the branches and interchanged cheques drawn on our local four banks, Barclays, the National Provincial, the Midland (our greatest rivals) and ourselves. This daily meeting of juniors was a chance to share our common moans.

Making morning and afternoon tea for the manager and the staff was another facet. Grandad Vaughan, recently widowed, was now living with us at Park Avenue and I knew he liked his tea strong: one teaspoon for him and 'one for the pot'. In the light of this ratio, and faced with making tea for a staff of fourteen, I decided to put a mere *eleven* teaspoonfuls in the large bank teapot. Mr Mashiter the manager was delivered of his morning tea but he instantly returned the tray. "I want *tea* next time" he ordered, "not *syrup!*" My tea duties lasted a day and I was promoted.

I had also begun the protracted process of professional examinations. The Institute of Bankers required passes in eleven subjects which made up Parts One and Two of their exams. The first batch included a wide diversity of subjects, ranging from a basic English course to Commercial Geography and a smattering of Economics. Part Two was more banking-specific: Accounting, Law Relating to Banking and more Economics. Most men, but by no means all, who decided to do the exams chose to study through a correspondence course, or 'distance learning' as it is labelled today. Some dutifully went to Night School. I tried my hand at both but easily preferred the former. It was rare, then, for women in the bank to contemplate doing the exams. Not only were there so few of them, those who were employees seemed content to be secretaries or 'machinists', operating those early computers.

Much more important to me was the sending and receiving of letters to and from Ann. Often the delay of a much-awaited letter caused me deep misery. It was all too intense. We saved all our letters – several hundred – and had a ceremonial burning of them when Ann finally finished her course.

Meanwhile, the Young Christians group was doing wonders for me. I had grown in confidence, enjoyed learning about the Faith and how it impinged on everyday life. I had become a natural leader of the organisation, whose activities were by and large from my initiative and ideas. I took on the occasional preaching engagement at some of the local chapels. It had to be the chapels, of course, since the Church of England had a much more defined strategy of who could lead worship and preach. To be the Sunday preacher invariably meant doing the whole service: choosing the lessons, the prayers and even the hymns as well as the sermon. I did not undertake the task many times but I always found it exhilarating after the early nerves. It's quite an experience to be exposed, up there alone in the pulpit. The minister does everything from there. The architecture of dissenting chapels during the Victorian age insisted that the pulpit was centrally placed. And because most of the buildings boasted a gallery, the pulpit rose like some giant sea-creature to the level of the upper deck. The Ministry of the Word was all-important to Non-conformist worshippers. Consequently the Word must emanate from the focal point of the chapel. By contrast, the holy table, upon which Holy Communion was administered, monthly or even longer, was a small affair *at the foot of* the pulpit. I have no idea what subjects I preached on but I do recall spending hours and days in my attic-bedroom on sermon preparation. I dread to think of what I said!

Wayside Pulpits still do exist, though they are a dying phenomenon. In my youth every chapel had one fixed near the main gates and adjacent to the road. They were the Protestants' Calvaries. The Wayside Pulpits were basically a notice board in two halves. An Orthodox diptych! On one half, in large print, was the week's scriptural text – a pause for thought for the passer-by. The other half contained information about the coming Sunday's services and the preacher. I was to lead and preach at one of these chapels on one particular Sunday. The Wayside Pulpit announced: "This Sunday EveningWorship at 6pm. Preacher: Mr Trevor Vaughan." The corresponding other half proclaimed "Man shall not live by bread alone." In the light of my family's baking and confectionery business, some folk wondered whether this was a sly advert to promote our vanilla slices!

Ann and I planned our Wedding for July 25th 1964 at the new Holy Trinity. After all, it was *our* church. We had both taught at Sunday School there and enjoyed the nurture and care of church people belonging to that place. We could legitimately have chosen two other Anglican venues within the parish. St Mary-le-Ghyll was the quaint, picturesque, mediaeval ancient parish church of the town; St Michael's Bracewell was equally picturesque, equally ancient and was the sister church of the united benefice. Society weddings, "posh do's" always took place at one of these buildings. Edward was to marry Brenda at Bracewell, Stephen Elva at Ghyll. But we belonged to Holy Trinity. We'd been there from the start: our spiritual home, despite its youth.

If there were any progression to priestly vocation at this time it was subconsciously put on hold. I was still a guiding force in the Young Christians. One Sunday evening, the final half-term week-end before Ann finished her course at Cheltenham, I felt I was committed to the agenda of the Young Christians. Being the last evening before she returned, Ann felt we could both give it a miss and spend the remaining few hours together. The upshot of it was that I went to the meeting and Ann went home – after an enormous argument. We patched things up: in retrospect it would not have been the end of the world if I had not attended the group. I ought to have given it a miss.

I suppose the episode gave Ann an insight into what was to come in the way of divided loyalties. It was the all too familiar picture of my grandparents Vaughan: Grandad was never at home: always out at Council meetings in the Town Hall. When he was Chairman of the Council the family's Christmas celebrations were put on hold until he returned around mid-day from his civic duties in the local hospitals. It was against all this which my father vigorously rebelled. Ann, however, *did* understand and was already a marvellous encourager on my spiritual journey. In fact, she was the catalyst for all that was to happen. We both knew of the eventual likely outcome and she never wavered from that position.

Catalyst was the right word! Once we were married, my religious feelings were given free rein. Once in our new home in Barrowford Road, Colne, we decided not to return to Holy Trinity – a great temptation – but to launch out and find the Christian community in our new parish.

St Bartholomew's Colne had a young rector, Kenneth Whittam, whom I knew slightly from dealings with him over the bank counter. He and his wife Margaret were most kind and welcoming to us. Then there was Sarah Ann Dixon. Mrs Dixon was probably in her seventies when we became acquainted with her. She had made a determined effort to befriend that young couple who had started coming to church. She invited us for coffee after the morning Eucharist and we had several afternoon teas at her home. We took her (or did she take us?) to a variety of church functions. Come Christian Aid Week, she and Ann shared a round of house to house collection. It was so bitterly cold that they emptied an unsealed envelope and bought a bag of chips with the contents! They reimbursed the bag afterwards. Mrs Dixon was a wonderful worker for the Gospel. Her overwhelming love and kindness, accompanied by a constant smile and twinkling eye, belied her own private grief and troubles. Widowed when young, she had brought up her daughter single-handedly and got her through College. She loved the Lord – and the Lord's people – with an old-fashioned evangelism, warm and wise. When she learned of my vocation, she proved a stalwart of spiritual support. Despite nearing eighty years old she made the long journey alone to Coventry for my Ordination. "Are you in the Mothers?" she asked a somewhat startled Joyce, my Vicar's wife. Joyce and Ken were not able to have children of their own and adopted a boy and girl. Mrs Dixon, of course, was referring not to any biological ability but to membership of the Mothers' Union, of which she was an ardent, life-long adherent.

There was a host of friendly folk at Colne Parish Church, including William Whittle, a solicitor in the town. William dealt with the purchase and subsequent sale of our first home. There was a thriving Twenties Club – of about twenty members! These were, on the whole, young- or nearly-marrieds. Tom, the curate, had general oversight. He was one of a new kind of curate in the Church of England. These men were priests who had spent a good deal of their working life in another sphere. In Tom's case he had been a sales rep. for the local brewery firm. Tom and his like brought a much-needed dimension to the ordained ministry. What they lacked, perhaps, academically was made up by their experience in the university of life. They were usually local men who spoke the local dialect, knew the local situation. In most instances these curates were as old – or even older – than their vicars. That was the case here: Tom's former work experience, indigenous background and age was counter-balanced by Kenneth's academic qualification and training and youth (he had studied both for his degree and ordination at Oxford).

Tom also had a very attractive, much younger wife, who worked as a beautician in a neighbouring town's departmental store. Most of the young men in the Twenties Club were secretly attracted to her. If you asked any chap to picture in his mind 'the vicar's wife', I doubt if he would conjure up some Sophia Loren, seated on the front pew at Evensong. Totally irrational of course. Why shouldn't clergymen marry attractive women? The answer is, of course, that they do! (*We* do!) Men in particular associate the Church, and all that belongs to it, with what is old-fashioned, strait-laced and mundane. Oddly, that latter adjective originally meant 'of this world rather than a heavenly one'. Modern man means to use the word pejoratively but in fact conveys the very opposite, because in this day and age to be 'of this world' (i.e. 'with it') is to be taken as a compliment. Nonetheless, this dim and inaccurate view of all things 'Church', includes its womenfolk, be they Mothers' Union members, runners of coffee mornings, sorters at jumble sales or vicars' wives. Because of her job, Tom's wife was always immaculately dressed and strikingly made-up. Sadly, she too discovered that those general preconceptions, those misguided expectations of ordinariness were only too real and accurate. Within a couple of years we were to read with great dismay is some seedy tabloid newspaper that she had left her curate- husband. For a man of more substantial means? I do not know. Tom remained at his post and later became a vicar in the same diocese until his retirement.

It was on March 9th 1965 that I declared my inner thoughts about ordination to the rector. I don't know why I remember the date but it's one I especially note each anniversary and thank GOD for my vocation and opportunity to work for him in this particular way. I suppose the date was that on which all that had gone before was placed on track and that the calling, if it were real or imagined, could begin to be properly tested. In all this, as I've said before, Ann was totally behind me. The rector seemed quietly thrilled by my news and advised that I must continue to pray about it. At the same time he would arrange for me to meet Bishop Charles Claxton, our Diocesan, who conveniently was the visiting preacher in a few weeks' time.

This meeting, held at the rectory, was quite a low-key affair. The Bishop had been invited by the Whittams for lunch and he 'squeezed me in' before his meal. However, it was a chance to meet my Father-in-God, whose Father Christmas jollity (and appearance) was somewhat daunting but encouraging. It was nothing more, nothing less than a pleasant chat. Strange to record, I never met my bishop again in either official or unofficial capacity. Undoubtedly he must have supplied various documents about me on my journey to College, my training and first parish. But that's what Directors of Ordinands are there for and I'm sure that Canon Schofield did everything but sign "+ Charles Blackburn." As for the latter, the next time I met him was at our friends Peter and Beryl's party at their vicarage in St Luke's Blackburn, when Charles was simply Charles Claxton – looking even more like a jolly Father Christmas and having had far too much to drink!

Ann had begun her teaching career at a small primary school in Salterforth, a village set between Barnoldswick and Earby. Despite being only five miles away from home, her journey to work involved a mile walk on North Valley Road in Colne, a bus to Kelbrook, from where another bus took her to Salterforth. Being newly-marrieds we had no car. A vehicle was far down our wish-list. A washing-machine topped that list. In order for Ann to reach school in good time, she had to leave home each morning at half-past seven. That was after a cooked breakfast!

In the first few months of our marriage I worked in our Colne branch, ten minutes up the hill. Colne was built on the steep incline of a hill. Many years ago, so I'm told, one of the candidates in the local election, promised in his manifesto that, if he were elected, he would abolish all the up-hills – but keep the down-hills! Needless to say, it wasn't long before the Bank moved me to Burnley branch – "the factory," as it was called. Whether at Colne or Burnley, however, I had plenty of time to wash up the breakfast pots and get on my knees to say my prayers.

"Cactum"

Before there could be any real progress, of course, I had to be accepted for training for the ordained ministry. Thus began a series of interviews with the Diocesan Director of Ordinands, Canon Schofield. Once every six weeks or so I would catch an early evening bus to Blackburn and make my way to the Diocesan Office in Cathedral Close. The Office was an old, dark stone building: a Victorian Church or Sunday School, erected adjacent to the parish church, which had become in time the Mother Church of our Diocese. The Diocesan Office itself had been refurbished internally to house various departments – those of the Diocesan Secretary, Surveyor, Registry and so on. I don't think the DDO had a purpose-built office, though I saw him in the same room on every occasion. Over the course of these interviews I received guidance and encouragement from the kind Canon. He was a small, thin man with bony features, a balding head and twinkling eyes with a smile to match. Naturally these chats were a process of assessment. It was normal policy for a candidate to be recommended for selection by the Director of Ordinands. The Bishop could intervene and override his DDO's recommendation, especially if the candidate did not meet the latter's expectation. Usually, however, once the DDO had made up his mind as to the suitability of the candidate, the wheels were put in motion for the candidate to be officially interviewed and assessed. This event was known in the trade as one's "Cactum" – the selection process organised by the Church's Advisory Council for The Ministry, hence the acronym CACTM.

CACTM was the Church of England body whose task was to advise on the readiness and suitability of men for the Church's ministry. There are almost as many variables of ministry in the Church as candidates. A dozen, perhaps twenty, such men were bidden to attend the CACTM Selection Conference. This was a three day affair usually held at some Diocesan Retreat House. 'Conference' is not the word I would use to describe the event, though there was plenty of conferring and talking. This was rather contrived in so far as it was very much initiated by the selectors as they listened to our contributions and examined our reactions. Age, academic ability, domestic situation, character and personality were all taken into consideration. Overarching these criteria the advisers (a more accurate term than 'selectors') had the exercising work of trying to discern whether Almighty GOD was indeed calling such a fellow to the full-time ordained ministry. Looking back on my rawness and that of the others, I am reminded of the lovely prayer which asks Christ the Master Carpenter of Nazareth " who on a cross of wood and nails wrought man's salvation" to wield well His tools in the workshop of the world, so that we – and here, especially, I'm thinking of those offering themselves for the priesthood – who come to Him *"rough-hewn...may be fashioned according to His will..."*

As a consequence of these selection conferences, some men were advised to gain more 'O' levels, some to wait (and to continue to pray) for a length of time, some to consider other aspects of ministry, such as Lay Readership, specialist pastoral or evangelical work. Those, however, who were discerned by the panel to fulfil the criteria were given the green light to pursue their priestly vocation. There was, however, even for these chaps, a long way to go!

My CACTM letter asked me to present myself at Morley Rectory in Derbyshire for a residential selection conference beginning on a Wednesday afternoon in November 1965. I caught a train from Colne station to Blackburn. I vividly recall the journey: I was seated facing front in a two-coach diesel. There was a stray dog on the track and no amount of warning signals from the driver had any effect on the creature, who was summarily mowed down. From Blackburn another train to Derby, from where a slow country bus to the village of Morley. There had been the customary delays on the rail journey and I arrived at the former parsonage, now Retreat House, well after the appointed time. Fortunately I was not late for any of the programme and was able to have a much needed cup of tea and sandwich before Evensong, dinner and the first session.

There were about twenty candidates of differing age, background and churchmanship. There were four advisors from CACTM. The chief one was the youngest of the quartet: a handsome thirty-something, yet an experienced priest who was the convening secretary – and destined for higher things; a senior parish priest who was Vicar of Gateshead; the suffragan bishop of Huntingdon (who was to succeed Charles Claxton at Blackburn – and eventually to be my Bishop) and the lady Governor of Her Majesty's Prison Askham Grange, a women's establishment near York. Their job over the next two full days was to interview individually each candidate. That's *eighty* sessions of concentrated probing whizzing round the old rectory, permeating the atmosphere with tension and fretfulness. Interspersed with these half-hour cross-examinations were group discussions, in which we did most of the talking whilst the panel observed and noted...

And yet I enjoyed it. I believed that the four good folk would discern if God was really calling me.

I arrived home on Friday with a spring in my stride. Then there was the waiting. The letter came some three weeks after the Conference and advised me that I could begin training for the ordained ministry at the start of the next academic year. About nine months' time. One of my interviewers, Canon Hugh Corden, the Vicar of Gateshead, also wrote to me offering both his congratulations and a curacy in his parish after my training. That in itself was a boost for my confidence. Needless to say, the joy of all this wonderful news was tempered by my having to break it to my family. Being the messenger of such news, however, was tantamount to being shot. Let me put this seemingly harmless act into some perspective.

Windows and doors

The Vaughans had been bakers and confectioners in Barnoldswick since the turn of the twentieth century. Martha, my grandmother, was the real baker. Born of farming stock she could turn her hand to most things practical. She was a cotton weaver when she left school in her early teens, weaving both at home (as the Census pointed out) and at one of the town's large textiles mills.

Her marriage in 1904 to my grandfather George Vaughan brought about a change of lifestyle for both of them. He had left the Chatburn quarry when he met Martha and took up employment at the same mill as she. He was quite politically motivated – one of the new Socialists – and his attitude to his employers ultimately resulted in both his and his wife's dismissal from the mill. Fortune shone on them, however. My grandmother's father, Henry Bradley, had an uncle who experienced a religious conversion. Overjoyed at his new-found faith he gave Henry four terraced houses in Rainhall Road, Barnoldswick. One of them, number 40, Henry gave to his daughter Martha to set up her own confectionery business. It was here that my grandparents lived and from where they baked, sold and delivered their bread, pastries and pies.

My father followed in their footsteps. My mother also worked in the shop both before and after her marriage to Dad. The business grew and a new bake-house was purchased. For my family their hard work brought wealth and not a little civic status. Grandad served on the Barnoldswick Urban District Council for many years, being chairman for two of those years; he was also Worshipful Master of his local Lodge. After the

Second World War my grandparents, now 70 years old, sold the thriving business to Redman's, the grocery chain store, for a substantial amount of money.

In 1957 my father returned to the confectionary trade when he bought a small family-run enterprise, Deakin's, in the town. The location of shop and bakery could not have been better. The latter was a mere fifty yards from our home and the shop no more than a five minutes' steady van drive away, when loaded with warm meat pies!

My father's forte was baking: or rather, his business acumen. I think he would have made a financial success at whatever venture he undertook. He had brilliant ideas and the skill and verve to put them into practice. He could not, however, be content with simply 'ticking over'. The business *had* to expand. To hold a steady line was tantamount to failure. Consequently my parents' business rapidly flourished. Another shop was acquired in neighbouring Earby. It was just like the good old days of the 1920s and 30s. We could do no wrong!

But there then followed a series of blows which affected my father. First, his mother, my grandmother died in March 1960. She had been the inspiration behind the whole undertaking for almost sixty years. Grandad had been the 'front' man in the first four decades: he oversaw both the buying of the materials and the selling of the finished goods. But Grandma did the baking. Advertisements in the local paper and journals heralded "G S Vaughan, Master Baker and Pastry Cook" but the truth was that it really emanated from Martha's hands.

She was also my inspiration in the long journey of my vocation. She was a deeply religious lady and I recall many moments when she would talk to me about God. One particular day I remember quite vividly. She and I were in her kitchen and she was talking about saying my prayers. "Always remember," she instructed, "to say 'if it be Thy gracious will'," since God ultimately knew what was best for us. I wish so much that she had been there in the traumatic events that were to unfold within a few years of her death in March 1960.

Grandad Vaughan died in June the following year, knowing that the second phase of Vaughan's the Bakers was well and truly roaring along.

In 1962 Dad's foreman baker, Arthur Lambert, an avid mountaineer and pot-holer, fell and fractured his skull in a week-end accident. He was to be absent from work for several months. My father, 48 years old at the time, had no option but to recommence his full-time baking. Latterly he had assumed a much more managerial role. The sudden reversion to five o'clock starts, all the late finishes, plus all the accounts and paper work sadly resulted in his having a cerebral haemorrhage, from which he made a good if not total recovery. Arthur, too, made a remarkable recovery and was able to resume his foremanship at the bake-house. Things appeared to return to normality.

At that time I was studying for my Institute of Bankers exams. One of the subjects I had to grapple with was Law Relating to Banking and it dealt with, among others, the laws regarding limited companies. A limited company – 'Ltd' after its name – meant it had limited liability. If anything should go awry financially and the firm become bankrupt, the nature of its being a limited company precluded any assets other than those of the company being seized to pay off the creditors. In other words, the private property of its directors would be safe. I suggested to my father that he consider this option for our family business – in the *very faintest* possibility that we should ever find ourselves in a financial difficulty. It would be a valuable safeguard. Much to my surprise and pleasure my father agreed and promised to consider it most carefully.

During this time of his deliberations Ann and I were married and it was in this wonderful security and love that I was able to discern God's will more freely. No more under the sway of my father, I was the master of my house and (as I truly ought to have been before) my destiny.

Dad's decision regarding my idea of a limited company coincided with the arrival of the joyous letter recommending me for training for the sacred ministry. He had decided to go ahead with the scheme. The relevant papers were already drawn up and were awaiting the signatures of the prospective directors, namely my parents, my brother Edward and I. There was one proviso, however. I could only become a director if I would "pack up this daft idea" of being ordained. Blackmail can sometimes have the very opposite of the desired effect. So it was in this instance. My father's conditional offer only made me the more determined to follow what I believed to be God's call, now so recently endorsed by the CACTM selectors. Taut with tension and a little anger I managed to spell out to him in very polite tones that I felt called to this work and would therefore forego any directorship of the family firm.

From that time onwards, Ann and I were subjected to almost daily visitations from my family. To be more precise, from my father with either Aunty Mary or my brother Edward in tow. Each visit took the same form: there was "no money in the Church," by which they meant that parsons were poorly paid and the work they did was equally poor. In other words "nothing". The whole 'Church thing' was doomed to failure. 'Making brass', earning money, was all that really mattered."When money goes out of the window, love leaves out of the door" added Aunty Mary, which became over the weeks and months her signature song. Our marriage just would not stand the strain, we were told in no uncertain terms. I reckon there was also another agenda, a secret irritation which never surfaced. Dad was still a Non-conformist at heart, suspicious of the Church of England. I once referred to him and my mother as 'parents' and was immediately cautioned by him for using such "High Church" phrases! Dad possessed a natural dissenter's mistrust of the Established Church. How could *ordinary* folk (bishops and the like) dictate who should and should not be ordained? How could *they* discern the will of God, let alone speak for him, and then proceed to arrange a young man's future? But money, love, window and door were the ever-recurring theme of these horrid nightly confrontations.

All their browbeating achieved nothing but distress. Possibly for them; certainly for Ann and me. It would have been much wiser if we had refused them entry. Just left them at an unanswered door. Remarkably, oddly, we somehow felt it was our duty to allow them into our home and allow them another round of their relentless ranting. My father even deployed the services of one of his best friends. Rennie had been a secondary school teacher, town councillor and regular churchman. His total support of my father's point of view and his antipathy towards the ordained ministry said nothing about his professionalism or his faith.

Mum never accompanied Dad on these sorties. She was never afraid to reprimand us boys for our misdemeanours when we were young but confrontation and prolonged assault were not part of my mother's make-up. I presume her lack of involvement was, in part at least, her defence of her eldest son. I always hoped so. Yet my father was so dominant that her compliance was for the best. She had to live with him.

My brother Edward said very little on these visits. Perhaps his participation was solely as my Dad's chauffeur (as Dad himself would be in too much of a pent-up state to drive). He did make one strange puzzling comment about the affair. "If God is like that," he stated, "then he's not what I thought of him." He could, of course, have refused to act as reinforcements.

My younger brother, Stephen, was a mere teenager in all this bad business and thankfully he sat on the sidelines. No doubt his opinions were shaped and coloured by the conversations at home.

No other member of my family *ever* uttered a word about the affair. Neither support nor opposition. Most of my eight cousins were too young but a remaining grandmother, four aunts and three uncles could and should have offered a word. Their silence revealed how forceful and persuasive my father was, even in the wider family circle.

One of my uncles *did* call. Weekly. He ran, as he had done in the years just after the War, an ice-cream business, which he called 'Clap Hands Charlie'. It was truly wonderful ice-cream. In recent years he had resumed the trade by acquiring a small custom-built van, with which he toured the cobbled streets of 'Bonny Colne on the hill' every Thursday night. Several streets away we would hear his van's mechanical jingle of a tune, advertising his presence. It was the signal for us to put on the kettle for his cup of tea, in exchange for two ice-cream cones. It was a pleasure to have him. He sat in our black vinyl reclining chair, cup in one hand whilst his fingers of the other drummed out lengths of Morse code messages, as he described his work as a wireless operator in the Merchant Navy during the War. It was odd that he never mentioned the 'ordination business', especially since he was my godfather. However his wife was Aunty Mary and she was a declared antagonist of the other camp. It was obvious that discretion was the better part of valour – even for a sailor who had outmanoeuvred the U-boats in the dangerous seas of the Atlantic.

So I broke the news of my 'success' to my parents. I did so with much fear and trepidation, since I am normally reluctant to initiate certain hostility and conflict. Dad's bribe – or 'bargain' – was still on the table. But so was my rejection. Vaughan's the Bakers became a company with limited liability and had three directors. I was excluded.

Within five years my father had died and the bakery business had gone into liquidation. The bankruptcy was a result of my father's undergoing several mini-strokes which increasingly affected his ability to make calculated business decisions. The creditors shared the spoils of a once-thriving enterprise. Every item from the bake-house and the two shops were sold off to pay them. My mother's home and contents remained intact. The loss was limited. It goes without saying that nobody, but nobody, acknowledged my instigation of this damage limitation, which would have devastated, if not destroyed, my mother.

Onward

I continued, of course, to see Canon Schofield. One question which I needed to be resolved reasonably quickly was over my banking exams. I had completed Part One and passed two of five subjects in the Final part. Would it be wise to obtain the professional banking qualification before embarking on training? Certainly it would be a tremendous asset should I fail in my studies for the priesthood. Tony Schofield thought not. He must have been fairly sure I would not only get through theological college but stick in the ordained ministry. He was a wise man and he was proved right.

Private prayer, too, continued and became more intense and urgent. I want to stress again and again that I experienced GOD's call in that whole series of prayer. Every single obstacle, every worry, was removed and erased. Every impossibility was made possible. Often against very high odds. It was certainly not plain sailing – it never has been. There were in those early days terrible pain and grievous hurt. Ann almost lost our first baby through all the trauma she had to suffer at the hands of my family. GOD does not promise a cushy ride. Stick with him, however, and he will get you there.

Recommended for training for the Church's ministry created an about-turn in my mind. Accountancy and the other banking exam requisites were replaced by some theological reading. Bishop John Robinson's best-selling book *Honest to God* was my very first book. This small light-weight paperback was certainly no light-weight in theological circles. It created shock-waves right across the religious world. Even the tabloids gave it coverage, though never in a positive light. Incredibly, the ordinary 'man in the street' had heard of this bishop with his liberal ideas. Born out of German and American theology, *Honest to God* was, in retrospect an odd book on which to begin my spiritual travel. It stood me in good stead, however, for future study. Bank lunch-times once revolved round hastily-eaten sandwiches and a cursory glance at the day's newspaper. Now, one bank clerk had his head in some liberal theology. Quiet lulls whilst on sub-branch duty at Habergham or Duke Bar in Burnley were spent learning the Greek alphabet and elementary vocabulary in readiness for New Testament subjects.

One of the ways I discovered GOD's dealings in my vocation was in the sphere of my work. The manager at Colne branch was a good man but possessed, in all fairness, very little idea of things spiritual. Explaining to him about my decision to leave the Bank would have been extremely difficult. There would have been no understanding, no empathy. In fact, to have spilled the beans to him might have brought about my dismissal. I was certainly no future asset if I were to abandon ship: I might as well go now! But just as things were beginning to come to the boil, I received a letter from Head Office, requesting me to report to Burnley branch the following Monday. Martins Bank Burnley had a rather dubious reputation. Totally unfounded but rumour had it that the staff there worked far longer hours than anywhere else in the district. Not for nothing its nickname was "the factory". The branch employed four or five times the number of clerks than at Colne; it was a huge, modern building built to house hundreds of square feet of computers in its upper storey. It actually replaced *two* of our branches in the town. Strangely all that upper floor space was never occupied by machinery. In 1968 Barclays Bank bought up Martins and a whole new structure within the Barclays empire was created. It had neither plans nor need to convert our bank building into a district office. During my days at Burnley that huge space boasted a full-size table tennis table: the scene for many a memorable duel between pimple and sponge!

I turned up for duty on my first day at "the factory" with some apprehension. Derek Mudd was the manager. A short, stocky man, quiet and serious. He himself had been promoted from our Hereford branch some years back. He was, however, a licensed Lay Reader in the Church of England. When the time came for me to disclose my intentions of leaving the bank to begin theological training, he was the ideal person in whom I could confide. GOD was definitely at work! Derek Mudd was so enthusiastic for me. He explained that he, too, wanted to try for the sacred ministry but was too fearful to take the necessary steps. He trained as a Reader as some compromise. Mr Mudd made my last eighteen months in banking pleasant and tolerable. In and around the bank he would not say anything about the matter but when the opportunity arose for a confidential minute, he would enquire, most interestedly, about developments. What wonderful encouragement!

Some eleven years later I had just become Vicar of Sabden, only four miles from Burnley. I had heard that Derek was very ill, having retired prematurely for this reason some years earlier. I drove over the hill to his home in Colne Road. Audrey his wife met me at the door: he had died the day before. "Come and see him" she invited. He was laid in his open coffin in a small reception room off the spacious hallway. He was robed in his cassock, surplice and the light blue Readers' preaching scarf. I was devastated not to be able to speak to him. To have missed him *by a day!* I wanted to thank him for the support he had given me – far more than he could ever have realised. Though I was unable to speak to him, I saw him: typically composed, serious and perfectly at rest.

"Being recommended for training" was the C of E's bureaucratese for allowing someone to commence the protracted progression to Ordination. During my final term at Theological College I devised a silly, harmlessly satirical board-game, which I called 'Ordinopoly' which I attached to the Common Room's free-for-all Day Book, whose usual contents were letters from disgruntled students about meals or the tiresome time of Saturday night Compline. The game was a 'snakes and ladders' concoction, involving the ups and downs, the kismet and karma of the path to ordination. It caused quite an amount of merriment, a necessary diversion to all who were revising for their Finals.

But I'm jumping the gun: the next task for me was to choose a theological college where I could commence the training. And then, having chosen one, hope that it would offer me a place to start the study. Then there would be a book-list to consider and grants to be applied for. A black cassock had to be purchased, along with a surplice. All these extras to be squeezed in to a busy schedule of being newly-married, looking after our home and – from early February 1966 – our first little son Matthew.

Let's start with Matthew. At the first meeting with Canon Schofield, after my CACTM letter of acceptance, I was told that I would receive a small grant from the Church, sufficient for my student needs. There might also be some additional grant from *The Church Times*, whose readers every Lent sent in donations to support wives and families of ordinands in training. Some counties also looked favourably upon the further education of their population, others didn't. Studying for a qualification for a specifically religious profession was often deemed inappropriate. Today it would definitely be regarded as politically incorrect to make grants to students preparing for the Christian priesthood. However, Lancashire County Council *did* grant some such financial awards and I was able to benefit. A godly county, Lancashire!

The sum total of all these bursaries did not amount to a fantastic figure. The Church grant did not take in to account the fact of a wife. The Church presumed that she would work – to keep herself and subsidise her husband. This arrangement was inflexibly based on the student's situation as he entered training. If I began my theological course married but childless my grant would reflect that circumstance throughout my three years' of training. No matter if we produced six children in that time: there would be no grant towards family. On the other hand, if I were to begin College with a wife and one, two or three or six children, I would receive an increased grant, which (to some extent) took into consideration my parental responsibilities.

There lay the dilemma. Ann and I did not want to wait to start a family a full three years on from the commencement of College. That would be 1969 – and far too long to wait! The alternative answer was to go to College *with* a family – and thereby qualify for CACTM's 'millions'. Like everything else, the dilemma was prayed about. And Matthew duly arrived six months before the new adventure. 'Matthew' means 'Gift of God'. He certainly was – in more ways than one. Yet again, another sign of GOD's opening doors, of showing us his continual guidance and commitment. Yes: *his* commitment to us. We often forget that it is a two way process.

The choice of theological college was not an easy one. I was a Low Churchman, without ever realising what that really meant. Barnoldswick did not have any other kind of Christian, so I was a natural son of the firm.

I suppose I was Low because I was, above all other things, suspicious of High Church. Its pomp veiled the real issue, I reckoned. There were in the mid-60's no less than 25 Anglican establishments which offered training for the priesthood. From Edinburgh in the north to the several London places in the south. From Llandaff in the west to Ely in the east. A wonderful choice. One could study in an urban or a rural setting. In addition to the English colleges, your training could take on a Scottish or Welsh flavour. There were seminaries to suit all spiritualities: 'High and crazy', 'Low and lazy', 'Broad and hazy.' There were also varieties of places within the great centres of university learning: Oxford and Cambridge and London. Many other establishments operated under the shadow of great cathedrals, though independent of them and the dioceses they served. Falling into neither of these categories was St Aidan's College, Birkenhead, on the Wirral. It was the nearest to our home and nearest in my then-perceived churchmanship. I applied and was invited for an interview by its principal the Revd Arthur Widdess. The College and its setting were the very antithesis of, say, Christ Church Oxford. It stood inconspicuously among several other dark stone edifices. Nor was the architecture the only grey item on the agenda. The course of study seemed uninspiring, even to a complete tyro like me. The weather, too, did not help matters. It was a typical North West grey day. But the greyest of all the greyness was the fact that the College did not cater for married students. And since Ann and I naturally did not want to be apart, I quickly but politely turned down the subsequent offer of a place.

Not many Colleges in the list of twenty five provided accommodation for students with families. The training of married, family men was never commonplace up to the end of the Second World War. Many men who had won University places postponed their studies and joined the armed services at the outbreak of war. When the War was over, a number of these wished to resume their courses. Some of them were now married and had families. They picked up their studies but in the majority of cases lived as single men during term-times. By the 1960's, however, the Church was encouraging men to come forward for ordination whose background was not academic. Those who had been out in the big wide world, who had experienced the 'university of life'. These men, naturally, would be older. The majority of whom would have a wife and children and would require, if they were accepted for training for the ministry, larger housing than the staple college bed-sit. Men in their forties, and even fifties, were beginning to take up places in our theological colleges. But only in those who had planned for this radical change. Why *all* theological establishments hadn't prepared for this beats me.

One College which had understood this new development, and acted upon it, was The Bishop's Hostel in Lincoln. Its governors, over recent years, had wisely purchased a number of cottages and small houses which snuggled around the College, Cathedral and Castle. They had also built up an even larger list of landlords who would look first and favourably upon applications from Lincoln Theological College. Looking at a map, Lincoln lies almost off it! It is not an easy place to reach. West to east. Like Barnoldswick, it's almost off the beaten track! And yet its information pamphlet sounded attractive, particularly because it could provide housing for Ann and Matthew and me. The snag was – and there's always a snag – Lincoln was *High Church!* The pamphlet described its long reputation for "Catholic Worship and Radical Theology." I had no idea what 'radical theology' was but the word 'catholic' made me very dubious. However, having our own accommodation – and near to the College to boot – counter-balanced the doubt. Canon Schofield spoke highly of Lincoln. He *would,* of course, being a High Churchman! Saddled with the dilemma I decided to apply. What followed would not be the last of the many conversions I encountered on the journey.

CHAPTER THREE

Training for the Priesthood

Making my Mind Up

My interview at The Bishop's Hostel was to be spread over one night. I arrived one Saturday afternoon, was welcomed and shown to a single room by a student. I was to meet Canon Alan Webster, the warden (Lincoln's name for its principal) after tea for a chat. He was tall and thin with a most disarming smile and genuine friendliness. I remember he invited me to browse at his book shelves whilst he collected some papers, asking me to pick out something that caught my interest. I was aware of some possible ploy: would he then question me on the subject of the book? I therefore steered clear of theology. I reckon now that I was too suspicious but then I played safe. I chose a book of poetry by John Keats. At least I knew a little bit about the poet from my English 'O' level days.

There was no grilling: just a delightful conversation about College life, my family, work and interests. After which I must have had an informal supper with the resident students. My mind is a complete blank as to what occurred in those late afternoon and early evening hours. By contrast, I vividly remember the ensuing hour. At ten o'clock every Saturday night in the College chapel Compline was sung. Compline was the seventh and final daily Office performed by the monks in their monasteries. It still is. At the Reformation, some 450 years ago, Archbishop Cranmer had reduced the daily round of worship to Mattins and Evensong. Compline is often used as an additional fare to complete the day. Especially so in Christian communities: monastic, clerical or where lay people gather in parish study groups. I was shown to a seat in the narthex, a kind of 'overspill' space at the back of the chapel, where visitors like me take unallocated seats. The seats in chapel, eight rows of pews divided by a central aisle, were reserved for members of the College. The staff (Warden, Sub-Warden and fellow tutors) sat, stood and knelt at larger seats, not dissimilar to cathedral choir stalls, on a raised dais behind the students. This elevation seemed solely to exist so that the Sub-Warden could make a note of absentees, since every student had his allotted place for the term. If an absentee was not absent but rather had arrived late, he was to take a seat in the narthex. For a late college member the narthex had this additional role of a sin-bin.

I had never heard of Compline until that Saturday evening. A short service, it is sung to the haunting mediaeval music of plainchant. The psalms are sung antiphonally by each side of the congregation and the whole act of worship is led by a cantor, with the rest of us singing our response to his versicle. The music, the words, the altar candles amidst the dim lighting, the periods of silence were to me electrifying. I had never been so moved by an act of worship. The silence continues after the worship. No one is allowed to speak after Compline, certainly not in the College precincts. I was thankful to be able to return to my room with that numinous experience unbroken by chatter or other frippery.

I had made my mind up to come to Lincoln.

Sunday morning's breakfast in the large refectory gave me a chance for more general conversation with other students. The College boasted both a football and cricket team (though it was usually a difficult task cajoling someone to make up the eleven!). It had a clay tennis-court. Down in the bowels of the building, labelled 'Sheol', the Hebrew for hell, was a full-sized table tennis table. It was somehow squeezed into the constricting vaulted arches of a cellar. Like Sheol, I assume, it was always hot. The chief sport, however, was croquet, played on the manicured lawn at the front of the old house. Croquet had by far the greatest number of adherents.

The College's Sunday Eucharist was a revelation. It was a complete contrast, yet total complement, to the previous night's worship. The chapel – and narthex – were packed solid as we sang our way through some five or six hymns, as well as the Kyrie, Gloria, Creed, Sanctus, Benedictus and Agnus Dei. The congregation included the 'College wives', the other halves of the married students. What was incredibly unusual was the *age* of the worshippers. Almost all under thirty! This was an inevitable situation. Never again would we aspirants to the parish ministry experience this majority of youth and vitality.

This Holy Communion, as I would undoubtedly have called it then, was yet another eye-opener In truth, the word 'Eucharist' was certainly not in common vogue. Perhaps the College used it in equal measure with 'Communion' simply because we were a *theological* community and we would want to show off our Greek. As proof of this, the College lavatories were never called 'loo' (after the French 'lieu' or 'place') but τοπος 'topos' – the *Greek* for 'place'. I think it sounded extraordinarily crude to visitors.

This Eucharist, Holy Communion – call it what you will – was a revelation to me. My own blinkered church-going had never been exposed to such liturgical flamboyance. The priest celebrating Holy Communion back home in Barnoldswick – and he would almost certainly have preferred the title 'minister' – would have worn cassock, surplice and preaching scarf. To witness in the College chapel the splendid vestments of celebrant, deacon, sub-deacon and servers, with all those candles, processions and music was for me a taste of heaven! The joyfulness of the worship led naturally into the jollity of the college breakfast, where staff, staff wives, students, students' wives and children joined together for a meal and a chat. A couple of hours later the clatter of cutlery on crockery suddenly subsided as a couple of wives took charge of a crèche of all the children, allowing their parents to have a more sedate and civilised Sunday lunch.

A final meeting with the Warden concluded my twenty four hours stay. I would hear from him soon, he promised, as to whether he could offer me a place. His letter arrived quite quickly, inviting me (and our family) to Lincoln, where I could train for the ministry. With great excitement I replied and accepted.

God's Own Exams

We had sold our home in Barrowford Road before advertising it. Most loose ends were tied up: bank resignation signed and sealed, mortgage arrangement redeemed (which was via Martins Bank Ltd) and all the bills that could be paid then, were paid. The only blot on the landscape was that the house allocated to us in Lincoln would not be vacant until September, since the current occupant was not to be ordained until Michaelmas. I, therefore, had no option but to leave Ann and Matthew at home for just over a month and live in College, as a 'bachelor' for that period.

Saturday August 13th was a bright, warm sunny day. Even in Colne! Our first full year of married life contained 256 days of rain, the weather experts informed us. But the day of my departure thankfully bucked the trend. Two large suitcases and a holdall were tightly packed with books and clothing. How I was to carry these loads was anybody's guess. Mr Richardson, our next door neighbour, kindly took me in his car for the first leg of the journey. It's never easy in this country travelling horizontally, that is on an east-west axis. North to south, by contrast, is plain sailing. That's an exaggeration, of course, but it is a far less frustrating and time-consuming activity if you can manage to arrange your movements vertically. I wonder if Julius Caesar had chosen Norwich or Aberystwyth for his capital, would all major roads strike out east or west? At least road atlases might be better orientated. Why is it that every book of road maps starts with *Cornwall and the south* and then steadily works upwards, northwards? Like most of the world, we English read from top left to bottom right, north-west to south-east. But no: we have to leaf over our gazetteers in an Arabic or Hebrew fashion: from bottom to top. Perhaps we should not be surprised, since weather forecasts, too, invariably start with the south and anything north of Watford Gap is a postscript. Still, the fishing forecast gets it right: "Viking, Forties, Cromarty..." *That* starts at the top and works its way down and round in a sensible clockwise direction. It is all Caesar's fault. If he had sailed into Skegness all would be different.

Lincoln, however, is not as east as Norwich. Nor Skegness. But it was still a tiresome 120 miles across country. I would have to travel by way of Skipton and Leeds. And since we had no car, public transport was the only option. The details of the journey are a total blank, though I do recall the excessive weight of my luggage. Anxious not to leave behind any book that might be vital, I crammed in the volumes of the entire College's recommended book-list. I must, somehow, have transferred the load from Mr Richardson's car onto the train (at Colne), then on to the coach (at Leeds). But I have no memory of doing either. My sole recollection of that important (I cannot say *memorable*) trek is suddenly spotting the awesome sight of Lincoln's great cathedral from down on the low plain, some twelve miles out of the city. As we approached Lincoln on the A57 the cathedral's mellow stone was bathed in the afternoon sunlight. Perched on its steep hill, it simply beckoned every visitor, be they returning residents, business folk, tourists, pilgrims or students like me. It was a contemporary picture of my favourite psalm, number 84, in which the Jewish pilgrims, on their way to worship at Jerusalem, suddenly espy the holy Temple. I deliberately kept my eyes fixed on that magnificent spectacle and felt an overwhelming pride and determination to do well.

Humping my baggage out of public transport for the third time at Lincoln's bus terminus, I hired a taxi for the final half-mile to The Bishop's Hostel.

The College's main entrance was technically the back door. To the original red- brick building a largely glass extension had been recently added. Great panes of glass made up the entrance porch which led in turn to a spacious reception hall. These huge panes reflected the magnificent twin towers of the west end of the cathedral. Because of the angle and obstructing buildings it was impossible to take a photograph of the towers from a more orthodox position. By using the reflection on the glass, however, a very pleasing image could be achieved. The porch was part of the new block, adjacent to which was the rather ordinary lecture room with two of its sides almost entirely made of glass. Above the lecture room were two storeys of three study bedrooms. Mine, I was to discover, was the middle one on the first floor, from which I had a wonderful view of part of the minster's west end.

Edward White Benson became Chancellor of Lincoln in 1872 at the invitation of Bishop Christopher Wordsworth, the nephew of the great Lakeland poet. During the final quarter of the nineteenth century several theological colleges were founded throughout the land. This 'redbrick challenge', as David Dowland's book on this subject is sub-titled, was an attempt, often by individual churchmen, to widen the opportunity for men of the middle and lower class to train for the sacred ministry. A High Church Tory, Benson had the support of Bishop Wordsworth and was able to found The Bishop's Hostel in 1874. Nine years later Benson was to become Archbishop of Canterbury accepting the gift from the Prime Minister William Gladstone. Though in opposite political camps the two were good friends and it was on a visit to Mr Gladstone's home at Hawarden that he died in 1896. As I described earlier, I was to stay at Hawarden myself for a study week towards the end of my parochial ministry. The rise of red brick colleges was a tremendous success in that the mission of the Church took on a seriousness hitherto lacking. With the huge rise of urban populations at this time, the need for priests to minister in these seemingly God-forsaken areas was immense. The Bishop's Hostel was a red brick college, literally and metaphorically. The main – and original – building was a fine symmetrical edifice. It stood on high ground overlooking the city, which in Benson's day was fast developing into an industrial centre, chiefly in engineering. Those who worked in these engineering factories lived with their families in the myriad of rows of tiny terraced houses down in the bottom of the city. The Brayford Pool, once a busy Roman port, still employed a large workforce in the latter part of the nineteenth and early part of the twentieth centuries. The railway, too. Lincoln was the hub of the agricultural hinterland. Farmers and their wives would come from the outlying countryside to do their business and their shopping. And Lincoln had its hospitals and prison. So much work-experience for the man who wished to serve God in the ordained ministry.

In the very middle of the red brick building were the front, main doors of the college. They opened on to a large south-facing lawn, which ultimately sloped down to borders, beds and vegetable patches, which were intersected by many pleasant paths. Often the warden would ask a student to accompany him on a walk along these paths: a sure sign that he had something rather serious to say to the man in question! To either side of the front door the building stretched itself. Bursar's office, kitchen and refectory to the west; Common room and library to the east. Above these were the students' rooms: the smaller ones, naturally, for the married men who could legitimately escape each evening to wife and family. Tacked on to the end of the external eastern end of the college was the small chapel of St Hugh of Lincoln. Despite its very modest proportions the college chapel was the source of a great wealth of teaching. Above the chapel doorway St Benedict's maxim was carved in stone: "Orare est laborare: laborare est orare". Prayer is work; working is praying.

The weekly rhythm of College life quickly enabled a newcomer to feel settled. This is especially so when a Christian community is bound by a regular pattern of prayer and worship. I felt very much at home, as did the twenty other freshers, fashioned as we were by 7.30am Mattins, eight o'clock Communion (voluntary), Evensong at 5.30pm. and late night Compline on certain nights of the week. Tuesday night Compline included a sermon by one of the staff. There were always a handful of visitors who came for this, one of whom was a very elderly priest. He was extremely deaf and wore one of those very conspicuous hearing aids with wires leading to a control box, which, in his case was clipped onto his chest on the convenient overlap of his sarum cassock. The aid's volume control was on this box. When the sermon began, he would settle back into his pew and surreptitiously turn the control to 'off'. Unbeknown to him, but to our great delight, whenever the hearing aid was in the 'off' position the contraption emitted a quiet but distinct high-pitched whistle. As soon as the sermon was over the whistling stopped. He obviously hadn't come for the preaching!

My supervisor was Ivor Jones, a Methodist minister, seconded to the permanent staff to give the College the correct ecumenical dimension. Ivor was certainly worth his salt: a brilliant theologian who read much of his theology in German – the language of modern Protestant theology. He was a gifted musician, a fine cricketer and an agile, splendid goalkeeper. He set my essay topics, which he duly marked, criticised and discussed with me. It was rather awe-inspiring to sit at such a prophet's feet every week.

I had never ever read so much before! So much so that I began having severe headaches, verging on migraine. A visit to the optician meant I was to wear glasses solely for reading. I was, however, still experiencing dizzy bouts both inside and outside our home. Attempting to follow the scriptures at morning prayer was often a frightening feeling. It wasn't long before I was compelled to wear spectacles all of the time. Within a couple of months I had gone from perfect vision (as I thought) to being utterly and permanently reliant on spectacles. Mind you, I discarded the things when we played football!

At any one time there were just over forty men at Lincoln but there was no simple pattern as to their studies or length of time of training. A graduate would normally spend two years, whilst a graduate in theology might just get away with one. A student over thirty was labelled an 'older man' and, as such, embarked on a non-examination course but with continual assessment throughout a two year period. Others who were under thirty but had no degree but had undertaken a two years programme of pre-theological study at places like Brasted in Kent also did two years. I, together with David Mackenzie and Christopher Owens, did not fit into any of those categories. We were neither graduates nor 'older men' and were required to spend three years. Graduates or not, all under 30's sat the General Ordination Examination. The G.O.E. (also known as *God's Own Examinations*) consisted of thirteen papers.

The first year topics covered various Old Testament books, the epistles, modern Church History from the nineteenth century and Worship. New Testament Greek was also compulsory but many –and there were *many* who could not cope with it – were allowed to drop it. It was so much like the Latin of my schooldays, which I loved, that I romped through it. We were on holiday when the results were to be published. Like some others I had given the Warden a stamped postcard with my holiday address, the reverse side of which I had written "Results of May Exams" and listed the four subjects (I had already passed the Greek). The postcard duly arrived. The Warden had *typed* in the marks. All passes! Opposite the New Testament II mark (75%) he had *written "an excellent mark and should give you real confidence. Hope the sun shines. Congratulations. Alan."*

It wasn't that I was unconfident, though it may have appeared so to my superiors. I was, in fact, very fearful of failing. Having taken your family away from regular employment and your own house, this was no silly venture. I had to keep my head down. Those results, however, did give me much more assurance for the following years. For that New Testament mark I was awarded a College prize: a book token to be spent at our local S.P.C.K. bookshop, which sold not only theology but Christian artefacts, including a ten-inch crucifix, the focus of my window-shopping for several months. I bought it. A metal Christ on a wooden cross, its purchase was yet another sign of my catholic conversion. I was certainly 'moving up the candle'. It has always had pride of place at my prayer-desk in my study.

I worked hard at my books. Chiefly because I enjoyed the study. The chance to discover what lay behind the Gospels, the authentic figures of the Old Testament, Christology, Church History and the rest. In my second year I was much more self-assured. Just as I was at Ermysted's when I reached the fifth form. My own individual – some might say odd – sense of humour was a tell-tale sign of this confidence. I recall one example which brought laughter and fun to both class and lecturer. We were studying the Gospels and had been introduced to the variety of sources behind the work of the four Evangelists. I volunteered a new rhyme to replace the traditional "Matthew, Mark, Luke and John, Acts and Romans follow on." My modern form-critical version went: "Matthew, Mark, Luke, John, Proto-Luke and Q, Acts, Romans, Corinthians 1 and 2."

In addition to the Gospels, my middle year's syllabus involved more Old Testament studies, Christian Doctrine and Church History from Wolsey to Wesley, from Reformation to Rome. I passed the exams with good marks, though no book-token this time. Many of the chaps did not fare too well and I was thrilled to receive a letter from David Lunn, the Sub-Warden: "I'm delighted with your G O E results. A well-earned consequence of much hard work!...You bring a much-needed ray of sunshine onto a gloomy scene." He ventured to suggest that I should have had a much higher mark in the OT paper. Of the examiner he wrote: "I'd like to get my hands on that man."

The third and final academic year was much shorter. Final exams were held in March rather than in June, since the frenzied activity of sorting out your first parish, moving house and arranging matters of an ordination service with your new diocese, all took most of the fourth term. My final subjects numbered four: a set book in the Gospels, which in our case was actually only *five* chapters of St John – 13 to 17. I knew these 155 verses almost off by heart. I had tape-recorded them and most mornings between Mattins and breakfast I would play the recording whilst following the Greek text. There was another paper on Doctrine, the OT set book was Jeremiah. And there was Ethics. My main worry, this. Ethics seemed so nebulous. "Situationism" was the ethical buzz-word, which simply meant that each moral problem depended on the individual circumstance. However, one of the paper's questions was about gambling. I had written an essay on this very topic some while ago with great feeling. I was *personally* only too aware of the consequences of gambling. Grandfather had lost a big fortune on the horses, Dad a somewhat smaller one. Yet I could not have convinced the examiners to any great extent since I just scraped a pass. Nevertheless, played 13, won 13. I had passed God's Own Exam and would receive a Certificate to prove it. Almost forty years on it is still waiting to be framed...

Outside the College Walls

Interspersed amongst all this study was my family. I have to admit that most married men probably spent more time at home than I did. They were less fearful of failing. Ann was a wonderful wife. She knew how I felt about not failing the exams. We had moved from the flat in Carline Road, with its damp walls and lack of basic amenities, two hundred yards up towards the College. Right opposite the College's main entrance, in fact. To number 4 Wordsworth Street (named after the Bishop). Unlike our former flat this house belonged to the College. The rent was two pounds ten shillings a week, with ten shillings knocked off for being in charge of stoking up the College kitchen's Aga every morning and night. Easy: it was just like being back home in Park Avenue when I had to fire up the bakehouse ovens each night. The College timetable meant that I was able to join the family after lunch and spend the whole afternoon with them, returning at 5pm for Evensong. There were the occasional evening lectures or tutorials, sometimes Compline, but normally I was free to return home in the early evening. This free time did not amount to much but it was always spent well and it was certainly a far better arrangement than that which most Colleges could offer.

Philip was born at Wordsworth Street. I could see our cottage from my study room, though Ann sometimes complained that whilst I was "up there with my books" she was busy mowing our small pocket-sized back lawn – and seven months pregnant into the bargain!

Ann and I and our two little sons must have been a splendid advert for family life at College. The warden asked me if we were prepared to pose for a family photograph which would be an illustration in the forthcoming edition of the College prospectus. A cameraman from the Lincolnshire Echo duly photographed us in the College gardens and subsequently we graced one of the pages in the new brochure. "Come to Lincoln to train" was the insinuation "and bring your family too!" It really was a delightful photo.

The Theological College was not the only centre of adult learning in the city. There was an Art College and a ladies' Teacher Training establishment, The Bishop Grosseteste College. The elite RAF training centre was at nearby Cranwell. With all these places a small number of "theos" (as the "Grotties" labelled us) collaborated. I played my fair share in this collaboration. Ann and I, with Bryan and Linda Hackney, attended the sumptuous Cranwell Ball in the Assembly Rooms. A smart, 'pucker' event for which Ann bought a new dress and Aunty Mary sent me £25 for a Montague Burton's dinner jacket and trousers. I have still got the suit and, what's more, can still get into it!

A number of us "theos" joined with the girls from "Grotties" in their Rag Week fun. The theme for the week was 'Roman times', an appropriate one since Lincoln had Roman foundations. The highlight of the fun was to infiltrate the busy town centre on the Saturday morning. So there we were, toga'd or armoured, generally making a nuisance of ourselves and extracting money from the shoppers. It really was a jolly 'do'.

Lincoln possessed its very own mediaeval cycle of Mystery Plays. Freda Mitchinson, the wife of one of us students and a drama teacher, persuaded both the College and the Cathedral authorities to allow us to perform the play. Permission was granted and, using the huge canvas of the cathedral's west end, the play was performed with huge success – and not a little expertise from Freda and some of the main characters. Sam Marsden played Jesus and suffered long-term back problems as a result of his time on the cross. Another student played Adam, whose Eve was a rather young and attractive actress. "Adam" found his permanent erection somewhat of a hindrance as he strutted his stuff upon the stage in his body-stocking! The fig leaf helped! I played the prophet Isaiah, whose copious biblical prophecies were reduced in the play to a couple of lines.

The College, unusually, kept four terms: mid August to Michaelmas; early October (when we all went on our allotted 'parish visits' to see how the other half live) to just before Christmas; then early January to Easter Day – unlike most theological establishments which close down before Holy Week and so miss out on the most important and influential week of the whole year. The final term began after an Easter break until the end of June. For us married men, whose homes were where we trained, the vocations were an opportunity to go out and earn some money. Jobs were not easy to come by. One holiday all I could get was with the City Council laying flag-stones. I lasted one day, suffering a slipped disc!

I don't know how it came about but I met Dave O'Connor. He lived in a most interesting house set at right-angles to Steep Hill, right on the incline. Dave was a cost accountant for one of Lincoln's largest engineering firms, Clayton Dewandre. He told me that his department was always looking for clerks to carry out the great welter of mundane tasks and, since I was an ex-bank clerk, I'd find the work a doddle. I worked at Clayton's for three vacations and earned a lot more money than I would heaving paving slabs. The job mainly entailed adding up columns of figures, checking them and then double-checking them. I managed to get Sam 'Jesus' Marsden some work there. Office work was not too taxing on his back.

Ann and I became friends with Dave and his wife Anne. When they were expecting their twins we were asked to be godparents and we duly accepted. Eventually two more godchildren were added to our list: Lois and Rachel. How Anne managed to negotiate the terrible slope of Steep Hill with her double-push-chair every time she went out was a feat in itself. I suppose we were all a lot younger then! Steep Hill was steeped in history. Its sharp and lengthy gradient separated the industrialised, commercial part of the city from the almost village aspect of the community set around the cathedral and Roman castle. Hugh of Avalon had been persuaded by the English King Henry II to leave his monastery and take pastoral charge over the huge diocese of Lincoln. Hugh was his own man and was not afraid to admonish the king if he thought he were wrong. His great far-reaching talents were responsible, among others, for the building of the glorious Gothic cathedral. When he died in 1200 the kings of both England and Scotland helped bear his coffin up Steep Hill to lay his body to rest in the east end of his great edifice. After the twins' Baptism at the little parish church of St Michael, on the opposite side of Steep Hill, we repaired to the O'Connor house for refreshments. I discovered that I knew Dave's father-in-law: he worked for Skipper's, a large motor car outlet in Burnley, and he came in regularly to our bank to pay in. I had served him on numerous occasions over the counter.

Just before we left for Wyken, Dave and Anne and their family also moved house. Sad to say, we quickly lost touch. We haven't seen our god-daughters since then: I reckon they are in their forties now.

Lasting Impressions

What part of Lincoln's training left a lasting impression? It would be far easier to list what *didn't*. I certainly enjoyed biblical studies: form criticism and other methodologies which took one behind the New Testament writings. Whilst we might only have skimmed the surface of such investigative work, I derived great pleasure from it. The Old and New Testaments are together the story of God's people and any student of such readily becomes aware of his own part and place in the sacred story, the continuing narrative of His chosen folk. Our time, if you like, is a mere few verses in the never-ending series called the Book of the Acts of the Apostles.

Very much linked with all this biblical baggage was preaching. We were not allowed anywhere near a pulpit until our final year, when we were allocated various preaching duties. We were, consequently, thrust upon very tolerant congregations of neighbouring rural parishes. We were let loose on such kind people chiefly at Evensong, where we not only preached but – equally important – sang the versicles, collects, the lot! We had, naturally, received instruction in both the singing of the Office and preaching. My chorister days at St James' Barnoldswick stood me in good stead. I could easily hit the right note and pitch, though every student had the College's 'G' tuning-fork tucked into his cassock pocket, just to make sure. Amongst these congregations of country folk one person had been asked – by a member of staff – to make notes and to complete a questionnaire on the competence or otherwise of the day's preacher. It was no good trying to fathom out who the spy was: you just had to get on with the task in hand..

As for homiletics (we never called it that, thank goodness), we spent the first term learning the rudiments of the art of preaching. And it *is* an art. At our very first sermon class we listened to Alan Bennett's parody of a sermon in the magical show *Beyond the Fringe*. Bennett's brilliant, perceptive analysis of what *not* to say and how *not* to say it is a magnificent tutorial in itself. His (silly) text "My brother Esau is an hairy man but I am a smooth man" sets the scene for a plethora of parsonical faux pas.

Preaching had, quite suddenly, become the fashionable topic in the Church of England. Whilst congregations were not having to endure hour-long diatribes, as had our Victorian ancestors, nevertheless sermons were still far too long and far too complex for the average person in the pew. To make matters worse, it had to be admitted that since the end of the war in 1945 new (and decreasing) generations were attending church or chapel with very little knowledge of biblical stories, let alone any Christian doctrine. The preacher could not assume that everyone knew about Abraham or Jacob or any of the prophets. The Old Testament in particular was a total mystery to most. The Church had become to many people rather like a bookmakers' betting office or a lap-dancing club: you had heard rumours of what went on behind the doors but were never really sure. And you had never gone in to find out. Schools, also, sensitive to what might be deemed politically incorrect, steered away from the bible, replacing it with a mishmash of sloppy moralisms. All too quickly a great gulf had been fixed between the preacher and his hearer.

Of course, sermons have always had a bad press. Years ago The Times ran a prolonged series of correspondence from its readers about the usefulness or otherwise of them. It began by a letter from some reader who said he had gone to church twice every Sunday for forty years and in all honesty he could not remember one single sermon. The editor allowed his readers to debate the topic for quite some time before drawing it to a close with a letter from another contributor, which simply stated that his wife had cooked him two meals a day for forty years and he, in all honesty, could not remember one of them. The point he made was that without his wife's cooked meals he would have starved to death. Equally, without the sustenance of the sermon his soul would have gone the same way!

Nevertheless 'preaching' was the Church's new plaything and rather like a Jack Russell terrier the Church would pull it, shake it, rip it and rag it until it found a new formula. In all fairness there had to be a radical re-appraisal of the preached word. Radio, and more importantly television, were attracting increasing audiences with their short, precise sentences and clear-cut vocabulary. The sermon was fighting for survival. It is true to say that many important figures in the Church in the early 1960s were advocating its being laid to rest. If the sermon were to survive – and it jolly well ought to, since it is a very intrinsic part of the Gospel's proclamation – then the theological colleges and seminaries had to be responsible for a more vigorous approach to its effectiveness and relevance.

Roughly around the same time as this angst about preaching was the growing apprehension regarding church language and liturgical language especially. My generation had been brought up on the Book of Common Prayer. So had my father's generation. In fact for three hundred years there had been no alteration to the texts of Holy Communion, Morning and Evening Prayer – the mainstay of Anglican worship. In 1928 there had been some attempt at revision but Parliament (as it could) threw the Book out. Despite the fact that the Church at every level had recommended the changes by huge majorities, and that three-quarters of the peers in the House of Lords had also passed Archbishop Davidson's motion, the House of Commons rejected the Bill by 238 votes to 235. Church historians explain the defeat as the work of a staunch and militant minority of Evangelicals.

But it was the same old story: to be repeated so often in the history of the Church of England, and never more poignant than in the aftermath of the dreadful vote on the ordination of women to the priesthood in 1982. How can the House of Commons, made up of atheists, agnostics, other

Christians, Jews and Muslims dictate and decide the internal musings of the English Church? Way back in 1928 there were many in the Church who began to speak ever more loudly about disestablishment. It's odd, really, because I recall asking my teacher at primary school what as the longest word in the dictionary. "Antidisestablishmentarianism" she replied. I used to brag that I could spell the longest word in the English language. I hadn't a clue, however, what it meant. During most of my ministry I would nail my colours to that mast: I've changed sides now.

The simple argument about the Church's language was that it was archaic, unintelligible to the ordinary person and often misunderstood. When I 'persuaded' the PCC at Bolton-by-Bowland to try – experimentally for six months – a service with the new language, the following morning I was astonished to see four households displaying a large poster in their windows which cried out, in bold letters, "Save our Prayer Book". I actually devised, as part of that PCC discussion, a short questionnaire, in which I asked the councillors to write down the meaning of some of the phrases used in the Prayer Book. "Whither the twain shall meet.." and "...may prevent and follow us..." were two such phrases. There was not one correct translation. There was indeed huge misunderstanding and incomprehension amongst the members of the Church of England.

Tentative experiments were made. More, initially, to do with the *order* of Communion, since a recent discovery of an early second century liturgy had prompted revisers to return to this more authoritative outline. The Church of England's Series One Holy Communion Service was published in 1967 – at some point during my first year of training. The College used it almost exclusively. Mattins and Evensong were still according to the 1662 Book of Common Prayer. In short, the main emphasis of the new Series One was to bring together the entire age-range of the Family of GOD into one corporate act of worship. There was a growing popularity among church folk for this Family (or Parish) Communion. The quiet 8 o'clock Communion and the rather wordy Sung Mattins at 11am were making way for a new act of worship at a more convenient time mid way. And with this change there just *had* to be a radically new approach to preaching. At this juncture the two movements met and the onus of teaching practical preaching was even more heavily placed on the staff of seminaries. The total lack of communication between priest and people at the eight o'clock would not do. Neither would the complicated, technical, boring, lengthy verbosity of Morning Prayer.

"What shall I preach about?" the curate asked the verger. "About five minutes" he replied. "And if you don't strike oil in the first two minutes, stop boring!"

Instead of the sermon, therefore, the homily! Was there, is there, a difference? Yes. With the ushering in of the Family Communion with its wider age-range and backgrounds, the familiar "conversation" style of the homily was better suited. 'Sermon' has its derivative in 'speech' or discourse'; 'homily' on the other hand reflected a more informal, almost chatty, talk. Not that informality meant an empty, worthless content. On the contrary, the homily was to provide dynamic teaching: 'understanded of the people', as the old Book of Common Prayer prefaced its publication. The homily, therefore, because of its insistence on an intelligible vernacular and a relatively shorter time, demanded greater preparation, finer tuning and minimal wastage of words from the preacher. The skill of the preacher was to teach his people something of GOD's word in seven or eight minutes. That demanded scholarship and a deep knowledge of both theology and the listener. It was said of John Wesley that if he were asked to preach for one hour, he would do it straight away; for half an hour he would require a day's notice; for five minutes a whole week!

For me and my contemporaries sermon preparation and technique were taught within this climate and context. "Preaching at the Parish Communion" was a brand new approach but one whose challenge I have always loved. We were taught to begin each homily by writing where and when it was preached, the biblical text (if any) and, most importantly, the *aim*. At the conclusion of the sermon we were then bidden to ask ourselves if we really had fulfilled the aim. Quite sobering. Sermon classes were on Tuesday afternoons.

We missed out on some family time for the privilege. The whole group would troop off to the tiny church of St Mary Magdalene almost built in the wall on the corner of the castle square at Bailgate, next door to the famous White Hart Hotel. The student preacher would climb the pulpit steps whilst we, the critical congregation, positioned ourselves in various parts of the church, to ascertain whether he was audible. Armed with pen and paper we astonished ourselves in discovering how vitriolic and cruel we could be to our fellow-student, as we later met to dissect his sermon piece by piece. We were all rather raw and our performances pathetic. We could only get better.

I asked what part of my training held a lasting impression. All of these things: but surpassing them all was my experience of the College's Holy Week Liturgy. For three times in three years I was spellbound. Perhaps it was because I was new to this 'Catholicism thing', though by 1968 I was truly dyed in the wool. The worship from Palm Sunday to Easter Day was utterly moving. It touched my heart, my mind and my soul. I tried in the ensuing thirty seven Holy Weeks following my Ordination to imitate as much of the content of Lincoln as I could in my parish.

The Week at Lincoln was exacting. Palm Sunday, as one would expect, was a joyous and boisterous affair. Students, their wives and children processed around the college bearing their blessed palm crosses. All academic lectures were cancelled, of course, and were replaced with meditational addresses, delivered by various members of staff. There was much time given over for our own silent meditative reading. Even we married men had to stay and sleep in College: it was in effect a week's silent retreat, whose silence was broken only by our voices raised in worship and praise. Mealtimes, too, were silent. As we ate, we were read to: extracts from the spiritual classics which, perhaps surprisingly, contained some very jolly and humorous episodes. The Commemoration of the Last Supper on Maundy Thursday evening was held in the College chapel, after which we departed, like the disciples of old, across the Kedron Valley of Castle Square to hide ourselves in some remote corner of the vast cathedral. There, snuggled up in our cassocks and heavy serge cloaks (we all possessed one: £16 from the ecclesiastical tailor Noel Vasey of Wolverhampton) we endeavoured to keep watch with Christ for one hour. At the end of that hour a bell was softly tolled, Compline was said and we silently filed our way back to the College. A cup of hot soup was laid on in the kitchens. I had to go there, in any case, to perform my nightly duty of stoking up the large Aga.

On one Maundy evening there was much hilarity in the kitchens from us "disciples". It was all very untoward and inappropriate but sometimes the seriousness of the situation just makes it all the more silly. The housekeeper, Miss Pontefract, had thoughtfully left a great pan of soup on a low heated plate of the Aga cooker. She had, however, also inadvertently left behind two rather large pairs of her bloomers, which were drying on the stove's front rail. Regrettably the solemnity of the previous three hours was somewhat tarnished by the scene of ribaldry in the kitchen. 'Ponty's panties' was definitely one rite I would not be taking with me into my future parishes!

The whole College underwent "Choir Practice" in the chapel one morning each week. Whether you were a singer or a groaner, it was compulsory. We learnt splendid new hymns; we were taught the rudiments of plainchant and introduced to settings, both ancient and very modern, of the canticles and psalms. The contemporary music of Joseph Gelineau to these was very much in vogue. It was true to say that almost the whole of the French Church, both Catholic and Protestant, was using his new translations and music. He came to College to lecture and I still have his autograph, sellotaped into the back of my Bible, from that visit. The music and liturgy of Good Friday was exceptionally moving. Holy Saturday, too, continued the theme of being with the crucified Christ. After the morning devotions the afternoon was given over to some physical exertion. Staff and students alike were detailed with a variety of jobs. The College chapel was thoroughly spring-cleaned, de-Lented ready for the Paschal Feast the next day. The College gardens also were tidied and it had become tradition that a couple of students went to the churchyard of St Mary's Riseholme, a nearby village north of Lincoln, to spruce up the grave of Bishop Christopher Wordsworth, so that he, neglected during the year, might also be groomed for the coming celebrations.

Saturday evening and we were back in the chapel for the Easter Vigil, the lighting of the huge Paschal Candle and the renewal of our Baptismal promises. Then, next day, the celebration. And what a celebration! The College chapel was teeming with its usual family of students, their wives and highly excitable offspring, who had obviously got wind of a windfall of Easter eggs. At the Easter Eucharist lots of incense; magnificent music, all rehearsed, all thoroughly learnt; altar linen crisply laundered and vestments dazzling in their gold and white. Immediately after the Mass, the College children were out of their starting-blocks and into a frenzied search among the shrubs of the College garden for tiny Easter eggs, hidden by the Warden and his family some time before breakfast. Then a happy, noisy lunch for all. And the end of term.

The Holy Week liturgy was both hard work and easy. It was Anglican tradition at its best: our doctrine spelt out, played out, prayed out through our worship. That's how we Anglicans do it. Or used to.

Sporting Life

Sport has always been a large part of my life – in childhood, adolescence, youth and early manhood I kicked and passed and tackled and served and batted and bowled and ran and hopped and skipped and jumped. Note, they were all performed on terra firma. I was not one for water. I was an average player; I never made the first XI or XV at Ermysted's' but I had a good cricket average in the seconds, captained the third XV and always, it seemed, represented my school house in all the sprints and relays. I played soccer when not required by the school on Saturdays. By contrast, Lincoln Theological College sport was a very fringe affair. As I said, croquet was the major sporting interest. Lincoln was hardly Loughborough or Carnegie. We did, however, have a cricket team and we were privileged to play on rather fabulous grounds. Lincolnshire County's Lindum, for example, was a Minor Counties ground. Some Cambridge College grounds were set amidst the tall towers and trees and spires of that city. We played on immaculately-kept pitches of several RAF stations, which dotted up the Lincolnshire coast. There were several West Indians serving in the RAF and I imagine most were cricketers. Their spin bowling bedazzled us and we were always lucky to get fifty runs in an innings. I remember once at the crease trying to cope with the leg-breaks of such a bowler and at the same time being conscious of a huge dark cloud over the pitch, as a massive bomber flew across the sun from the nearby airfield. But they were always gracious in victory. Wherever we went we were royally entertained with massive teas for us and our supporters, which usually comprised of our families. Of course, we played on less attractive grounds – a local school staff gave us an annual fixture – and there were always the usual couple of 'pastoral' matches against the young energetic lads of the Borstal Institutions.

For my final two years I captained the College cricket team. Being Captain of Cricket was not as glamorous a rank as one might think. It meant corresponding with an opposite number to arrange a match; a fixture list had to be published; if we were playing another theological college then extra meals were ordered, as the fixture often evolved into a full-blown 'College Visit.' This worked both ways, of course. I recall a handful of visits to the Society of the Sacred Mission at Kelham and to the College of the Resurrection at Mirfield, where post-match Festal Evensong in their respective glorious chapels made pale our sporting antics on the field. Being Captain of Cricket also entailed having a neat catering hand, as I unfailingly and single-handedly buttered and filled several loaves-full of sandwiches for the team and our opponents.

Similarly for my last two years I was elected Captain of the College soccer team. (A funny word 'soccer'. It comes, of course, from 'association', the type of football which distinguishes it from rugby football. As a small boy I was always fascinated by my Grandad Vaughan's pronunciation of the word: 'sosser' he would say; and since it derives from 'association' I reckon he was correct). Since there were under fifty men from which to select a team it was always a nightmare trying to cajole someone to fill in the gaps on the team sheet, especially when the east wind blew and the rain was doing its very worst. Strangely, though, we always managed to field eleven players. The College even had its own football strip. The shirts, at least: purple with gold sleeves! Are they the Queen's racing colours? They were certainly very ecclesiastical. Very 'catholic'. We invariably played the same teams we had met the previous season on the cricket square. The results were invariably the same as well.

We had six or seven keen footballers, some quite good. Ivor Jones in goal; Jimmy Wheatley a sturdy, Geordie defender; fellow-Geordie, ardent Socialist Ron Mitchinson, strong and built like a tank; John Crust, a rosy-cheeked farmer's son from rural Lincolnshire, over six feet tall and mighty. In the forward line three East Lancashire lads: Peter Grierson, quick inside right and loyal Burnley supporter from Nelson; Peter Wilson, equally quick inside left from Accrington and, sadly, a Manchester United supporter; and me. Oddly, though we three came from neighbouring towns and the same diocese, we never met until we arrived at Lincoln. The chief task of Captain of Football, as you can deduce from the afore-mentioned team-sheet, was to cajole and bribe four others to wear the gold and purple! Never an easy task but I did it.

The Borstal boys were fleet and cunning in their play. We normally lost to them. We almost always beat Anglo-Catholic theological colleges, these games played in a most friendly and charitable spirit. Evangelical colleges, however, were a different kettle of fish. These teams would enter into a pre-match ritual around the centre-circle. A tamer version of the All Blacks' 'Haka': a time of prayer. After which, at the first blow of the referee's whistle, they would proceed to hack and kick and chop at us with the ferocity of the previously described Maoris. Kelham was our bogey team. It always had been. No one knew if we had ever beaten them. We probably hadn't. Past records indicated losses of 12-nil,13-1. Kelham Theological College was part of a working Anglican monastery and seminary. It trained young men of sixteen on a lengthy academic course, consisting of GCSEs and 'A' levels and ultimately leading to a qualification in theology and Ordination. Consequently its football team was made up of energetic, over-active and often frustrated young men, whose turn of speed and general athleticism left us thirty-somethings somewhat gasping.

We were due to play this young old enemy one February afternoon. For the life of me, I could only persuade nine players from our College to turn out. Rumours of 12-nil drubbings do nothing for one's confidence, especially if one turns up merely to make up the numbers. In desperation – and technically against the rules, I suppose – I accepted the help of two chaps from the teacher training college up the road. We were playing on their pitch, so they had not far to travel! The match plan was exceedingly simple. We had eleven men behind the ball. When the opposition challenged we put our entire weight (which was quite substantial!) fairly but squarely into the man. Thus winded, bruised, and battered the Kelham boys were not unnaturally put off their game. Midway through the second half we scored a goal and then proceeded to deploy every time-wasting game tactic we could conjure. The final whistle blew. We had won a magnificent historical victory. The young lads could not believe it. Neither could we. It was akin to winning the FA Cup. We returned, skipped Evensong and celebrated in the pub.

As was tradition at College, special notices were always announced before formal dinner. I informed the Sub-Warden of our first-ever glorious triumph over Kelham. The news was greeted by College members with disinterested amusement. By comparison, we jubilant conquerors of Kelham, like naughty schoolboys, were brought down to size and severely reprimanded for missing Evensong.

Early in the New Year, the beginning of the Lent term at Lincoln, final year men began to consider the exciting prospect of their 'first parish'. The move was a very important one in terms of future ministry. Since 'serving one's title' – being assigned to your first parish – was to be seen as a continuation of your training, it was essential that a good 'training vicar' was found. Equally essential was a good training parish: one where there were lots of opportunities to learn one's trade, lots of activity, plenty of lay involvement and encouragement, faithful worship and a positive attitude to the mission of GOD. Much prayer, therefore, to the Holy Spirit. His guidance was vital in this auspicious step on the vocational journey.

One winter's morning I received a letter from Arthur Lawes. Arthur had been a curate in Barnoldswick at the time of our Wedding. It was he who had asked us, amidst the furore with my father, if we were giving up enough! Arthur was now rector of two small villages in the East Riding. He wrote to say that there was a vacancy for a new deacon at St Mary's Beverley, that he had mentioned my name and, if I were interested, to get in touch. Ann and I were both elated by the news and decided that I should see the Warden, seeking his permission to pursue it.

As soon as I entered his study and before I had time to explain my visit, Alan said that he had received that very morning a letter from a Vicar in the Coventry Diocese seeking a new ordinand. He thought the parish ideal for me. It had been previously decided by Canon Schofield, my Director of Ordinands, Blackburn Diocese and my College, that I should not return to my home diocese, because of the pressure from my father and members of the family.(I had actually, inadvertently, been given a copy of such a letter by the Warden, hidden in some other correspondence addressed to me).

At that time Coventry Diocese was widely known and highly admired. Had we not seen television pictures of the construction of its brand new cathedral in 1962? I vividly recall seeing on TV the fixing of the final tall metal spire, carried aloft by a RAF helicopter. The zigzag shape of

Sir Basil Spence's new cathedral had literally grown out of the ashes of the old cathedral, destroyed by German bombers on November 1940. His new building was a fabulous amalgam of so many materials. At the Consecration in May 1962 the Archbishop of Canterbury had referred to the building as "a house in which all the arts and craftsmanship of our time have been united: stone, wood, glass, metal; the designer, the builder, the painter, the sculptor; a generation has made its offering of beauty in the service of God." With the birth of this new Mother Church came a whole host of exciting ministries: industrial mission, a chaplaincy to the polytechnic and initiatives into schools, an ecumenical venture and even an international enterprise with the establishment of its Cross of Nails links. Graham Sutherland's tapestry of Christ in Glory, the Baptistry windows, the Chapel of Gethsemane, Epstein's bronze sculpture of St Michael and (my favourite) John Hutton's enormous west screen, a vast wall of glass panels carved with an array of angels and saints. All symbolised a brand new beginning, a dynamic impulse to the proclamation of the Gospel in our time.

The whole College had spent a couple of days in October 1968 at the John Kennedy House, a purpose-built centre adjacent to the cathedral for mission to youth. We students had explored there in those two days the whole canvas of Christian mission, as Coventry exercised it. It was a memorable time for most of us and certainly for me.

"It's a parish called Wyken" the Warden explained, "on the north east edge of Coventry. Thirty thousand people. Vicar and three curates. The Vicar would like you to get in touch." Arthur's letter about Beverley never came out of my pocket. Thrilled with the prospect of Coventry, I said I was very interested and would await contact from the Vicar, the Reverend Kenneth Bradford. I dashed home to tell Ann the even latest of latest news. This, I believe, was yet another indication of the Spirit's prompting along the route of God's calling.

Mr Bradford wrote to me in positive terms. I replied. He said he would like to see me, talk things over, and in this respect would bring along a small group of parish representatives to meet me, Ann and the boys. The day he chose was a Saturday in early spring. The same day as the College's Open Day.

'COCKTAIL' SHAKER!

Young Christians' smut
angers the elders

"COCKTAILS" with a kick like a mule — and a risqué mule at that — have angered members of the Barnoldswick Independent Methodist Church.

When a revue called "Cocktails" was presented in the Sunday school by the local Young Christians, several members of the audience walked out in protest against the show.

They say the show was "disgusting," and that the church should have had nothing to do with it. And they allege that the script was drastically altered after it had been vetted and approved by church officials.

The show — which was modelled to a large extent on "That Was The Week That Was" — referred considerably to Christine Keeler and her associates. It made a parody of the 23rd Psalm, and poked fun at local churches and clergymen.

But the Young Christians, who staged the show on Friday and Saturday night, don't agree that the show was in any way disgusting. They deny altering the script, but admit that the show "probably made some people angry."

Barnoldswick & Early Times reports on our revue,
"Cocktail" of 1963

Barnoldswick C E (Controlled) School, where God's prods began

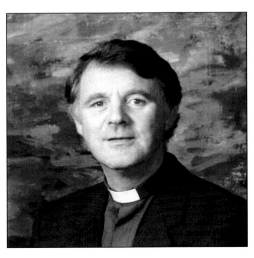

A picture of me in 1988

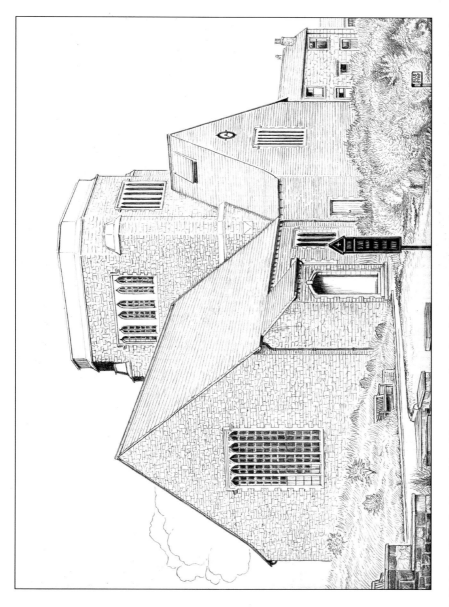

Holy Trinity Church, Barnoldswick. From a drawing by local artist Frank Cunnington showing the original tower.

Clergyman explains opposition to women priests

RECTOR'S NAME ON SHOCK LIST

The Clitheroe Advertiser's front page headline on December 22nd 1988

A RIBBLE Valley rector put his name to a national campaign this week against the ordination of women priests.

Fr Trevor Vaughan, rector of SS Peter and Paul's Church, Bolton-by-Bowland, is one of 1,500 clergymen who have openly refused to accept the ordination of women into the Anglican Church.

The shock list, published in the national press this week, includes the names of 20 bishops, 11 archdeacons, and the Dean of St Paul's Cathedral.

Fr Vaughan, who is also priest in charge of St Ambrose Church, Grindleton, is the only Ribble Valley clergyman in the list.

Fr Vaughan (47) spoke to the "Advertiser and Times" about why he is against the move, even though observers claim that it may cause the biggest split in the Church of England for hundreds of years.

"I am not a reactionary, but I call upon all Christians in the Ribble Valley to pray earnestly so that we may reach the right decision in what is going to be a grave and confusing time for us all," he said.

Fr Vaughan pointed out Grindleton parishioners had told him they were against ordination, while Bolton-by-Bowland was more evenly divided.

by JOHN DOVER

Opponents of ordination of women say they will risk their careers and livelihoods fighting the move, while others have intimated that they intend to work from within the existing church to oppose it.

Fr Vaughan said he could see a time of tribulation and considerable confusion in his parish if the church ordains women priests.

"Things would be more complicated if the diocese appointed a woman bishop. Alternatives would have to be found, but what they would be I

● continued on page 16

76

With Ann, Philip and Matthew showing the family side
of college life for the new prospectus

Lincoln Theological College staff and students in 1968.
The warden Alan Webster is seated front row centre. I'm 3rd row up and 2nd from left.

Life-like caricature of Bishop Cuthbert Bardsley who ordained me.

The Collegiate Church of the Holy Trinity
Stratford-upon-Avon

Shakespeare Sunday

29th April, 1973

11.00 a.m.

Front cover of the service for Shakespeare Sunday during my time there. RSC actors Richard Pascoe and Brenda Bruce read the Lessons.

Aerial view of the parish of Monks Kirby. The vicarage is in the copse near top left of picture.

The Open Day was a new initiative for the College. Perched on the top of the highest hill in the county, we looked down on the seething city in our comfortable surroundings. It was quite rightly felt that the city's theological college should make itself more widely known to the people of Lincoln. We were engaged in some aspects of civic life but really we were only skimming the surface. To be fair, we students had limited time: study was the priority. But some of us were involved in the county-wide Industrial Mission, which had a presence in Lincoln's larger engineering firms; college men did visit the youth offenders' institutions and some of us were weekly prison visitors; we all experienced a smattering of teaching practice at local schools and each Sunday, groups of us students would work the wards at both the County and St George's Hospitals. Yet the rank and file of city folk probably had not even heard of us. The Open Day was to address this problem.

It would be a mixture of many things. Part Garden Party, part exhibition, part demonstration; a sort of day-time 'parents evening' where the townsfolk could come and see at first-hand what theological college students were doing and why they were doing it. People from parishes in the wider diocese were also welcomed. So there was an opportunity to inform people of the Church's mission. Much publicity was made of the event, many came and it was a success.

Because I had suggested a five-a-side football competition, it was left to me to organise it. The city's youth clubs were invited to join in a knock-out competition, which would take place on the College's clay tennis court. We had a good response and half a dozen of us students fielded a team for the fun of it...

The weather was fine and dry, ideal for football. The (few) tennis aficionados of the College were not at all pleased that we were kicking up the clay but needs must for the greater glory of God. The trouble was that the clay *did* kick up. Participants were like ancient Britons covered, not in the blue of woad, but in the terracotta of clayey clart. Sweat and perspiration ensured that the colour stuck. It was whilst I was looking like a Flower-pot Man that Ann appeared, with the Vicar and reps from Wyken in tow! She had been looking after them most of the afternoon. It was a crazy first meeting. I was exhausted (we had just been beaten in the semi-final) and could not properly engage brain and mouth for several minutes. However, the informal 'interview' must have gone very well, since I was invited to visit Wyken and stay at the Vicarage. Luckily Kenneth was a keen sportsman, cricket and rugby union being his chief interests. He obviously approved of some future curate, however, who could organise an event and get physically involved in it as well. Not that he ever said that to me. He would often refer to our first meeting at that College Open Day, "when Trevor looked a sight". With his dry sense of humour, he always insisted that it was *Ann* who had got me the job!

All was set for my new posting and for a brand new life for Ann, me and the boys. It wasn't, of course, the end of the story of my vocation. God's call continues. Even now in my retirement. The story so far, however, has indicated how God has guided and led us through many obstacles and hurdles to arrive at where we are.

CHAPTER FOUR

Parishes

A Magnum of the Holy Spirit

In my first chapter I used the metaphor of Christian ministry as a ship. It is not inappropriate. There are connotations of a church's nave with that of a boat from which our Lord preached and taught the crowds and revealed His miraculous power. 'Nave' and 'navy' share the same etymology. The Church is often portrayed as a ship. Both St Jude's and St Anselm's symbol is that of a boat, as is that of the World Council of Churches, in which the mast is the cross of Christ. Despite the maritime imagery, the voyage of my ministry was entirely landlocked. It took us to and from the Midlands. My story recounts the aspirations, the design and planning of this 'ministry' ship upon the drawing-boards of youth and early marriage in Barnoldswick and Colne. Then its building in the dry-dock of Lincoln. From there to its commissioning, its naming ceremony. Recently we enjoyed a holiday cruise on the new cruise-liner 'Ventura'. Only six weeks before our trip, the actress Dame Helen Mirren had named the vessel. Her portrait hung in one of the main areas of the ship. She was described as Ventura's *sponsor*. A word commonly used for 'godparent'. Ordination was my commissioning or naming. Some ordinands, like monks or nuns at their own professing, take on an extra name. I didn't go that far but the service in Coventry Cathedral was like the launching of a newly-built, newly-named vessel. I was sent, 'apostled', by the magnum of the Holy Spirit which broke upon my head at the hands of Cuthbert, my Father-in-God.

What a wonderful service it was! 'Awesome' is an over-used word today. It should only be employed in the context of the divine. This was. On Trinity Sunday, June 1st 1969, I, with half a dozen other men, were made deacons. A similar number of deacons were returning for a further laying-on of hands to be ordained priests. Would-be deacons and would-be priests together had shared three nights in retreat at Offchurch, the Diocesan Retreat and Conference House since the previous Thursday. Deep in the Warwickshire countryside, yet near to Leamington Spa, the House had been a Vicarage up to 1961. The surrounding countryside afforded the ideal criteria for a retreat: many lanes for the solitary and meditational strolls that retreatants could and should make. Since its development the former vicarage possessed an attractive, homely purpose-built chapel and its score of single study-bedrooms each carried a parish name on the door. Appropriately I was allocated 'Wyken'

Our pre-Ordination retreat began on Thursday afternoon. We had reported to the cathedral and were put through our paces in a very thorough rehearsal for the real thing on Sunday morning. The Precentor, Canon Joseph Poole, was a skilful liturgiolist and he tackled every conceivable aspect of the Ordination service. What I vividly remember in what was generally a tense, excitable blur was our entrance up into the great building from the Undercroft. As we nervously climbed the steps in pairs we had to align ourselves, once on the level surface, with a line of pennies set in the gleaming granite of the north aisle. In Coventry the north aisle was actually west, since Sir Basil Spence's cathedral had been designed and built on a south-north axis. In the huge majority of English churches the altar is at the east end. Because of the lie of the available land adjacent to the mediaeval cathedral, which suffered devastating bombing in 1940, the new High Altar was situated almost due north. The coins, dated 1962 the year of the Cathedral's consecration, were placed in two parallel lines every few strides. These were a guide, a railway track almost, an aid to all who formed liturgical processions. A simple but great idea! The last time I visited the place of my ordination the coins were still there, bright coppers honed with the continual tread of crucifers, choirs and clergy. After our exacting rehearsal we were driven to Offchurch and our silent retreat commenced in earnest. Bishop Cuthbert Bardsley himself conducted the sessions, seven in all, from Thursday evening to Saturday night.

I recall, too, the dread thrill of the several hands which were laid – quite heavily – on my head. And the accompanying realisation of the duty now bestowed upon me. Despite all the emotion – the fears, frustrations and the fun – that preceded that moment which brought me to the Bishop and his cathedral, I felt that this was the beginning of the beginning. God had got me there. I'd give it my best, my very best.

We deacons were presented with a slim leather-bound copy of the New Testament. Those ordained priests received the full Bible. Father Mark Meynell, the Vicar of Leamington Hastings and my new Diocesan Director of Ordinands, preached the sermon. His text was from St John's first epistle. By some strange coincidence the red ribbon marker in my new gift was inserted on the page of his text. I mentioned it to him at a Post-Ordination Training Day not long after. He didn't seem surprised at all by this fluke: he simply smiled as if minor miracles happened every day. Or had he furtively 'fixed' every deacon's scriptures with the book marker?

Toughening up

Wyken had been a small village off the A46 trunk road to Leicester until the 'back to business' 1950s, when post-war Britain slowly began to finds its feet once more. An immense building project resulted in thousands of homes being constructed around the tiny ancient church of St Mary Magdalene. The church was a quaint edifice, having a pitched tiled roof set on its tower, and a narrow nave with a central aisle. Its stone structure predated its surrounding red brick brood by over eight centuries. The development, all to the west of the main trunk road, must have amassed a population of some twenty thousand. On the other side of the A46, to the east, a daughter church had been built to serve the people there. On the very day that the Second World War broke out, September 1939, the Church of the Holy Cross was hallowed and consecrated. The two churches happily served the parish of Wyken until this explosion of population. The Holy Cross 'side' itself was by no means static in this explosion. It also grew at a great rate. So much so that when I arrived in the parish in 1969 there were some 30,000 souls. To cope with this influx a new church complex had been built adjacent to the old church. The Church of the Risen Christ was a splendid plant. Its open-planned rectangular nave had a spacious sanctuary shaped in a hemisphere and bordered by an altar-rail which emphasised the faithful gathered *round* the Lord's table. The pews themselves were set in the round to complement the motif. This 'church' section was one side of a square of buildings. Classrooms, and meeting rooms formed one other side; a huge hall yet another, whilst on the fourth side stood a welcoming glass entrance foyer leading down to a well-equipped kitchen and toilets. In the middle of this square arrangement was a landscaped garden with several seats. Unfortunately this area was much under-used but a fine idea, nevertheless. The parish was magnificently organised. There were provisions for four full-time clergy – the Vicar and his three curates, though this never materialised as far as I knew. I became the junior member of the staff of three in June 1969. However, the ministry of the laity was superb. Men and women were committed leaders of every uniformed organisation; there were two choirs and dedicated organists; a huge, active youth club; bands of servers and hosts of hard-working people of every age. The Mothers Union members were like an extra curate in the amount of work they performed. It was, in every respect, an excellent training parish. I have counted myself indeed fortunate to have learned my trade there.

When a student leaves his place of theological training he is assigned to a parish. There he is about to put into practice all the theory he has hopefully amassed at college. A good 'training vicar' is therefore essential. Kenneth Bradford had the task of converting all my biblical knowledge, doctrine and worship into an effective and functioning parish priest. He had become Vicar of Wyken in 1967, succeeding a man who was destined for preferment and who did eventually become a suffragan bishop. Kenneth was a Bristolian who had left school in his mid-teens and worked in the insurance business in that city. He felt called to the ordained ministry in his early thirties and studied theology under Michael Ramsey at Durham University, where he gained a First

Class degree. There are not many graduates in theology in the Church of England, let alone those with a First. He loved Durham and despite his South West roots always referred to Durham as "God's own county." He served all of his early ministry in the North East, including the industrial towns of Pallion and Shildon. He became a Governor of the High Church college of St Chad's in Durham and relished the academe. His chief focus, however, was always the parochial ministry. An ardent parish visitor – " a house-going parson means a church-going people" – who went out every afternoon in all weathers. This visiting had its source in the daily Eucharist and the holy sacraments. His background was non-Conformist. He told me once that his aunt, a faithful Baptist lady, attended his first ever celebration of Holy Communion after his priesting, but he refused to allow her to receive Communion because she was not an Anglican! I think he would act differently today but that was the seriousness of his vocation. He was a clever man, a spiritual priest, a fine teacher and possessed a gentle if somewhat idiosyncratic humour. How he was never offered preferment – even Rural Dean or Canon – I do not know.

Kenneth fell ill with tuberculosis which left a permanent disability in his right arm. His supportive wife Joyce sewed long zips into the right sleeve of all his jackets, coats and cassock, so that he could get his arm into the clothing. The Durham diocese, along with his medical advisers suggested he move to warmer climes 'down south'. He therefore left his beloved Durham and was inducted into the living of Ratcliffe and Rearsby in the Leicester Diocese. Joyce's sister Peggy was Headmistress of the Girls' Grammar School in the city and it proved to be a good move for the family, as Peggy, too, was able to provide all kinds of help to Joyce and Ken and their children Michael and Helen.

Before long, however, Kenneth's health greatly improved and he itched to take on a larger challenge. From a few hundred parishioners in rural Leicestershire he travelled some 30 miles south on the A46 to minister to an immense suburban parish of 30,000 in Wyken on the north-east edge of the city of Coventry. I know that Joyce would have preferred the quiet calm of the countryside – but who am I to talk? Like Joyce with Kenneth, Ann has followed me, started up again, wherever I have felt moved to go.

Our arrival in Wyken coincided with the Vicar's day off, Friday. He had written and apologised to me about his being "ruthless" in his observance of his 'sabbath' but, he said, it was necessary. Even then, he always conducted Friday morning School Assembly before starting his day off! He had, on this particular Friday, the day of our arrival in the parish, arranged lunch for us all at Mrs Terry's, an elderly widow in whose home the other curate lodged. She would also look after our two boys. It was most kind of her but we neither needed a meal nor a baby-sitter. In his letter he also enclosed a list of activities in which I would be involved during my first week after Ordination. He didn't waste any time! The list, which I still possess, was as follows:

June 2   your day off

June 3   Chapter meeting in morning for Trevor

June 5   Mothers' Union Outing for Trevor (pastoral necessity. No expense – clergy go free!)

June 7   Wyken Carnival. Trevor carries a bucket to collect en route – but so do the other clergy!

June 8   Trevor preaches at Evensong H Cross (& takes service)

June 9   your day off

Kenneth would often hand me notes or written instructions concerning work. *"Staff Meetings,"* he headed one such set of briefings, *"necessary to prepare for this: 1. Bring last sermon. 2. Bring any fees. 3. Bring (1) Baptism forms collected from Mrs Francis (2) Marriage forms – banns read and published (3) Funeral cards (4) List of people visited (5) Any reports of meetings attended (6) Special comments.*

He would also write letters to mark very special occasions. I arrived at the Diocesan Retreat House at Offchurch to begin my retreat before my Priest's Ordination to find a letter from him waiting for me.

"My Dear Trevor, So you come to the last lap before being ordained priest" he began. He advised that I relax in the presence of God and lay aside *"all parish worries and even family worries...in the silence which can be so fruitful and satisfying. At priesting we come naked of soul*

before God who knows us through and through and yet there is the terrifying thought that He is prepared to accept and use us."

He went on to say that I had "served faithfully in my diaconate with a humility and loyalty that is too uncommon these days...[and] brought a sense of ministering more deeply than just the passing popular fashion. So often youth work is so shallow."

He had one criticism of my short ministry: that of my use of time. "You are so willing that you get into a jam and you must think over your priorities, which will be ever more important once a priest. Pressures of time and work and family will come upon you...particularly when celebrating the Eucharist you will just have to be on time...[just as] the factory worker...even if he has a wife and three children." He reminded me that discipline of time is vital; funeral calls must not be made at the last moment. I must also limit pastoral calls to twenty minutes.

Kenneth warned me that my first year as a priest would be "toughening...harder perhaps than you ever imagined when you offered yourself for ordination...but the tougher the job, the greater the grace of God." He knew me well and he was brave enough to spell out the negatives among the positives. I hope and pray that I practised his sound and pastoral advice in the priesthood which was to follow. "Ann is such a grand wife and mother" he added and concluded by asking for my prayers and "God's forgiveness for my many faults which must hinder and exasperate you." He assured me of his continual prayers every day. He signed off the letter "Yours sincerely in Dno (Domino), The Boss."

It was indeed a 'toughening' year. The whole of my three years in Wyken was an incredibly steep learning curve. The operative word being 'learning'. Learning the work of a priest: marrying that which we assimilated in our studies at college with the practical everyday experience of the parochial rounds. Within months of my priesting John the senior curate left for his second curacy. For quite a while no one was appointed to replace him, which meant that my Vicar, with me as a very inexperienced assistant curate, had to run this huge parish. The Sunday schedule was a heavy one: a said Holy Communion at the little ancient church at 8am. We alternated with that. Kenneth mainly celebrated at the 9.30am Parish Eucharist at Holy Cross, whilst I did the equivalent at our modern church of The Risen Christ. There were also two evening services in the parish; the vicar officiated at Risen Christ with the Book of Common Prayer Evensong and I was allowed the privilege of conducting experimental worship at Holy Cross. There, Sunday by Sunday, we encouraged scores of enthusiastic teenagers to participate in new forms of worship, in which they contributed by singing, playing their instruments or drama. It wasn't all modern fare: we learnt plainchant and sang the Compline Office to that haunting music for several weeks. We were blessed also with a group of older, regular worshippers, who by their very presence were a source of support to the younger element and were, naturally, extremely pleased to see their church so lively and so full.

The parish ultimately did receive another curate. An American priest who had decided to serve in England. There was an obvious 'gap' in his c.v. but Kenneth did not query it too closely. After a year with us he was suddenly hospitalised. Our new curate had been very badly beaten up in the gents' toilets in the city centre. He had given the police my telephone number (rather than Kenneth's) and, in the hope of by-passing the Vicar, requested that I visit him as soon as possible. In reality I had no other choice but to inform Kenneth. Consequently we both went to the hospital. In the ward we passed by his bed, failing to recognise him on account of his severe injuries. It was abundantly clear what had transpired. The Archdeacon advised his speedy exit back to the United States. So it was that four days later I drove him in his spacious Ford Cortina estate car to Birmingham Airport, where he left our shores. He also left the folk of the parish to clear his flat, pay his bills and sell his car.

His replacement arrived from one of our country's former African colonies. Sadly, he too had come to us under a confidential Archbishop's Licence, indicating some past misdemeanour. Within months of his arrival it was time for me to move on. I did hear, however, that he was embroiled in some incident in a Children's Home. The Diocese of Coventry did not play fair with Kenneth, or with the parishioners of Wyken. Its efficacy in parish mission and worship was second to none. Wyken ought to have had a steady stream of young ordinands, who would have been guaranteed a splendid training – by both priest and people – and gone on to serve the Church of the future. Yet again the

Church of England showed itself to be completely inept in its forward thinking.

My last Sunday in Wyken featured a joint Parish Eucharist at Holy Cross, when the two halves of the Great Divide (the A46) got together to say 'Farewell'. May 14th 1972, the Sunday after the Ascension. Kenneth preached about the Ascended Christ, Who is both King and High Priest.

Towards the end of his sermon he made reference to me: *"This parish has been very fortunate in those who have served it as God's priests. In that succession Trevor Vaughan has taken his place and earned our gratitude by the sweetness and diligence of his ministry. He has been humble enough to learn and therefore God has been able to raise his ministry to great heights."* The last sentence was a quotation from Cardinal Heenan, which Kenneth wrote out on a separate sheet and enclosed it in his gift to Ann and me: Pevsner's book on Warwickshire, in The Buildings of England series. An appropriate gift as we were heading off southwards (still on the old A46) to Stratford upon Avon.

Steamed up

Stratford was a very different kettle of fish. The ecclesiastical parish of Holy Trinity contained the whole town. There was, I understand, another Anglican parish in the town but the church of St James was demolished as an unsafe building many years ago. Included in the parish was the village of Bishopton, where there was no church. Also the two villages of Shottery and Luddington. Shottery was a mile west of Stratford and the home of Shakespeare's mother, Anne Hathaway. Her cottage, part of which is C15th, remains a firm 'must' for the thousands of tourists who come to 'do' Shakespeare. St Andrew's church there was built in 1870, of light coloured brick. Luddington All Saints was erected two years later and is situated some 3 miles south west of the town. These made up, with the town's church, the trinity of Holy Trinity parish. Within this ecclesiastical patch – and therefore in its care – was the very ancient Guild Chapel. Founded before 1269 it continued to hold divine service, albeit reduced (in my day) to one mid-week weekly service of Holy Communion. The chapel had a small regular congregation. As they knelt there each week they were surrounded by the magnificent wall-painting over the chancel arch, which dramatically depicted the Doom. There Christ stood reigning in majesty, flanked by Our Lady and His beloved disciple St John. Hell was painted on the right and Heaven, with St Peter, on the left. Numerous resurrection figures completed the vibrant scene.

These four buildings of worship were served by a Vicar and three curates. The senior curate in the group was John Panting whose chief concern of pastoral care was St Andrew, Shottery. John was a jolly chap who, I seem to remember, laughed loudly and laughed a lot. Sadly he died at too early an age. Only very occasionally did he venture into town and assist at Holy Trinity.

John and his wife Harriet had three small daughters of primary school age. They were rather a handful. The Vicar labelled them "the girls from St Trinian's." The lasses were outrageously eccentric but rather fun to be observed. One week-end, I recall, the three of them set up camp – tent, sleeping bags, food – on the roundabout on the busy Stratford to Evesham road. On another occasion Ann and I called on their parents only to discover the girls hurling all manner of their mother's dressing-table items out of the upstairs bedroom window. To make matter worse, their mother was outside the front door completely in the full range of fire. Her protestations only seemed to encourage her offspring in their practice of field events.

Clifford Robinson was the remaining member of the team which I joined in May 1972. He had the responsibility of All Saints', Luddington, though there were only monthly services there. Clifford was a kindly man who had been ordained in his early fifties, a year after me. In fact I first met him at our ordinations, when I was priested and he deaconed. He had owned his own engineering business in Coventry and found it most difficult to concede that I, some twenty years younger, was actually the *senior* curate at Holy Trinity. This attitude made teamwork somewhat strained and laboured. It was equally testing for the Vicar, for he and Clifford were of a similar age. On a brighter note, Clifford owned a Labrador puppy which he began to train. Part of that training was for the dog to accompany him in his car on his parish rounds. After one visit, however, Clifford returned to his car to discover that the puppy had eaten the steering-wheel: completely and utterly. A mere stub of a hub, where the horn would be, remained!

Peter Barnes was our Vicar. An outwardly peaceable man, composed, courteous and capable. A Cambridge graduate he had trained for ministry at Ridley Hall in the same University city. His was a middle-of-the-road churchmanship and, whilst he was most tolerant, he obviously had little time for any Catholic externals. Despite this suspicion he was obliged to wear vestments at the Parish Communion. It was the tradition there. I suppose he could have changed the practice but his good tolerance and common sense let things be. He was certainly broad-minded as regards my ever-escalating High Church views. I began to miss the daily Mass at Wyken: sometimes I would not be on the rota to celebrate for over a week and I longed for some of the Catholic ambience of my former parish. Absence made my heart grow fonder!

Yet Peter Barnes allowed me to hear my first Confession, encouraged me with the Youth Club, the membership of which was made up of very bright boys and girls from the town's two grammar schools. He also commended my work with the lads from the 'down town' area in Stratford and my weekly children's Lent course, "Good Food" which I ran in conjunction with Oxfam.

The town was endowed with an immense variety of organisations, some sacred, most secular. Guilds of this, Companies of that, Associations of the other. These titles were so given, I am sure, because of the mediaeval temper which ran through the town. These, along with many other such bodies from further afield, were always requesting to hold their special celebratory events with an act of worship in 'Shakespeare's Church'. The Worshipful Company of Cordwainers asked to stage some special service there. Peter Barnes welcomed the members from all parts of the country. The text of his sermon for these gentlemen manufacturers of shoes was from St Matthew's Gospel chapter 20, verse 16: "The *last* will be first." That perfectly summed up Peter. Amid the serious demeanour lay a bright, twinkling humour. He was, inwardly, something of a contrast.. He must have taken on board lots of parish hassle, mentally and spiritually. Almost every Tuesday morning he was absent from Morning Prayer: the recurrence of his migraines. I hope his curates were not responsible, since Monday afternoons were Staff Meetings at the Vicarage.

As Vicar of Stratford he was asked to serve on a plethora of committees, civil as well as ecclesiastical. Stratford, of course, had more than its share of very able people. The town attracted many intellectuals, as did the parish church. Parochial Church Council meetings were therefore brimming with expertise but these, I would suggest, did not enhance the task of the chairman, the Vicar. Moreover, he had his own 'private war': not with the church folk but with the townspeople at large. He conducted an endless campaign against dog-fouling in and around Old Town. This lovely area included Hall's Croft, the splendid parish church and the delightful leafy road between them. And his Vicarage. He would regularly write to the local weekly 'Herald' urging dog owners to pick up their pet's deposit. And he practised what he preached. Beyond the call of duty, he would probe the pavements, 'poopers' in hand.

In the Church's liturgy he appeared less pro-active. His sermons were thoughtful and learned, though I recall his saying, much to my horror, that the Church ought not to expect the faithful to be at worship every week. The laity had other leisure commitments to fulfil, he said, so that once a fortnight would be acceptable. I trotted out the old argument that every Sunday was a celebration of the Resurrection and that, whether we like it or not, it came round every *seven* days.

The Americans, especially, who visited the church for Sunday worship, lapped up everything on offer. The ancient church building with the River Avon flowing behind it, the first-class music of our church choir, the actual grave of the Bard within the sanctuary: they genuinely delighted in everything. And because a great many American tourists are Christian, they equally loved the hymns and prayers and sermons. Often they would comment on the sermon at the church door to the preacher – always favourably. Sometimes the day's preacher would receive in the post a letter of appreciation for the spoken word. I received one such complimentary letter once. The notepaper was headed "The Stratford upon Avon Hilton" and signed by somebody who was "The Third". We were one of the first churches to install a radio microphone. For several weeks after this technical innovation Peter Barnes' sermons were 'on the hoof ', as he walked and talked his way down the aisles and transepts, stopping at various pews to ask questions or glean comments on the particular theme of his sermon.

There was one visitor who occupied the same pew at the very back of the church. He was a regular worshipper and was conspicuous amongst the hundreds of worshippers because he always entered the church after the first hymn but before the Gospel reading. In addition, he was always the first to leave, moving quickly towards the door as soon as the final hymn was announced. Who was he? I asked the Vicar. "It's a former Bishop of Bradford" he replied, "He arrives late and leaves early, so that he doesn't have to speak to people!"

All of this took place within the wondrous setting of the parish church of the Holy Trinity. Even without the Bard's connection the building would still be an essential focus of pilgrimage for the tourists and trippers. Like most of this land's ancient churches, Stratford's is an amalgam of additions and later additions. The transepts and narrow aisles betray its C13th Early English origins; the tower its Perpendicular period of English architecture. The spire was once of timber but now, since the middle of the 1700s, built of stone.

Walking up the river bank from the Memorial Theatre the pale stone chancel is a sight to behold as it rises majestically beyond the river displaying its clerestory and many windows. From the town side and the north west gate there used to be (I hope there still is!) an avenue of limes, their siting enticing the visitor to explore inside. Beyond the church door is a trove of treasures to delight the pilgrim and the student of history, literature and architecture. The C14th font in which Stratford's favourite son was baptised; the sanctuary wherein lies his tomb. Each and every 23rd April hundreds, if not thousands, flock to this spot, bringing bouquets, bunches or even a single stem of flowers to mark his birthday. We clergy were deputed to receive these floral tributes and arrange them around his memorial. Naturally, the sanctuary was full to over-flowing. The entire sacred space was carpeted in blooms of every hue. The words on the tomb contained a curse: "Bleste be the man that spares these stones, and curst be he that moves my bones." The alabaster half-bust of the playwright also stands there. Sculpted in 1616, the year of his death, it is reckoned to be the most accurate, life-like image we possess. With quill in hand, the bard appears, according to Pevsner, as a scholar or divine.

It was strange, our living in Stratford. In July 1964 Ann and I had our honeymoon at Cheltenham and spent a most memorable day in Stratford at the Shakespeare's Quatercentenary Exhibition. We purchased a wall-hanging of Henry V's Battle of Agincourt, dynamically painted in brilliant blues and gory reds, full of men and horses meeting the impact of sword or arrow. I am ever amazed how many full circles we humans make within our life.

Dozens of extra-curricular events took place in the town. The Literature Festival attracted highly appreciative audiences. Ann and I heard Mr Laurie Lee, author of 'Cider with Rosie', among other writers.

On a less glamorous scale, though equally thrilling, the annual Edwardian Steam Fair made its visit each July. Most of the 'travellers' who ran and managed the fair possessed a deep-seated religious faith. It was, therefore, customary to commence proceedings with a short act of worship. Traditionally, one member of the parish church staff led this opening service, and like St Matthias two millennia ago, 'the lot fell on me' to kick off the 1972 Steam Fair. A couple of prayers, the 'Our Father', a hymn bashed out on the steam organ (what else?) and a very short pithy homily from me was all that was required. It went exceedingly well and Ann, the children and I were treated royally by the Fair management. Afterwards we explored the myriads of rides and slides, the gaudy stalls selling candy floss, ice cream and pop. We tried our arm at Hook-a-Duck and Try Your Luck.

This latter was an intriguing contest. "Roll up!" the lady shouted to no one in particular. "Three darts to win a pound!" To the side of her stood a large board covered in £1 notes. They were worth something in 1972: most church collection plates were still buckling under the weight of *coins*! To win one pound sterling the thrower had to land his dart not only on the note but directly and precisely into the middle of the number "1" on the note. You might recall that there were two number ones on the old 'green', top right and bottom left, so technically the thrower had two chances. If it touched the edge then it didn't count. "Come on, Vicar!" she called "let's have a go!" I protested but only half-heartedly as I reckoned joining in these competitions would be a bit of kudos for the Church. "A quick prayer!" I jokingly replied, as I accepted her invitation. Rather flamboyantly I made a rough sign of the cross over my three arrows. My first throw struck the pound note. More than that: it firmly embedded itself exactly and unerringly within the aforesaid number. A 'clean 'dart, as they say. "You've won a pound!" the lady cried in disbelief. She handed me a £1 note. I, too, was dumbstruck. The sudden remembrance of my flippant blessing of the darts had made me realise that we should not mess about with the sacred. It rather scared me and I have never ever acted in similar fashion since. As we meandered our way around the ground, I could hear the voice of the lady on the dart stall. "Roll up! Roll up. Three darts to win a pound" she called, adding: "even the Vicar can do it!"

Where Wyken was *pastorally* organised, Stratford was *bureaucratically*. Within its brand new purpose-built parish hall, set opposite the church, was the Parish Office. Here worked a full-time Parish Secretary. She typed out and printed the weekly pew-sheet, the parish magazine, the church council agendas and minutes and even organised the publishing of banns of marriage and the writing up of the marriage registers. This reduction of work load, normally executed by the clergy, did allow much more time for outreach. Or so one would think. To my mind there seemed to be lots of areas in the town which were untouched by the Church. I suggested that we should make inroads into the two theatres. "I'm the theatre chaplain" the Vicar informed. "What about going into the factories on the edge of town?" I ventured. "That's my responsibility" said Clifford. It did not appear to me that the Church of God either set one foot back-stage or on the factory floor. Yet I got the message loud and clear that neither these areas were any concern of mine. I stuck to the ministry of young people – the Youth Club, Junior Church, Primary School and five-a-side football. Even in this sphere I always felt I was treading on clerical toes. So much so, that in frustration and desperation, I went to see Jesse Proctor, the saintly Archdeacon of Warwick, to air my problems. He listened carefully and with kindness. I reckon he was instrumental when, a few months later, I was asked to consider going to Monks Kirby and being priest-in-charge of the Wolvey Group. On the A46 yet again!

A Littlewood's Pools plan

'The Wolvey Group of Parishes' was a name dreamt up by someone in the Diocesan office. If you had asked any one of my future parishioners to describe it, they couldn't. Besides, nothing was official. When invited to go there I was informed by the Archdeacon of Coventry that these eight villages were to work together and form a united, unified whole. Easier said than done in the countryside. Then, whilst this plan was in process, I was to work steadily to effecting a large rural team ministry, More of that anon.

My new parish was already an amalgamation of several parishes. In times long ago, possibly four; certainly three in more recent history. Thus in the autumn of 1972 I was to have pastoral responsibility of two large rural parishes. One centred on Monks Kirby, the other on Wolvey. The Bishop of Coventry employed a strategy of placing his new young incumbents in large rural benefices, where they could cut their teeth and learn their trade. I consider it to be a wise policy. It was decided that we should live in Monks Kirby's parsonage. Eventually, when a new vicarage had been built, we would transfer to the other centre at Wolvey.

St Edith's, Monks Kirby, was a giant of a church. As the village name infers, it was the site of an C11th Benedictine community, a priory church and buildings. Though in our day not one single stone of these monastic dwellings remains.

Amended, added to, rebuilt, the red sandstone church held some 700 folk. Twice the size of the entire village population. It was a cold place. Impossible to heat. In winter our congregations of twenty or so shivered and shook. 'Many are cold but few are frozen' to misquote the Gospel. Mrs Wotherspoon always sat on the front row. Most of the year she swaddled herself in her tartan car rug and hot water bottle. Like peas on a drum the faithful few fought bravely during the Eucharist. We had a talented organist, Julia, who was music teacher at Brockhurst, the local Church Primary school, and a dedicated body of wardens and sidesmen.

It's fair to say that all the sheep in my new flock were not used to vestments and catholic worship. I made an uneasy decision before my very first Sunday service to bite the bullet. There's no time like the first time: if I had deferred the strategy I might never have plucked up courage to initiate it in the future. And the people might justifiably say that we were content to do it that way: why change now? So I took the plunge and appeared in alb, stole and chasuble, a simple white one kindly purchased for me by David Scott, the Team Rector-elect. Forty years ago the priest in full eucharistic vestments would normally have raised eyebrows, if not alarm bells, especially in conservative areas like my group of parishes. Today not many would blink. Even Low Church Anglican clergy are now wont to wear all kinds of paraphernalia. I am reminded of the true story of a C19th Low Church bishop, about to be consecrated in his new cathedral. Not wishing to offend any of his High Church predecessor's congregation, he decided to wear all the items of clothing which the sacristan had laid out on the vestment table. He recognised most of the garb, though one piece did baffle him: an embroidered piece of ribbon, rather like a stole but only eight inches in length. To be on the safe side, he wore it round his collar. After the service the bishop remarked how glad he was to get all the robes off and enquired as to the nature of the small item around his neck. "Good heavens, my Lord!" exclaimed the sacristan "that's the last bishop's bookmark!" Despite *my* sartorial anxiety at some possible back-lash, no one objected in the least. If truth were known, no one actually *commented!*

Historically linked to Monks Kirby was Pailton, a mile away to the south east. This village, too, was small but possessed its own simple yet delightful red brick church of St Denis, built in 1884. In addition to its unusual dedication – were they trying to outdo St *Edith's*? – it possessed a small apse. Pailton had few amenities, though the local doctor Eric Killey had his surgery there. His ancient basset hound, Oscar, used to catch the bus outside the surgery and travel to nearby Rugby, where, it was rumoured, he met his canine lady-friend. He never failed to catch a bus back home, though. Pailton also boasted a potter who worked and sold her wares there. We bought six fine-looking goblets from her.

Withybrook was situated a mile away from Monks Kirby in the opposite direction. A hamlet containing some luxury houses, some of which were crowned with thatch. The pub had a good reputation as an eating-house, though why it changed its name from The Half Moon to The Pheasant is a mystery. Both names are rustic but there are many more 'Pheasants' than Half Moons. In the deep, dark countryside the moon is called the 'parish lantern' and conjures up the picture of real country folk knowing their way with only the moon for light. All Saints' church sat round the corner from the pub, adjacent to the stream where willows grew. Hence the village's name. These three villages, together with Stretton-under-Fosse, where no church existed, made up the former benefice.

Mentioned in the Domesday Book and in records of 1285 Stretton Baskerville was no more. It was one of England's disappearing villages. Its death probably occurred as a result of the Enclosure Act when landowners, preferring flocks to folk, fenced off the land and turfed the villagers and their households off it. Sometimes the deadly plague decimated a village population. Either way, all that remains of lives lived many centuries ago is a series of radiation photographs taken from the air which clearly delineate the foundations of our ancestors' dwellings in this place. Burton Hastings is close neighbour to this ghost village, whose title still remains on the diocesan lists. St Botolph's at Burton Hastings is another old Warwickshire church, a small, sturdy C14th edifice.

St Botolph was the patron saint of gateways – and so many buildings dedicated to this Roman saint stand at the entrance of a town or village. Boston in Lincolnshire derives its name from St Botolph. Boston, Massachusetts, was so named by its founders who hailed from England's eastern county. And this Boston, USA, is home to our daughter Rebecca and her family.

I suppose St Botolph's stands at the old gate into Burton Hastings. It is such a small village, it is difficult to know where you are entering – or leaving. Like all the villages in my care, farmsteads, often a few miles outside the natural centre, made up the rest of the parish. And added a substantial number to the electoral registers. 'Burton' had an enthusiastic cricket team and arranged an annual trip to Scotland to play a few matches with the Scots. As most of the team were farmers, this excursion was squeezed in around the various harvests. It possessed a good mix of population: big houses, council houses and well-kept cottages. We had the Smiths and the Smithies. Alan Smith, ex-farmer was churchwarden. Alan Smithies, ex-teacher wrote brilliant poetry and articles on plainchant, church history and especially of Margaret of Anjou, his heroine. He never came to church but had the deepest Christian faith. Avoided by most of his fellow-villagers as an eccentric, he and I got on well. I warm to eccentrics.

Copston Magna was even tinier than Burton Hastings. Many villages and hamlets, particularly in neighbouring Leicestershire, carried the substantives Magna (meaning 'Great') or Parva ('Little'). In Copston Magna there existed a couple of farms and a short row of cottages. I'm not surprised there was no Copston Parva! Copston means a settlement on a hill and it went back to the days of the Roman Empire. At the crossing of the two famous Roman roads, the Fosse Way (the A46) and Watling Street (the A5), the high settlement provided the appropriate site for soldiers to keep look-out on possible enemy movements upon the highway. Despite the paucity of parishioners the village boasted a small church, St John's, which was devotedly cared for by the small faithful band who were determined to keep their early Victorian building open for business, whatever the cost. And they succeeded.

Wolvey was the chief and centre of these last three mentioned communities. It was the centre because it was by far the largest village – and it was where the vicar lived! Its parish church of St John the Baptist was a solidly squat building. It had a delightful Norman doorway, though the rest of its structure was a blend of 13th, 16th and 19th century additions. Its position, on the top of a high mound, made it the highest edifice in the village and stood as a token of greeting to travellers motoring on the Leicester road to Coventry, Stratford and beyond. I have given a fuller description of Wolvey in my chapter on Parsonages.

From an ecclesiastical point of view, it was the right choice in which to base a plan of mission and pastoralia in this northern part of the diocese. The whole parish – my 'empire' – was roughly a five-sided shape, not unlike a small child's outline drawing of a house, with inward sloping walls and a high pitched roof. It stretched six miles SW to Stretton- under- Fosse, one and a half miles NW to Pailton, whence 4 miles north to Copston and from where it was a further three, west, to Burton Hastings. An area of approximately 30 square miles. As in Roman days another two main modern arterial roads inpinged upon the united parish. The M69 motorway, constructed during our time there, dissected Burton Hastings and Wolvey. I remember Christmas Day 1975 when we walked, children and dog in tow, up the unmade stretch of this motorway, very recently excavated and revealing the rich red-brown Warwickshire clay, a marked contrast to the white seasonal frost on surrounding land and trees. The lengthy southbound M6 suddenly veered eastwards to link up with the M1 and by doing so split little Stretton and Pailton. We were always rather proud of a large green road sign on the A5 which announced "Copston Magna 1 mile; London 100". Wolvey was situated geographically on the western edge of the child's 'house', at the juncture of roof and wall. Not central but very accessible.

The new motorways were not the only thing creating a split in my patch. The whole parish was schizophrenic regarding its internal bureaucracy. It was split between education authorities and health authorities. Monks Kirby and Pailton were nearer Rugby, so my Church Primary School came under that town's jurisdiction. All my secondary school children were bussed to several schools there, also, including a good Church of England Secondary School. Parishioners who became ill were admitted to one of the hospitals in Rugby. On the other side of the parish all the under-elevens attended Wolvey CE Controlled School. After which they were usually transported to Nicholas Chamberlain School in Bedworth, or further on to Nuneaton. Hospital provision for these parishioners was at The George Eliot in Nuneaton. Farmers, too, had the choice of auction marts, though they invariably bought and sold at the one nearest to them. The great big 'family shop' was either in one of the supermarkets in Coventry, Rugby, Nuneaton or Bedworth. The latter's establishment preferred the Greek epithet: *hyper*market, which was dubiously named "Shoppers' Paradise". More like Shoppers' Hell!

With a population of eleven hundred Wolvey provided a challenging mix of parishioners, ideal for a first-time Vicar. When, in the autumn of 1973 I accepted the living – though technically I was to be priest-in-charge – the diocese envisaged a large rural team ministry based on the small town of Bulkington, three or so miles south west of Wolvey. David Scott was its Vicar. He was, like Kenneth Bradford at Wyken, from the Durham diocese. In fact he stayed with the Bradfords when he travelled down for his job interview in late 1971. I was introduced to him after the 7.30am Eucharist at Holy Cross. Little did I know then that our paths would cross again in four years' time. David was a most amiable, gentle man and priest. On the creation of a Team Ministry he would be designated Team Rector, I and David Penney, who was priest-in-charge of Shilton and Ansty and churchless Barnacle, as Team Vicars. David took on one of my five churches, Withybrook. There would be eleven 'satellite' villages circling round Bulkington. An establishment of eight churches, three priests and a Lay Reader, Alan Gray. We took up the challenge towards this projected Team at once and began monthly Staff Meetings.

David Penney drove an old ex-Royal Mail van. It was still coloured red, though all the wording had been erased. Nevertheless, whenever he drew up you always anticipated a parcel! Times were hard for clergy in the early 1970s. Stipends were low, though I always felt sorry for the likes of Kenneth, who taught me in my first curacy – or even David Scott – both of whom had twenty years start on me and yet still received the same Church Commissioners' stipend at the end of the month. Experience counted for nothing for the thousands of parochial clergy who had not obtained (or who had refused) preferment. It did not seem fair. Since things were so tight financially, my fellow Team Vicar-designate reckoned he could not afford an *annual* Church diary, The Parson's Pocket Book.

This item, I believed, was absolutely essential on every Anglican priest's desk – and pocket! It contained priceless information: Saints days, whether red or black, commemorations, a table of readings for every day in the church's year, a long list of Church Societies and various Institutions, holidays and even moon phases. Each page was a week but there was adequate space in which to write the daily memos. Like all good Church calendars, it ran from Advent Sunday, the start of the Church's year. It also went one better than most secular diaries in that it provided a much needed overlap to the first week in January. This gave those clergy extra time to purchase their next year's Pocket Book! I bought my first Parson's Pocket Book whilst at College in 1969 and have bought one ever since. Forty up to press, almost as many as my News of the World Football Annuals. Both publications make fascinating retrospective readings, especially my diaries which have been an invaluable source throughout this book. The Parson's Pocket Book, always a deep burgundy colour in my day, invariably began its Preface with the sentence "Memory has been defined as the faculty in which we forget things." Since 1990 it has always carried a text from scripture on its frontispiece. A quotation from St Paul's first letter to the Corinthians, chapter 14, verse 40: "Let all things be done decently and in order."

Which brings me back to my colleague David Penney. Feeling unable to purchase the said PPB (it even cost extra to have a small pocket glued to the back cover, ideal for Compliments cards etc), David consequently divided each weekly page into two: one for the current year, one for the succeeding year. This, naturally, caused endless confusion, both for him and his colleagues. When planning well ahead, David would frequently enter, say, a Thursday July 10th appointment in the Thursday July 9th space; sometimes a Tuesday meeting would find its way pencilled in for a Monday. At Staff Meetings he would often take his shoes off. Not because of the holiness of the ground but simply because they were too tight. "I got them at the Church jumble sale," he would explain. His purple pullover, short in sleeve and body, also emerged from the same source. In spite of these eccentricities he was a good and caring priest and the team worked very well together.

Many joint parish events were staged. The chief one for me was our annual "It's a Knockout!" competition, held for a couple of times in the expansive grounds of Monks Kirby Vicarage. Five villages 'sent' teams of men, women and children. They were a brilliant success. The games required all types of talent. Brain, brawn and brute strength were essential. Certainly many of the games favoured the strong-in-arm farmers. Competitors tossed hay bales over an increasingly highered bar; a tight grip of hand and heel was the essence of the tug o' war; filling buckets of water on a soapy, plastic floor; shinning high up a pine tree to ring a hanging bell, fighting with sacks of hay whilst seated on a greasy pole, under which was a paddling pool full of water, and much more. There was food, prepared by church folk, drink and ice cream – and equally importantly several hundred parishioners trampling, jumping, running, cycling over our garden. Burton Hastings, the smallest of the five competing villages, won both years' contests convincingly. This fact helped enormously in the confidence stakes. It certainly was not a case of 'biggest is best'.

Liturgically my monthly service schedule was like a Littlewoods Football Pools plan. All five churches could not possibly have a weekly act of worship. Or could they? Not if they were to have the Eucharist, since I was the only priest in my patch. But if some churches were to have Mattins or Evensong then it might just be possible. Thanks to Alan

Gray's Reader ministry we were able to ensure that there was an act of worship in every village church every week.

Like a sensible football pools plan, I deployed two 'bankers': the central village of each of the two parishes before I came. I have always insisted that *times* of worship should not fluctuate. I cannot cope with an arrangement which includes "8am on the first Sunday, 10am on the second; 10.45am on the third..." and so on. It's confusing for the priest and even more so for the poor worshipper. My 'bankers' would hold the Parish Eucharist every Sunday at a fixed time: 9.30am Wolvey, 11am Monks Kirby. Then on varying Sunday evenings I would celebrate Holy Communion at one of the other churches. I had, in essence, become a mass priest. Not that I minded one bit. That was part of the job – *the* part. And Mr Gray filled in the non-sacramental gaps with much devotion. Christmas and Easter, of course, meant an even harder workload. I vividly recall returning home one Christmas Day at 1 pm, having done five morning Eucharists. The children had opened all their presents and were busy on 'other things'. I had failed to witness any one of my children excitedly ripping wrapping paper off a Christmas parcel. We decided that in future *some* presents would remain unopened until Dad returned home.

That situation, however, was destined to improve from another source. The Littlewoods Pools Plan of services had purred along quite sweetly for two years when I received a telephone call from the relatively new vicar of Brinklow, the neighbouring parish on the east of my group. "Just to let you know," he stated, "that I'm taking on Monks Kirby and Pailton." He went on to explain, somewhat triumphantly, that the diocese had decided on this new scheme. Neither I nor David Scott had been consulted, nor had any such decision been communicated to us. It was rank bad manners. In fairness, the Brinklow vicar might have assumed I knew, though he could have spoken to me rather more sensitively. The diocese had no such excuse. I was so angry that I phoned Bishop McKie, the assistant bishop, with whom I got on well. He too was extremely annoyed at the blatant breakdown of information and tore a strip off the chap from Brinklow.

To lose Monks Kirby and Pailton was a blow. We had made lots of friends 'over there' and we were suddenly separated. There was no official farewell, no acknowledgment of the two years of ministry. It was as if it had never happened. Throughout my entire ministry I have always felt that people were the last thing on a diocese's agenda. 'Flock' is the right word: so-called Diocesan *Pastoral* Committees move their sheep at a whim, like a snapping dog at their heels. Nevertheless a reduction in the number of parishes in my care was also a relief. With two 'selections' less in my 'pools permutation', I was able to celebrate the Eucharist more often in my Wolvey group – and to lead Sung Evensong, which I dearly loved. Particularly at Wolvey, where we had a small but capable adult choir.

Sadly, the demise of St Edith's and St Denis' seemed to end all hopes of the projected Team Ministry. It slipped out of the agendas of the relevant Diocesan Committees. We three clergy continued to meet but the lack of impetus from Coventry intimated a dead duck. As in Belshazzar's palace, the writing was on the wall – though a *written* memo from the Diocesan office would have been appreciated.! David Penney and I both felt in no man's land and within a short time of each other in 1977 we departed. He to two mining villages in Durham and I to Lancashire. Thirty years on, these small North Warwickshire villages have still not officially entered into a united team, though the Vicar of Bulkington now has responsibility for Shilton and Ansty.

Debit swings and parish roundabouts

It would be reasonable to say that up to the beginning of the Second World War the great majority of the incumbents of the Church of England would have their own private means, sufficiently substantial to enable them to lead a comfortable life. After the War things altered. Drastically. Yet the Church, being the Church, somehow did not adjust to the huge changes in society. Normally external events only produce necessary reaction after several years. Take clergy expenses, for example. Vicars and rectors in the first half of the C20th would probably not dream of putting in a claim for expenses of travel or administration. These costs would automatically, happily and generously come out of the pocket of the well-endowed clergyman.

Most of the men ordained in the second half of that century were certainly not of that ilk. Yet many began to subsidise the Church's ministry out of their own very meagre stipends. The majority could ill afford to do that. Urban parishes were more aware of this increasingly serious situation than their rural cousins. By the late 1960s it is true that Parochial Church Councils were paying their clergy expenses of office. Country folk either had not heard of such practices or assumed that their vicar would not require such expenses. Rural people used to have a deep suspicion of their clergy, almost a holy fear, inherited from the days when parson and people didn't really mix. Certainly the parishioners would not have any clue whatsoever as to the parson's finances. He lived in a big house, so he must have a big income...Rural folk could be obstinate. They often knew that it would pay them to keep their head in the sand. Thankfully, things have radically changed in this respect. And this phenomenon has occurred in the period of my ministry.

That ministry, however, began when things were rather tough. And parishioners somewhat stubborn. When I first arrived in the parish I earmarked certain days when I would be in such and such a village, where I would do house-to-house visits and say Evensong. Unfortunately it rarely worked in practice, since funerals and meetings would often intrude and mess up the arrangement. But the thought was there! Evensong requires a prayer book for the Office and a Bible for the reading of the lessons appointed for the day. Wolvey church, for some reason, did not possess a Bible. There ought to be one under every parish priest's stall! But not at St John the Baptist's. Rather naively I asked the Treasurer of the PCC for the money to purchase a Bible for my stall. The cost was 95 pence. The most up-to-date Bible one could buy: The Common Bible, an Ecumenical Edition, approved by the leaders of the Protestant, Roman Catholic and Orthodox churches. "Ninety five pence!" exclaimed a flabbergasted treasurer, "Ninety five pence!" I thought I'd asked for an all-expenses paid trip to the Holy Land. "*And what do you want a Bible for?*" he asked. With the patience of Job, I did my best to explain.

When I arrived in the parish I did receive a token amount from my five churches. I was also sent an annual grant of £90 from Trinity College Cambridge, who were the patrons of St Edith's, Monks Kirby. But these sums were becoming increasingly deficient in the actual amount expended. My banking experience taught me to open a separate bank account purely for expenses of office. This was often in debit and

Barclays Bank in Bedworth had somewhat kindly turned a blind eye to this occurrence. However, things were worsening. "The peaks of the debit swings seems to have been going higher and higher and the account is remaining overdrawn longer," the manager would eventually write. By mid July 1975, not quite two years into the job, I was in desperation. I decided to address the situation once and for all with my churchwardens. To the ten of them, and to the treasurers, I sent the following duplicated letter, to which I appended an Income and Expenditure Account for the previous year:

I am sorry that I must write to you in the form of a duplicated letter. Time, however, does not permit me to write twelve personal letters of this nature, which is really what I would like to do.

The purpose of my writing to you is to bring to your notice the state of my financial affairs. I have kept a record of all my expenses since becoming priest-in-charge of this area. I have produced an Income & Expenditure Account based on the year 1974, which shows an excess of expenditure over income of £266. Since the end of last year inflation has raced on to unprecedented heights and already this year I am providing parish expenses out of my own pocket of £135. That is £5 a week. Travel is the biggest expense. I try to cut down on the use of my car whenever possible. I use my moped when I can, though often time and/or load do not permit it. The Diocese and the Church Commissioners have approved a rate of 7.8p per mile for car expenses – your allowance does not anywhere near cover my real expenses. My car needs all new tyres (£30), an engine de-coke (estimated at £80) and a new silencer (£30). My Expenses a/c at the Bank is overdrawn.

May I suggest that my Wardens and Treasurers get together to discuss my expenses. I am sorry that this initiative had to come from me but I cannot continue to subsidise the parishes any longer. My family and I are very happy in this area, but unless the churches here can grant me adequate expenses, I have no alternative but to seek a new job in a parish which allows me full expenses.

The Diocesan Board of Finance and the Archdeacon of Coventry suggest that incumbents and priests-in-charge should submit an expenses claim form every month. Could this be done in our plurality of parishes? I believe it can, providing you can agree on the ratio between each parish. May I suggest that the basis for such ratio should be Church Electoral Roll membership. This would give the following percentage ratios: Wolvey 45%; Monks Kirby 23%; Pailton 16%; Burton 12%; Copston 4%.

I estimate that I need £600 per annum to do this job effectively. The figure ought to be reviewed, say, once each year. On the above ratios my required expenses granted by the parishes would be as follows:

Wolvey   £270 (£156) Copston Magna* £24 (£12)

MK *   £138 (£120) Burton Hastings £72 (£24)

Pailton*   £96 (£24)

*The MK united benefice can take into consideration the £90 from Trinity College.

I trust that you will all meet as soon as possible and endeavour to ensure that all expenditure incurred by me in carrying out the duties of your parish priest may be met by the churches.

Yours sincerely,

Trevor Vaughan

The wardens and Treasurers *did* meet – in my absence, of course. In true Church of England prevaricating style they decided to look into the matter further. They appointed a church member, a kind of ecclesiastical ombudsman, to discuss the situation with me: to see if I were spending extravagantly on my wife and four small children, to say nothing of my car and moped. I thought it a dreadful affront to my integrity and a most questionable method of procedure. However, beggars cannot be choosers and I allowed the humiliation to progress simply because I was most anxious to make these local churches aware of the cost of ministry. A ministry, it ought to be stressed, carried out by me *on their behalf.*

An ombudsman was chosen. 'Chas.' – not his real name – was presumably elected because he was from the north of England, like me. He was a 'Trotter', like my mother, born in Bolton. His accent, that central Lancashire rhoticism, betrayed him. But he had lived, I imagine, the greater part of his life in North Warwickshire, where he had done his farming. "Farming" is probably too grand a word for Chas. He was a cattle and sheep dealer. And a successful one at that. On at least a couple of days a week he would go down to Banbury market, where vast amounts of money changed hands. Our Parochial Ombudsman threw himself into the Inquisition with great gusto. He painstakingly examined our Bank Statements, our Joint Account as well as my Expenses Account. He probed into our pay slips and household bills. And yet not for one moment did I feel that his mission was caring and genuine. In our innocence we had felt obliged to divulge private items which were totally irrelevant to the task in hand.

By contrast we clergy were very poor. If there were such things as "clergy expenses," Chas. hadn't heard of them. Backhanders, under-the-counter, a wink and a nod: yes. His obvious antipathy clearly showed he did not reckon much to my job.

As he left the Vicarage, Chas. reached into his back pocket and pulled out a thick roll of banknotes for us to see. "Two hundred quid!" he chortled insensitively. "A bit o' 'luck money' I got at Banbury today."

The parish, however, did introduce Clergy Expenses. Somewhat reluctantly. Chas. would have made my annual sum in three good days at Banbury Market.

Two years later we were moving north to Sabden. David, the churchwarden, had organised a mini bus to take a dozen parishioners the 150 miles to see me inducted. He told me that he had asked Chas. if he wanted to go – since he too was a northerner. "Nay, lad," he replied, "me and the vicar, we weren't *that* chummy!"

All sorts of succession

Looking back on my first two years as a minister in charge I now realise how tough they were. The battles were all mental or spiritual ones. There were mind games to be fought and won. There existed a few families over the eight villages who had wielded all the power in church circles for quite some years. They had even bossed the vicars. There needed to be a wider canvas on which their power could be reduced and their responsibility shared. I too felt those constricting forces as these people attempted to run me. I was able, relatively quickly, I suppose, to replace these 'power' people. I have always implemented a strategy of replacing churchwardens every three years, so that no one could claim the job for life, which is death for the Church. Similarly I have always tried to ensure that official Church posts were spread out among as many people as possible. I learnt the art there in my first living. Within a short while, by totally legitimate means (though rather political, I admit) many new and different faces appeared on the scene of church government.

Henry Hobday was my choice of churchwarden at Wolvey. He had worked all his life, apart from his army service, 'on the track', the assembly line, at the Humber, then Chrysler, car factory in Coventry. Henry was a very quiet man, self-effacing, genuinely humble. His garden was his greatest love: possibly equal to his love for his wife Bertha. Best of all, Henry said his prayers. "How can *he* be churchwarden?" the 'powerhouses' cried, "He has no car, no telephone." And whilst they did not say it in so many words, they implied that he had neither leadership qualities nor gift of communication. But Henry said his prayers every day. And made his Communion every Sunday, plus all the Saints' and other Holy Days. He was my choice and my pre-AGM lobbying resulted in my getting my man.

All churchwardens hold their office under the licence of the diocesan bishop. Only he can sack them. The incumbent is powerless to do such a thing. So every year the wardens are obliged to attend a service, usually under the aegis of the Deanery, to make a solemn declaration that they will be loyal and diligent in carrying out the mission of God's Church in partnership with the incumbent. This promise is usually made in the presence of the Archdeacon at a special service called the Archdeacon's Visitation. At the Visitation the Archdeacon preaches a sermon. Only once, in Morecambe, have I heard such. It is usually a chance for the Archdeacon to lambaste the parishes for failure to raise sufficient funds and to make broad generalisations regarding the Articles of Enquiry, completed by churchwardens prior to the Visitation. These generalisations normally consist of progress, or otherwise, of parishes' efforts in attending to the downspouts, drains and dilapidations of parish buildings. It is nearly always very boring and to an outsider, at least, it seems very far removed from the proclamation of the Gospel.

Henry, as warden-elect, duly attended the Visitation, faithfully making the required promises. The following Sunday morning – his first as churchwarden – he came to church even earlier than normal. "Can we begin with a prayer at the altar rail?" he asked. And so we did. He was the one and only warden in my entire ministry to make this simple yet essential request. Henry was truly authorised and, despite having no car and no phone, increasingly grew in stature and benevolent authority. He was always first to church; welcomed every worshipper individually; prepared much of the church building for worship. Henry could always be relied upon to advise me of any newcomer or visitor in our midst. Bertha laundered the altar linen, bringing the freshly-starched and ironed cloths before each Eucharist. Henry, too, always brought the water for the chalice and the ablutions, since we were not 'plumbed in' at Wolvey.

One dark evening in early January 1977 he was uncommonly late in arriving at church for worship. It was a Sung Eucharist for the Feast of the Epiphany. A loud commotion in the church porch minutes before we were due to begin revealed that Henry had collapsed there. His plastic bottle of water still in his hand. Doreen, a retired nurse in the congregation, ministered to him; Bertha comforted him; Ann ran to phone for an ambulance; I said a quiet prayer over him; and the choir, having taken it upon themselves to process into the chancel, began to sing the opening hymn, partly to conceal the anxious activity in the porch and partly to offer some praise and prayer for Henry. They continued right through their Christmas and Epiphany carols repertoire, as Henry was carried away to the hospital in Nuneaton. They said he died 'on the way to hospital.' They nearly always do. In truth he died in the porch of his beloved church. An untimely end to his short but splendid ministry as churchwarden.

Henry's co-warden was the complete opposite: exuberant, gregarious, a physically energetic captain of our village cricket team, a businessman – and young! He and I got on very well, though he did not attend church very often. David was a farmer, specialising in pig-breeding but diversifying into everything from champion sheep rearing to developing a caravan park on his farmland. He was just what the parish needed. I knew he had a deep faith (which was to be severely tested in the near future). If you want a job to be done, they say, ask a busy man. So I invited him to consider accepting the post of warden. He would, naturally, have to be elected at the church's Annual Parish Meeting. But I would do the necessary politicking. Fortunately for Wolvey, he agreed.

David Eglin's farming meant he was always busy but that never put him off from being busy for Church. He ran Bingo drives for church funds. He advertised them as 'Pork Bingo', since all the prizes were varying cuts of pork – from his piggeries, of course! He put his boundless energy into his organisational skills. He was an inimitable impresario, plunging the Church into the very centre of the community. He and Henry complemented each other wonderfully. Like body and soul. Like the running of a good theatre, they represented front- and back-of-house management splendidly. No wonder St John the Baptist's grew and grew. It was David, as I mentioned, who drove the mini-bus on a 300 mile round trip one March evening to my Induction at Sabden.

Within a couple of years of that event a series of disasters struck him and his farm. The chief of these calamities was a fierce fire that devastated and destroyed much of what he had built on his farm. He telephoned me for advice and consolation. I was fairly useless on the advice bit: apart from assuring him of my prayers, my only recommendation was for him to read the Book of Job, in which countless catastrophes overtook our God-fearing hero. Like Job, David would have to remain faithful and all would ultimately work out for good. He did just that. And it did.

Wolvey was a good village to begin one's parish ministry. The worship at church was attractive and reverent. I had introduced vestments and, particularly at Wolvey, brought people 'up the candle' to a much more 'catholic' form of worship. Very few objected. We formed a small band of young altar-servers. We had a thriving Youth Club, led by some admirable young folk, notably the Rusted girls, Nicola and Verona. We had a memorable trip to the Wildfowl Trust at Slimbridge. The Miles family gave wonderful encouragement to me. From their home at Armswell, across from the church, our growing Sunday School developed. We were all thrilled with the burgeoning numbers.

One year on in my ministry I was very privileged to spend four whole days at the feet of the saintly Michael Ramsey. He had been installed and enthroned as the 100th Archbishop of Canterbury in June 1961, the first time any such event had been televised. After more than thirteen years in the post, which included a visit to Pope Paul VI in Rome and to Patriarch Alexei in Moscow, his resignation took effect on November 15th 1974. After two weeks' respite, his first task in retirement was to conduct a Priest's Silent Retreat at Offchurch. What a coup for the diocesan organisers! "The Archbishop encouraged the practice of retreats," Owen Chadwick would one day state in Bishop Ramsey's memorial address, "He loved spaces for silence and places of silence. He was an inspiring conductor of retreats." He did not fail us.

The Retreat was to commence at 7pm on Monday December 2nd and would conclude after breakfast on the following Friday. It was totally and utterly oversubscribed. In good biblical fashion lots were drawn for places. My name was drawn out, as was Kenneth's, my Vicar in Wyken. About thirty very fortunate clergymen were led into otherworldly realms by our former Primate.

Bishop Michael had taught Kenneth at Durham when he was Professor of Divinity at the University. Kenneth obtained a 1st Class degree in Theology and always spoke of his great debt to Michael Ramsey, whose teachings fashioned his priesthood. They became good friends and I was often regaled with his story of the time Kenneth attended some important service at which Archbishop Ramsey was the preacher. As luck would have it, Kenneth's seat was adjacent to the central aisle. All were standing as the processional hymn began. At the very end of a very long procession of clergy walked the Archbishop. He spotted Kenneth, was genuinely delighted to see him, and duly stopped to have a chat! The Archbishop's verger continued to process down the aisle leading no one, unaware of the hiatus.

After the Retreat's final Eucharist on the Friday morning we were allowed to talk. An excitable clutch of clergymen began extolling the substance of the retreat conductor's words. I happened to eat breakfast on the same table as Kenneth. "I'll take you up to meet Michael," he promised. After their exchange of greeting, Kenneth introduced me to the great man. "Michael," he said solemnly, "this is Trevor Vaughan. I've taught him all that you taught me." Bishop Michael smiled and nodded, his incredible eyebrows rising and lowering at their accustomed speed. He mumbled some encouraging words to me. I asked him to sign his autograph for me and he obliged. He unhesitatingly wrote "† Michael Cant-," then realised he was no longer 'Canterbury'! "Oh dear," he mumbled. Crossing out his half-completed episcopal surname, he signed over his error the simple surname "Ramsey." This signature was a piece of special history. The cross and one and a half words told a tale! I kept it safe for several years but, regrettably, it seems to have vanished. I still possess the notes I made of his magnificent talks at the Retreat, which I treasure. If only I could find that singular signature to accompany them.

That encounter, coming so early in my parish ministry, was one of the defining moments for my future work. That sentence "I taught him all that you taught me" has been my maxim, the basis of all that I did as a priest. I can truthfully say that I was always conscious of my training Vicar's words – and the gentle affirmation of the 100th Archbishop of Canterbury, whose orders and authority are in direct succession to Christ's chosen apostles. A close encounter of an apostolic kind!

Or was it? Was all that hand-me-down teaching a delusion? Was I just the next one down in a long line of misguided pretenders? Despite our sincerity, were we merely peddlers of a ministry of nothing?

'Witch' Country!

'Apostolic' is the adjective of 'apostle', which means 'one who is sent'. The twelve apostles were sent out by our Lord in mission to preach and to do and to be the Gospel. After just over two years since my memorable encounter with Bishop Michael Ramsey, I too felt 'apostled', called and sent by God to serve in the Blackburn Diocese, who had sponsored me for Ordination in the first place.

Sabden was a village of some 1600 people. It once possessed five large cotton mills working to full capacity – and employing a great majority of the inhabitants. When we arrived in 1977 cotton was no longer woven. Its mills were still standing but housed a plethora of small industrial units. Pendle Furniture, Propax (a packaging manufacturer) and Marbill, whose inventive owners had developed a special plastic for a variety of uses, one of which was the linking foot-plates between the corridors of railway carriages. Sabden was still a busy village. A handful of shops, two garages, two pubs and *four* churches. The eldest of these, rather surprisingly, was the Baptist chapel. One of its deacons, Mr Moorhouse, a chapel stalwart if ever there were one, would often remark to me, "Don't you forget, Vicar, that we were here first!" To which I would bite my lips but politely acknowledge, adding that the C of E – as part of Catholic Christendom – had been going for two thousand years.

Sabden St Nicholas was just the right sort of parish. When I began my ministry there in 1977 it was the only church I ever knew where *men* outnumbered women in attendances. The parish had a 'comfortable' population, which allowed me to get to know not only my flock but the remainder also.

Sabden's original name was 'Heyhouses', named after the small hamlet which pre-dated it by quite some time. It was famous for its 'witches' of the sixteenth century, poor simple women whose odd behaviour had them frog-marched to Lancaster Assizes and hung. Less historical, it was also known for its 'treacle mines' – a source of jokes for those who had the misfortune not to live in Sabden! The village nestled in a valley in Pendle Hill, some 1800 feet high, of which The Houghton Weavers sang:

> *"Oh Pendle, Oh Pendle, thou standest alone,*
> *'Twixt Clitheroe and Burnley, Whalley and Colne;*
> *Where Ribble and Hodder, their waters do meet,*
> *And Barley and Downham rest content at thy feet."*

It was said that Sabden's geography kept its residents at home, as it was surrounded by steep hills. An accurate reflection before the Ribble buses appeared. But there were two by-products of this communal 'house-arrest'. A larger than average number of inter-marriages; and a marvellous ability to provide one's own entertainment. This latter was happily still evident in my day there. I know of no village or parish where there was such a hive of activity: socials, discos, bingo, coffee mornings, afternoon teas, snooker, parties, pantomimes and processions. The Queen's Silver Jubilee in the summer of '77 was just the excuse for another outrageous event. St Nicholas' was just one of scores of participants who manned a decorated lorry: "The Girls of St Trinian's," no less!

We shared a couple of Parish Week-end Conferences at nearby Whalley Abbey, the Diocesan Retreat House: who could forget Eileen Luckett, covered in a white sheet, roaming ghost-like among the ruins at midnight? Our darts team won the Deanery Tournament three years running. We were accused of practising beforehand! The congregation grew in numbers. Servers graced the sanctuary and choristers the chancel.

Out of the blue, after only two and half years, the Bishop asked me to consider a parish in Chorley. Its priest had been dismissed on some serious matter, though he had continued to correspond with the churchwardens and even publish a parish magazine "in exile," which served only to confuse the parishioners even more. The church's accounts were in dire straits and so, after careful and prayerful consideration, I declined. A year later, *another* Chorley parish became vacant. I knew the patron, the rector of the parish church, in which my T.A. unit was situated. Chorley again! Was the Lord trying to tell me something about this town? This time I accepted the offer. When I broke the news to the congregation at the morning service, our daughter Rebecca, then aged eight, ran out of church in tears. And from an unknown parishioner I received a white feather.

The witches had not altogether left Pendle!

Waterloo: theirs and mine

St George's Chorley was one of five Anglican parishes in the town. It had been carved out of the ancient parish of St Laurence. St George's was a huge, imposing edifice built in 1825, one of the so-called 'Waterloo' churches erected to house vast numbers of people so that the Word of God could be preached and thereby dissuade Englishmen from rebellion, as the French proletariat had done to their great discomfort and defeat in the Napoleonic Wars. It was a direct result of these wars that an Act of Parliament (popularly known as the Million Act) was passed in 1818, granting large sums for the building of churches. The moneys coming from the reparations exacted from France after the battle of Waterloo.

Despite its very grand external appearance the church possessed no noted ecclesiastical treasures. Its treasures were to be found in its church members. Like St Laurence the Deacon in third century Rome, who, when arrested for his faith and ordered to bring out the treasures of his church, obliged by gathering his faithful congregation before his persecutors.

The church people at St George's were like that. Numerous organisations within the church revealed scores of dedicated folk, 'treasures.' The extreme breadth of the Scouting movement was represented, from Beavers and Rainbows, through Cubs and Brownies, to Scouts and Guides and Venture Scouts. We had a Church Lads Brigade, again fully staffed by loyal enthusiastic leaders. A Scottish Pipe Band, splendidly bedecked in their Hunting Stewart tartan, a thriving Youth Fellowship, a well attended Sunday School, choir, altar-servers and a tip-top Men's Institute which boasted excellent facilities for snooker, bowling, tennis – and a licensed bar! The Vicar, needless to say, was Chairman or President of most of these bodies, which added to the work-load. Not that I minded: the potential easily outweighed the problem. Annual Confirmation classes always numbered over fifty youngsters. The annual Procession of Witness was a joy to behold. The entire membership of St George's would parade down Pall Mall and Market Street, led by our own Pipe Band. Folk would carry out their kitchen chairs onto the pavement in good time to get a grandstand view as we passed by!

The parish was thriving. It was upwardly mobile! To maintain this happy momentum an extra priest was essential. I reckon that when a business is building up it requires additional resources. I had witnessed this at first hand with my parents' confectionery business. Dad would bring in more staff as trade increased, even moving to newer, bigger premises. To stand still is to decline. So I wrote to the Blackburn Diocese, explained the encouraging situation, and asked for a curate. The parish had funds to pay for one and even owned a house in which to accommodate him.

Today, I would not be surprised at the Church's response. At the time, however, I was both dismayed and bitter. Blackburn was hardly enthusiastic. The powers that be begrudgingly stated that I could try to find my own curate. So I advertised in the Church Times. The usual details but adding the phrase "sensible Catholic." I'd come across a number of 'High and crazy' clerics in my time, who would *add* to the burden, not reduce it. The response was pitiful. Eight letters in all. Five were from clergy who took umbrage about the tenor of the advert. (the "sensible" bit); and three applicants, all of whom had telling gaps in their c.v.'s and were under their bishop's supervision for past misdemeanours. I decided it would make more work than relieve it. I abandoned the idea.

What made matters more difficult was the unwillingness of various office-holders to move on or stand down. Churchwardens in particular, but other key people in the mission of the Church, should not monopolise the office for ever. Besides, leadership is exacting and consuming. A personnel change avoids burn-out for the officer and allows fresh talent and new expertise to be injected. Good leaders who do stand down can still offer their past experience or bring it to another part of church work. The refusal of some present church officials to stand down *plus* the shying away of others from taking up responsibility made me realise that there was little chance of maintaining the momentum of growth. I remember arriving at this conclusion with much disappointment and frustration. Neither Diocese nor local church, it seemed, were interested in fanning the flames of advancement of God's Kingdom. Perhaps I took the rebuffs too seriously. But I was angry. I know I toyed with the idea of quoting St Matthew 10. 14 (the one about 'shaking the dust off your feet') underneath the Church Register entry after my last service. I'm not sure whether I did it or not. My incumbency at St George's was much too short. Yet I could not bear to be just a guardian of the status quo. Jesus calls us to be fishers of men not aquarium keepers! I had worked extremely hard in that short time. I felt I had been made to look foolish over the question of a curate. My successor was quoted in the Chorley Guardian as stating that the issue of a curate was not on the agenda. But, miracle of miracles, within less than a year the Diocese had found one for the parish!

Connections royal, religious and rebellious

It was Harold Rose who kept telephoning me whilst I was at Chorley. Harold was a Lay Reader in the Bradford Diocese who helped out at St Ambrose's church, Grindleton. And a great help he was, too. Especially to its vicar, Fr Malcolm Sidebottom. The village, along with the likes of Gisburn, Waddington, Hurst Green and Bolton by Bowland were now in Lancashire but were originally in the old West Riding of Yorkshire and thus ecclesiastically still part of the Bradford Diocese. Harold knew that we all missed the countryside and encouraged me to state my interest in the parish. A few months before his first phone call Fr Sidebottom had retired on health grounds. He was taken ill during the Remembrance Sunday service of 1981. He had written up the details of the day's service in the Church Register but never signed it. It was a sad and unfinished way to go. Harold told me that there were four candidates whom the Diocesan Pastoral Committee was considering but he promised to keep me in his prayers and would do his very best to dissuade the Archdeacon from selecting any other chap! The 'Rhodes strategy' must have worked because finally Ann and I were invited to meet Archdeacon Rogers and his wife at Long Preston, to be vetted. They, too, were country folk and had dogs and cats and hens – and we made a hit! I had briefed Harold on the impending interview. "If you get the job, Father," he said, "may I serve for you at your first Mass?" I readily agreed. But from that moment of my appointment I never heard another word from Harold. He completely disappeared from the scene and never set foot in Grindleton ever again.

It was to be a *united* benefice: a legal document was drawn up to create a united parish of Grindleton and neighbouring Bolton by Bowland. "I must point out to you," Mrs Wilkinson informed, "that it will be known as 'Bolton by Bowland *with* Grindleton', since we are the more ancient parish." It didn't count that it was only half the size of the latter! There had always been some rivalry between the two. Bolton folk described Grindleton as "a mining village." The united benefice also included the tiny village of Sawley. There was no church here but the ruins of a compact Cistercian Abbey.

Despite a small population of twelve hundred the united benefice had two Church Aided schools, of which I, as the rector, was chairman. Ann had previously taught at Grindleton Primary School, so that when I first embarked on my ministry there, it is true to say that she knew far more parishioners than I.

A church certainly existed in the ancient parish of Bolton by Bowland in the twelfth centaury. The present church, a fine building, is an amalgam of fifteenth and sixteenth century additions. The parish has royal links. The deposed King Henry VI took refuge with the Pudsays, the lords of the manor, after his defeat at Hexham in 1464. It was the King's architect who designed the church tower – a much more decorated style than the usual plain Craven ones. The parish which the church serves was and still is chiefly agricultural. Besides the Primary School, there operated two pubs, a garage and a Post Office-cum-General Stores. A thriving Young Farmers Club was the best in the district and a splendidly equipped new Village Hall was the venue for many a steaming Barn Dance, ceilidh or disco. And then there was the rip-roaring annual Pantomime!

Religiously speaking Bolton by Bowland was traditional in the extreme. A hard core of Prayer Book Society members were unafraid to defend their corner. When I persuaded the Parochial Church Council to 'try' the new Alternative Service Book on a once a month basis, the very next morning I witnessed three or four houses displaying bold "Keep Our Prayer Book" posters in their windows. On my way into church one Sunday morning I bumped into one of my congregation hurriedly retracing her steps to her car. "Ugh!" she snorted at me, "I'd forgotten it was *that* service!" "That's a pity," I remarked very politely, "because the Lord will be there in the breaking of bread." She muttered something inaudible and Protestant under her breath and I never saw her in church again.

By contrast St Ambrose's Grindleton was traditional in the Catholic sense of worship but happy to embrace the modern liturgy. I say 'modern', though in actual fact the 'modern' was based on a traditional liturgy of the second century. It was really the Prayer Book which was modern – by fourteen centuries. St Ambrose's was a quarter of the size of its partner St Peter and St Paul's and several centuries younger. It was of simple rectangular design with no noteworthy monuments or furnishings. What it did possess, however, was a superb, large, tastefully painted crucifix hanging from the roof above the chancel screen. The

Church School next door contained the Parish Room, of little use save for storage. The School Hall was the place for meetings, dances, Choir Club and the like.

Grindleton also had two hostelries, two shops, a village joinery-cum-undertakers run by the Reid brothers and a Methodist chapel. It once possessed a Reading Room, or Institute, but that now had been transformed into a house. The village was famous for its jam-making, especially the now almost-forgotten damson. It was chiefly a farming community but it was the headquarters of a large haulage firm, whose heavy vehicles would rumble and rattle through the main street.

Despite its historically insignificant parish church – and chapel, too – Grindleton parish had had a disproportionately larger share in the chronicles of English Christianity. It was there in the early 1600s that a religious sect called the Grindletonians practised and preached their own particular brand of Christianity. Apart from the Plymouth Brethren, Grindletonianism is the only other English religious group to take its name from a place rather than a set of beliefs. It was the arrival in 1615 of the curate Roger Brearley which gave the sect the impetus it required. Two years later, however, Brearley and some of his congregation were charged with fifty offences. They questioned the authority of ordination and also refused to pray for the King, since he was not an elected head. Their unorthodox creeds – some would say heretical – spread throughout the region of West Yorkshire and East Lancashire. Within this large area of northern England independent thought was widespread. Grindleton, tucked away amongst the hills, was a safe haven for many who held such radical religious views. It is worth noting that Grindleton, lying by the river Ribble, looked up to Pendle Hill. It was on the summit of Pendle that George Fox had his vision and set in motion the wheels of Quakerism.

Tiny Sawley, in the ecclesiastical parish of Grindleton, experienced a much longer lasting contribution to English Christendom. It was in Sawley – or Salley – that Cistercian monks founded their abbey in 1147. King Henry VIII's Act dissolving the monasteries in 1536 meant that monastic worship and ministry suddenly ceased. Its abbot, William Trafford, urged his fellow abbot, Paslew, at Whalley to join in the protest. This rising was one of a series which spread across Lincolnshire and Yorkshire and became known as The Pilgrimage of Grace. Its points of protests were varied but all shared a common hatred of governmental interference in church matters: the attack on the sacraments, on Saints' days as well as the dissolution of the monasteries itself. Sadly the rebellion ended with the arrest of two hundred protesters who were subsequently hanged under the King's order. This " fearful spectacle" being a warning to others. Our two abbots were hanged.

We in the Church of England could do with the raising of another Pilgrimage of Grace.

Sawley's ruins still reveal where the abbey church was. The skeletal outline of cloister, transept and refectory are evident.

In my time in the parish, as now, English Heritage manages the site. I wrote to them asking for permission to hold a service in the abbey grounds. Better than that: a Eucharist on the former chancel and sanctuary. They were very happy to oblige. As far as I was aware it would be the first Mass celebrated on that hallowed ground for almost 450 years. Rather uncharitably I reckoned it was "one in the eye" for Henry VIII! The 'Pilgrimage' (as we called it) to Sawley Abbey was planned for Saturday, May 26th 1984, the Feast of St Augustine. It was a happy coincidence that Augustine was a prior in a monastery in Rome who was sent by Pope Gregory the Great in 596 AD to re-evangelize the Church in these shores. The fact added something extra to the occasion.

A horse-box earlier that Saturday had delivered an altar-table and other sanctuary paraphernalia. Some church ladies had provided a spectacular fan-shaped floral arrangement as an altar-frontal. They came in good numbers. The folk from St Peter and St Paul's, after prayer led by our Reader Richard, set off to walk along the river to the abbey. St Ambrose's people formed up, after their own Pilgrims' Prayers, and walked in procession down the hill to join their fellow-parishioners. Quite a thrill to see crucifer, choir, servers and congregation 'sallying forth to Salley'. The weather was dull but our worship was bright. So memorable was the Pilgrimage that we repeated it twice more in the Junes of 1986 and 1988. These two events were held on a Sunday and the whole worship enhanced by the sterling sounds of the Slaidburn Silver Band.

In contrast to the exuberance of the Pilgrimage, I found the work of two Church Schools exacting. Grindleton Primary was earmarked for closure by the Department for Education. We organised a battle campaign to save the school, which resulted in four of us Governors presenting our case before Mr Bob Dunne MP, at the House of Commons. I recall that we were given exactly six minutes to present our case – not a second more. We had rehearsed it like a short play and finished with ten seconds to spare. And succeeded in our mission! Sadly, schools in Ribchester and Hurst Green were not so fortunate. I was subsequently interviewed on Radio Lancashire about our success. I mentioned how we had worked very hard on our submission – and that it had been in our constant prayers. "Does that mean, then," asked the interviewer, "that the others didn't pray about *their* situation – or that God preferred Grindleton to them?" It was a good question and one I struggled with in my not very convincing reply.

As chairman of two Church Schools I had two sets of Governors. There were, naturally, many interviews for many posts, both ancillary as well as teaching. With the short-listing and interviewing of teachers, I worked very closely with one Adviser from the Education Office. He told me that at one such interview in my parish the elderly lady Church Governor had asked a young teacher-applicant about her interests. "They are catholic," she replied. At the summing up the lady Governor refused point-blank to consider the young applicant on account of "her Catholicism". No amount of explaining the meaning of the word (with a small 'c') would dissuade her. Needless to say, the young applicant didn't get the job.

It was some of the teaching staff who were the real problems. A series of untoward incidents concerning one teacher was sniffed out by investigative journalists from a couple of tabloid newspapers. I confess that I had to tell a few lies to get them off our backs. On a brighter note, Bolton by Bowland had a delightful link with a school in Sweden. And Grindleton School, having been reprieved, went to town in celebrating its 150th Anniversary in 1988.

Un-settled

I was not the first choice. The Trustees met in the home of the local dentist to appoint a successor to Canon Ashby at Holy Ascension, Settle. Alan Wright was a member of the congregation and a Trustee. His splendid home was, until a handful of years back, the town's Vicarage. I never knew the name of the man they chose but Bishop Roy refused to ratify the appointment because of some ethical blot on the applicant's c.v. Or so I was told when he asked me to reconsider. Ann firmly advised me not to go. "If they didn't want you then, they won't want you now." But I agreed to go. In retrospect she was right. Apart from a few marvellously supportive souls the majority of the 'original' church folk were at best ambivalent to my selection.

The signs, I suppose, were there from Day One. We moved into Settle Vicarage on Friday, June 30th. It was most strange that no one, except for two elderly church stalwarts, Jack and May Bowker, came to call on us. Normally a host of people call, some with flowers or an apple crumble or just a "Welcome to Your New Home" card. But nothing. We discovered that the churchwarden had *instructed* people not to call. And they had obeyed. We felt very isolated and unloved.

Then I was almost late for my Institution and Induction – when I am legally and ecclesiastically made incumbent of the parish. Usually the incumbent-elect is waiting at the church for a good half hour or more before anyone else appears. I appeared in the vestry with ten minutes to spare, somewhat agitated. Jack, our grand Jack Russell terrier, had gone AWOL. On this evening of all evenings. A newcomer to the area, like his owners, he was probably exploring his new 'parish'. None of us could find him. Ann, together with Philip and Rebecca, were almost latecomers to the service themselves. So fine had they cut it, that if there were reserved seating for the new Vicar's wife and family, it had been re-allocated. They were bundled off upstairs into the constricted gallery. Jack (the dog, not Mr Bowker) was ultimately found by a passer-by outside the Fish and Chip shop. His identity tag on his dog-collar showed a *Clitheroe* telephone number. His considerate rescuer, assuming that the dog had been dumped by some callous Lancastrian, took Jack to the police station. It was late in the evening, when in desperation we reported our missing dog to the police, that we were reunited.

The foreboding continued four days later at my first celebration of Holy Communion a bigger than average congregation turned up. There is always a larger than normal attendance on this 'first Sunday', as many non-regulars give the new chap the 'once-over' and thereby establish a reasonable excuse not to alter their ways of absenteeism for the next few years. After the service I completed the Church Register, writing in the number of communicants for that particular Sunday (the Eighth after Pentecost, as it happened to be): fifty six.

"There were fifty *five*!" snapped my lady churchwarden.

"Fifty six" I calmly replied. "I had five wafers remaining from the sixty brought up at the Offertory."

"Exactly!"

"And there was me. I use the Priest's Host. Fifty five plus one: fifty six."

She harrumphed loudly and turned away. The episode, naturally, wasn't anything to do with mathematics. It was all about power. The battle lines had already been drawn and I hadn't been in the job a week.

The parish of Settle was the town itself. Just over two thousand residents. It was a small but delightful market town. It had most of the amenities you would ever want. There was a small Co-operative store, where Mr Alan Bennett, the famous writer, would skulk and eavesdrop on customers' conversations, thus collecting many of his pearls for his amusing books. The market-place, surrounded by a host of shops, banks, solicitors' offices, held a lively weekly market. It was a tourists' stop-over and consequently there were several pubs and cafés, a local tourist information centre and at least two well-stocked outlets for serious hikers. There were four churches, plus a Quaker Meeting House.

The Church of the Holy Ascension – a wonderful title! – was a most unusual building. To start with, it was built on a north-south axis, so that the Jerusalem and the 'East end' actually faced south! It was rectangular in shape with a tower onto the west side of which was stuck a taller, spindlier octagonal construction crowned with a spire. It had the distinct appearance of a minaret, complete with openings in order that the church bell, rather than the muezzin, could sound and call people to prayer. Inside, the chancel was divided from the nave by an oppressive wrought iron screen, which meant the choir was partially obscured from the congregation. The pulpit and font, both rather ornate, were of alabaster and had a rather pleasant marbled hint of pink or rose. When we decided to paint the interior I sought advice from my sister-in-law who had an art education background who suggested a similar, paler but complementary, colour for the walls of the church. The colour would be ideal, since it would bring some warmth to a rather cheerless, huge, ungainly space. When representatives from the Diocesan Advisory Committee came to discuss our application the rose colour was dismissed out of hand. I protested and supported my argument with the recommendation of my artist relative. A waste of time. It had to be *white*, they insisted (with not an art qualification between them). "Why white?" I asked. They gave no reason. I said it would have the appearance of a gent's urinal and render the place even colder. But white paint is cheaper...

Affixed to the wall of the church porch is a memorial to the 'navvies' who died whilst constructing the famously awe-inspiring viaduct on the Settle-Carlisle railway. It was in the church porch that I had a most bizarre and creepy experience. One evening I had forgotten to lock the main door of the church and it was after 11pm when I went down to rectify the error. Ann came with me with our dog Jack. The curving pathway to the door means that the porch receives no illumination from the street lighting. With key poised I stepped blindly into the porch. I trod on what I can only describe as a bundle of cloths, out of which sprang a man with a great wail as he sped off into the graveyard and further darkness. My immediate response was to shout at him with great severity. Not that he took much notice of me in his sudden flight. When I realised that he was sleeping rough and was using the church for shelter, I was sorry that I had disturbed him. After all, he could have found much warmer accommodation if he'd tried the unlocked door.

The congregation at Holy Ascension numbered about thirty on a usual Sunday. All were above sixty bar four ladies who were nearer forty than thirty (I think!) and who were labelled by everyone else as "the young ones". There was a great need to inject not only new but young blood. The trouble was that the church was choked by its own conservatism, suffocated by a few individuals who did not want or did not know how to share responsibility for the Church's mission. It was going to be a struggle. The majority of friends we made in Settle did not attend church, nor did they want to. But there were some – a few – faithful people who did hold a vision of what might be. With my encouragement these folk slowly began to unlock their reticence and bring some fresh air into the lungs of our church. Progress *was* made. Numbers improved over 50%. A Junior Church, the 'Sunday Goers,' was formed, as was a band of altar servers and a full-time organist to complement the small but loyal choir. It was here that I most enjoyed teaching my Adult Confirmation Group. The tentacles of Holy Ascension began to reach out and new families began to appear and participate in the communal life. We formed a Gulf War Support Group which met regularly in the upper room of the Surgery. Six local families had sons deployed in Kuwait or Iraq, including us, for our youngest son Bart, too, was 'out there.'

The 'war' on the Settle Church front had somewhat abated. Yet despite the progress I detected a deep resistance and resentment to me by those for whom I was not the first choice. My dentist friend, in whose house I had been interviewed, felt he could no longer face attending church precisely because of this reactionary attitude, shown to him as well as to me. I reluctantly gave him 'dispensation' to stay away –"for his soul's health". I don't believe he has ever returned. I, too, felt it was a losing battle. What brought it all to a head was one particular morning at our Church School's morning Assembly. I had taught the children a modern Advent hymn by the wonderful hymn-writer Fred Kaan. The song sings of Our Lord Jesus Christ in Mary's womb. The music teacher, a member of an extreme evangelical sect, refused to play it and walked out. To crown it all, a parent Governor, who was a Methodist, complained to me about the contents of the hymn. I explained that they were good orthodox doctrine – and besides, the author of the hymn's words was himself a Methodist! He wasn't at all satisfied and 'reported' me to the Diocesan Board of Education. A bout of total senseless pandemonium ensued. Not once did the Diocesan Director speak up in my defence. I decided, perhaps cowardly, to call it a day. Unlike the name of the local café, I truly found it impossible to 'Settle Down'.

Three in one

"A prophet is not without honour except in his own country." I was very mindful of Our Lord's saying as I applied for, and later accepted, the living of Broughton, Marton and Thornton. The Gospel tells us that Jesus' ministry was in full flow when He returned "to his own country" to spread His message. "Home" might have been Nazareth (as St Luke points out) or the locality (St Matthew). Be that as it may, Jesus preached in His local synagogue and the folk just did not believe Him. "Is not this the carpenter's son?" they asked. "Where did this man get his wisdom?" For seven years I travelled on the school bus which picked up and dropped off boys and girls in West and East Marton, sometimes Broughton and occasionally Thornton. The area was certainly my Galilee and almost my Nazareth. Would my ministry be acceptable so close to home? Or would they question? "Isn't that the confectioner's son?" "Didn't we use to see him with that Burgess girl on the benches in Victory Park?" St Matthew records that Our Lord "did not do many mighty works there" because of their unbelief. How would I fare on home territory? I knew the area. I understood (and sometimes slipped into) the local dialect. I shared its history. I was, after all, cradled in Craven. I weighed it all up and accepted the post with eager anticipation.

The old adage "small is beautiful" certainly applied to the parish. It was by far the smallest in the whole of the Bradford Diocese. Six hundred souls, all of whom could have been accommodated *three* times over in my church at Chorley. Small, yes. But beautiful. Set in the sleepy, sheepy folding fields of Craven. Five villages in all: Broughton and Elslack; East and West Marton; and Thornton-in-Craven. There were three churches, all ancent and venerable. All Saints' had served Broughton and Elslack for at least 870 years. It was constructed partly from the russet-coloured sandstone of the now extinct Roman fort, which had stood alongside the Ribchester to York road, the chief highway for both Roman trade and Roman military. Rome still has an abiding presence here today: Broughton is the seat of the Tempest family, strong Roman Catholics who have been most kind to Anglicans over the centuries.

St Peter's in East Marton is a solid, stumpy twelfth century building, hidden from the A59 but a mere stone's throw from the Leeds-Liverpool canal. Its sister village of West Marton, once the home to a thriving dairy and creamery, shares the church. Marton was one of the ancestral homes of the family of Bishop Reginald Heber of Calcutta, whose hymns we still sing.

St Mary's Thornton stands at the entrance to the village at the Barnoldswick end. Its foundations reach back to the twelfth century also, though the present church is from the mid-1400s.

Despite its tiny population the parish had bureaucratic overload. Each church had its District Church Council with its two churchwardens, treasurer and secretary. From these three Councils some members were elected to a *Parochial* Church council, again with its full complement of officers. In total there were six wardens, four treasurers, four secretaries, plus a handful of Deanery and Diocesan Synod representatives. A nightmare! The rector, of course, was Chairman of all four Councils. His annual tally of all such meetings numbered at least twenty – quarterly Council meetings *and* the four Annual General Meetings, when the merry round of elections took place and set the ball rolling all over again. The local D.C.C.s had been created to give each village a greater say when each lost its incumbent to become part of the united benefice. The scheme had its merits but I reckon the Devil had scored the winning goal, since all that hot air and paper bureaucracy meant less time in the mission field.

It is a known fact that every parish blessed (or burdened) with an ancient church has to spend far too much time in raising funds to maintain the building. In almost everyone's set of priorities this takes precedence over finding money to pay the Parish Share, whose contributions to the Diocesan pot do actually pay the priest his stipend and cover the insurance on the parsonage. I was determined from the outset that each former parish should have a fair measure of independence, so long as it was understood that the *united* structure had ultimate priority. On the whole it seemed to work. The two branches of the Mothers Union joined together quite amicably after a suspicious start; Gordon, our Reader, and later Denys, did the rounds of all three churches; several united projects were tried and tested both in worship and in teaching the faith. The weekly Lent study and worship was always well attended, though not so the quiet Saturday evening Advent meditation at the rectory.

Broughton's faithful decided to redevelop the old church hall which stood adjacent to the lych-gate. It had been the venue for some joyous, steamy Harvest Suppers – steamy because the smallish main room boasted two open-grate coal fires which were generously charged during and throughout such occasions. The heat was tremendous. We wanted to equip the hall with sufficient electrics for all kinds of audio-visual presentations. Improved kitchen facilities, toilets and a better access were all part of the Big Plan. As were very necessary repairs and renovations. It would not be cheap. The bulk of the money, we hoped, would come from a National Lottery grant. Churchwarden Annette sent off for an application form. It duly arrived, a thick wad of sheets, looking like an 'A' level examination paper. We realised that to be successful we would have to watch our p's and q's and be p.c. The *church* hall would have to be the *parish* hall – open and available for use by every member of the community, irrespective of ethnicity, creed, colour or name. Wheel-chair access, rightly, was mandatory. Health and safety considerations would sadly mean the demise of those burning hot coals spilling out onto tiny hearths at the Harvest Supper. Thanks to her headteacher's expertise and patience Annette succeeded in obtaining a Lottery grant. Building work commenced. We began to receive outside bookings from a variety of sources. The Church's wider ministry was much in evidence.

Rogationtide was very much a Broughton affair. Traditionally the fifth Sunday after Easter was the day set aside for the Church to ask God's Blessing on the land, its crops and animals. Broughton's Evensong on this Sunday, almost always in the lovely month of May, comprised of suitable hymns, readings and a guest preacher. After whose sermon the sizeable congregation would process up and down our aptly-named Primrose Lane. Here we would make several 'stations', or stopping-places, to recite verses from the ancient biblical song, the Benedicite ("O all ye Green Things upon the earth, Bless ye the Lord!" and so on), and bless, in turn, crops and grass, sheep and cattle – the latter usually obliging by coming to peer at us through the farm gate. We also turned towards the churchyard and prayed for the souls of the departed, who thankfully did not peer at us over the headstones. The fruits of all this Rogation prayer would be revealed at Harvest-time, when once again we'd be back in the hall feeding our faces.

'Marton' meant 'mere tun', a homestead near water. In the time of the Domesday Book a small habitation had indeed resided beside a watery area. The centuries have long since dried it up in our Marton but water still exists aplenty, as the Liverpool to Leeds canal wends its way around the mediaeval church. A notice on the tow-path invites both boaters and bargees to its worship every Sunday. I suppose 'water' was the apposite tag to describe much of my parochial ministry in this particular place: 'hot water' to be precise.

Since my arrival in the parish I detected in this corner of the 'patch' a lack of keen responsibility. I had heard tales of locum clergy during the interregnum unable to find any Communion wine. Someone had to volunteer to fetch a bottle of sherry from home. Often, when the wine *was* left at church, it was stored in the bell-tower rather than the vestry. But the bell-tower door, like the main door, was never locked. So even though the dark glass bottle of Vino Sacro was on site, it was invariably empty. Our resident Sabbath-eve tramp saw to that. Snuggling down amongst the old hassocks and pew runners, he would keep beautifully warm, outwardly by the church boiler, which automatically fired up in the early hours for the following day's worship, and inwardly warm by the amber nectar from our ecclesiastical suppliers. And with worship at eleven o'clock, he had ample time to make an unseen getaway

These hiccups were easily rectified. Not so the problem of one affronted churchwarden. He could rarely appear at church because of the heavy work-load of his business. I felt we needed both wardens to be at church every Sunday and I reckoned he would understand if I suggested he resign until his work allowed him more time for church responsibilities. I broached the subject on the telephone. I had tried to contact him with a view to meeting him in person but it had never materialised and now I was speaking to him only the day before the Annual Meeting elections. I admit the phone is a very poor instrument for such delicate matters.

"So you're sacking me, then," he said.

"No," I replied, "it's just that we need two people at church on Sunday mornings."

"You're kicking me out," he insisted.

I explained that I could not do that. Churchwardens hold their office under a Bishop's Licence. I had no authority to dismiss him. Only the

Bishop could do that. He put down the receiver with the matter still unresolved. Within one hour, however, I learnt that I had "sacked" him. The news was instantly all around the village. I don't suppose the majority of village folk cared one way or the other. Not many of them were church-goers. "Of course, I can't go to church, rector," one lady told me on behalf of the many, "because I haven't enough money." No amount of protesting on my part could convince her. It was a typical – and accurate – reason why ordinary villagers, or 'cottagers' as the opposition called them – would not attend.

The impasse created by that telephone conversation developed into full scale battle. The warden did not show up at the Annual Meeting and someone else was elected. Months of bitterness prevailed. Tensions never really disappeared for the remainder of my stay there. The congregations from the other two churches were a splendid support to me but it left a black mark on the Christian stewardship of all of us. My ex-warden and I separately met the Bishop and Archdeacon both of whom did next to nothing to untangle the tensions and clear up the chaos. Even my antagonists were appalled at the Archdeacon's behaviour when he chaired a meeting to hear their complaints. Apparently he sat on the table in front of the gathering, swinging his legs, and produced a banana from his pocket which he duly peeled and ate, declaring that he would have no time for his tea. The whole sorry affair sullied the Church's ministry in that portion of the parish. The underlying attrition sapped us all of any real progress in God's mission. It was badly handled by me and my accusers. Both of us, however, ought to have been able to obtain sound counsel and unswerving guidance from our superiors. That never materialised.

By contrast things at Thornton in Craven simply blossomed. With the introduction of vestments, altar servers, the keeping of Saints' and Holy days – and the occasional incense! – I had pushed the people considerably 'up the candle'. They seemed to relish it. Each Patronal Festival we started the Eucharist in the village centre at the Love Tree. Accompanied by the Earby Brass Band and protected by the local bobby, young and old marched up the steep main road (a dangerous hill-top) and swung sharp right into the Barnoldswick road, past the almshouses and onto the church to conclude the worship. The ever-increasing congregation was an encouragement and a support to me. We worked *together* in whatever we did. It was not surprising, therefore, that the suggestion of marking the Millennium arose. Could we raise enough money for a new church bell? A Millennium Bell? St Mary's belfry possessed four silent bells, unable to sound forth because of the weakness of the tower walls. A new addition would necessarily incur the cost of strengthening the stonework, installing a new frame and retuning the original four bells. Could we do all that? We reckoned we could and before long a "Bells of St Mary's" Fund was launched. It seemed a mammoth task for a small village of three hundred souls. Undaunted, we sallied forth. Every conceivable ploy was used to raise the funds. Bright 'Mary blue' sweatshirts were bought by the box-load – and sold. Each shirt bearing our logo. These shirts were not only superb money-raisers, they were a splendid advert for our endeavours. It was after the August Bank Holiday Car Boot Sale (no prizes for guessing where the proceeds were going) that Ann and I returned home to Broughton. We were exhausted – 'jiggered' as the locals would say – from our last visit to the Household Waste Recycling Centre. Or 'the Tip', as the same locals would say.

"Good afternoon," said a polite young man as we got out of the car. "Are you the vicar?" In my Bells of St Mary's blues I could have been anyone. "Yes, I am," I replied, "may I help you?"

"My friend," he said, pointing to a stooped figure by the church porch, "would very much like to see inside your church." I told him I would get the key and let them both in. As the young man and I approached the church I instantly recognised the friend: Mr Alan Bennett, the famous author and playwright. I apologised for my unkempt appearance, explaining we had just returned from a Car Boot Sale. I gave them a concise description of All Saints', pointing particularly to my favourite pieces which were the two mediaeval alabasters of Our Lady. These wonderful objects, one decapitated, one breast-feeding the Holy Child, had been buried in the church grounds in order to avoid the marauding hands of Henry VIII's men at the Reformation. They were rediscovered centuries later during the digging of foundations for a small vestry. I left the men to explore at their leisure. A few days later I received a letter from Mr Bennett thanking me for my time. He enclosed a generous cheque towards the Bell Fund and wished us well in our fund-raising. To my delight he records the episode in his book "Untold Stories," noting that the vicar appeared "dishevelled"!

It's not the only best-seller in which I receive a mention! Blake Morrison, who grew up in Thornton in Craven, recounted my pastoral involvement in his father's funeral. His book "When did you last see your father?" describes the life of his doctor father. Both his father, Arthur, and his mother Kim were general practitioners in nearby Earby and would undoubtedly be the physicians for most of the local villagers. Arthur was a dictatorial, rumbustious character, accustomed to getting his own way. When I heard that he was very ill and near to death I visited his house. I was forbidden to enter. He had instructed his wife and family that he did not want any visitors. For Arthur it was too much like admitting defeat. When he did die the undertaker phoned to ask if I would take the funeral service in church.

I therefore called at his home and this time gained a welcome admission. I spoke to Kim, of course, but it was his son Blake who took to managing the whole business. Towards the end of our arrangements I referred him to an article he had written many years ago in *The Observer*. Like me, Blake was a Burnley football supporter. His newspaper column described his childhood heroes who were also mine. We fantasised about the great teams of the past – and of Burnley's winning the Football League championship in 1960. Football is a marvellous common denominator. I suppose religion was way back in the Middle Ages, though not any more. The funeral visit therefore concluded on this brighter note. In his book I appear, nameless again, attending to his father's funeral plans. Mr Morrison has me dressed in my duffle coat, wearing a claret and blue football scarf around my neck. *Not* true on both counts. But it puts the 'fun' into funeral.

Meanwhile the Millennium Bell Fund continued to grow. A plethora of plans, plots and ploys were forever being devised to persuade the public to part with their money. The small Planning Group were wont to meet in The Tempest Arms: perhaps it was the Jennings beer which lubricated our fertile minds.

The firm of John Taylor, renowned bellfounders of Loughborough, were given the job of producing our new bell. A number of us visited the foundry first to see the casting and then the completion of our bell.

It was during this time that we were given the chance of purchasing a second bell. It's not only the supermarkets which come up with enticing offers. Taylor's offer of 'Buy One Get One Half-price' seemed too good an opportunity to miss. It was agreed to purchase a brace of bells. The fund-raising was intensified.

All this time, as rector, I had a depressing feeling that the two new bells might, like their four silent siblings, go unrung for many a year. We hadn't given much thought to the question of *who* would ring the bells. We would require a dependable team, plus 'reserves', and they would have to be trained. I need not have worried. Word went round the parish and quickly a dozen or so people eagerly volunteered. An experienced captain of a neighbouring bell-tower kindly – and literally – showed us the ropes. We had *two* teams of six ready and waiting for the Big Day.

It was a fantastic day when the low-loader arrived with our new bells. The engineers from Taylor's were greeted by scores of church folk. The children of the Primary School were present to mark this historic occasion, as were journalists and photographers from the local presses. The larger and original of our new bells bore the inscription from Hebrews 13, "Jesus Christ is the same, yesterday, today and for ever." A 'quiet' ringing rehearsal had taken place on December 31st, proving all was well for the dawn of a new millennium. At twelve noon on January 1st in the Year of Our Lord 2000 Thornton's six bells were sounded in jubilant celebration. The climax of a marathon community effort.

Another great source of parish pleasure was to be found in our Parish Weekends at Parcevall Hall, the Diocesan Retreat House. The imposing Elizabethan house stood at the cul de sac of a narrow twisting lane just outside Appletreewick. A modern wing of bedrooms complemented the old rooms. Together they could sleep a couple of dozen retreatants. Appetising food, comfortable surroundings and glorious gardens made these weekend get-togethers most memorable. Teach-ins, group discussion, sufficient time for reading or resting, snoozing or strolling, all sustained by worship and prayer in the upstairs chapel. Our visits to Parcevall took place at different times of the year, We shared a Bonfire Night celebration – fire and fireworks – with the Hall staff; we enjoyed spring and summer slots; and one in late autumn when I introduced a certain film for the Saturday evening session. "It's a film about a vicar's attempt to live out the Gospel," I outlined, with a deliberately deadpan face and downbeat voice. The flock, bless them, obediently took up their seats, fearing some non-Saturday night fare. Imagine their delight when Peter Sellers appeared on the screen, playing the hapless, generous, naïve, truly Christian, very foolish Reverend John Smallwood in *Heaven's Above!* Sellers' antics of creating multiple mayhem in the ecclesiastical circles of Orbiston Parva left us talking about it for months afterwards.

The event, however, which has left us talking for almost twenty years, occurred in 1992. It impacted on my time at Broughton, Marton and Thornton and significantly altered the course of the parish. It was the Church of England's General Synod vote on the ordination of women to the priesthood. Remembrance Day of that year was more poignant than usual. For most of the morning Ann and I sat in front of our television set as the debate concluded and the voting counted in the three Houses of Bishops, Clergy and Laity. It was akin to waiting for the football results. Being a Burnley fan meant that every Saturday afternoon in the season I would have a sickening, sinking feeling in the pit of my stomach as the scores came in. This was a Wednesday but the tension was no different. I knew the bishops and the clergy would give the motion a sufficient majority. It all hung on the laity's vote. The newspapers spoke of a close-run thing. And so it was. One vote – *one solitary vote* – gave the General Synod power to unravel not only 400 years of Reformation practice but two thousand years of the Church's doctrine on Orders. The result was worse than Burnley losing by an own goal in the final minute of extra time. I could quickly get over a football defeat. This other loss has stayed with me from that day.

It was true to say that most of my church congregations were equally dismayed. Several of us joined the newly-formed Bradford branch of Forward in Faith. Over the months we rallied and, thanks to the lay people, we eventually decided to apply for alternative episcopal oversight. The C of E, in a clear sign that it was still unsure of its latest foray into Church doctrine, made provision for those who in all conscience could not accept the new situation. We could, providing a certain percentage majority was in favour, choose to be placed under the pastoral care of a specially appointed bishop. These bishops, three in all, were labelled 'flying bishops' as they were constantly flying about England tending to their scattered flocks. Our Parochial Church Council voted to be placed under the care of the 'flying' Bishop of Beverley. The decision was met with astonishment and not a little irritation by the Diocesan hierarchy. I have no hesitation in saying that I suffered because of it. Preferment, promotion passed me by. No doubt about it: the Bishop and his senior colleagues were embarrassed that such a piddling parish could upset the apple-cart. We were one of only two full parishes in Bradford Diocese to take such a vote. St Chad's in Bradford's Toller Lane, the diocese's Anglo-Catholic flagship became our twin sister. Other parishes in the diocese ought to have grasped the nettle but didn't.

On that fateful Remembrance Day morning I could not bear to hear all the 'post-match' analysis. I sharply turned off the TV and got ready for an early afternoon funeral. As I was writing up the episode for this book I referred to my Parson's Pocket Book for 1992. The diary entry was ominously blank, except for the reminder that the vote was to take place. Howver, a tiny newspaper cutting was lodged in the page. I have no idea as to its author but it was a message of confidence to priests of my persuasion. The snippet simply said: "My advice to the parish priest who is shocked by the decision is to stand firm and not lose hope. There will be a delay now while the legislation is implemented, which will give us time for considering the options. During this time we must talk to each other and make our plans as best we may." Nearly two decades on and most of us are still "considering the options". Meanwhile the liberals in the C of E are increasingly more illiberal and less tolerant. I, on the other hand, more disenfranchised, more ostracised.

Despite this unsatisfactory affair – or was it because of it? – my three little churches had a combined congregation of almost one hundred every Sunday. Bigger than our two neighbouring towns! Because of our alternative episcopal oversight the Archdeacon was somewhat stymied in his grand plans to amalgamate us with adjacent parishes. This fact, too, irked the Diocese.

One small but beautiful parish was thriving. However, I began to feel rather guilty because of my comfortable situation. Not that I hadn't worked hard for it, nor was I taking things easy. I became aware that a downtown parish in Morecambe had been advertising for quite some time for a priest of my ilk. It was financially poor, set in a very deprived, drug-riddled area. Was I too old to handle it? I reckoned that I had 'another ministry' in me. So I eventually applied and in the one-horse race got the job. My appointment ultimately appeared on the usual page of the Church Times. Above this column was another set of names: those who had recently been made Canons of Bradford Cathedral. The following week I received a gracious letter from a former Assistant Bishop of Bradford. He congratulated me on my recent canonry and went on at some length about the *honour* of it. I wrote back explaining that there was no canonry: I was merely moving to Morecambe. I think he was so embarrassed that he never replied to my letter.

Honour? We priests do not do it for honour. Anyway, I was reminded of the thoughts I had had, at the outset of a ministry so close to my home town, that with prophets honour doesn't get much of a look in!

The Naples of the North

There was an old railway poster, of which I have a postcard, which invites travellers to go to Morecambe. The resort is described as "the Naples of the North". I have been to Naples (the Italian one). On the second day of our holiday there, a shooting took place in broad daylight, with a number of fatalities. I have motored on the Amalfi coast and wondered at Pompeii, Herculaneum and the little island of Capri, where a famous Lancashire lass made her home. And I reckon that Morecambe Bay is every bit as wonderful as the Bay of Naples. Gracie Fields could have saved herself all that bother... To gaze out across Morecambe Bay and see the snow-capped hills of the English Lake District is as good a panorama as anywhere in the world. The poster is absolutely right. Morecambe is the Naples of the North. Even the violence is the same. The trouble is that with the Lancashire model, when you turn your back to the Bay and look inland, it is grim. Very grim. This lost resort smacks of the last resort.

I had decided, after much thought and prayer, to give my last six years before retirement to a rather unknown challenge. The parish of St Barnabas was one of two central parishes in the town. A population of ten thousand people resided in a variety of housing. Some still lived in the fast-diminishing 'grand' houses of Morecambe's hey-day. There were scores of bungalows, many painted white as befits a seaside location. And hundreds of apartments which had been carved out of the large terraced houses which were once the thriving boarding-houses of a busy resort. My grandparents owned and operated one before and during the Second World War. Within the parish there were some areas which were deemed by the relevant Government Department to be of the highest social deprivation. Many young residents in these streets had Anti-Social Behaviour Orders stamped upon them. A great proportion of the bed-sits were occupied by men recently out of prison. Most were penniless, dependent on drink or drugs. Some of these were as dangerous in the daylight as they were in the dark. There existed – *subsisted* is better – a violent underworld which only came to life in the very late hours of each night. A Hades which suddenly disappeared at the coming of the dawn. If I couldn't sleep at night I would peer through the bedroom window overlooking Regent Road. What strange, bizarre sights! Men fighting men, men fighting women, women fighting women. People staggering crazily about like sleep-walkers. The answer to Blackpool's illuminations: Morecambe's *hallucinations!* In reality, not very funny. Truth to say, the streets of my parish were unsafe after 10pm. All our Church socials – and we had a lot! – finished at that time and everyone but everyone was offered transport home.

From the street-side the church building was quite insignificant. But for the large brightly painted church notice board fixed to the wall you would probably pass by without recognising it. Its length ran parallel to Regent Road and appeared more like the side entrance to Marks and Spencer. Inside, however, it was a different story. When you entered, the vastness and the expanse of it arrested you. Its light stonework, the pale oak chairs, the soft green glass of the high windows admitting the sunlight, all gave a feeling of airiness and space. The well-made solid chairs with the crimson seats were arranged in a slight arc, allowing for a wide central aisle besides enormously large areas around the margins. Magnificent for processions and ideal for congregations to travel the pilgrim way of the Stations of the Cross, which we did every Monday in Lent and on Good Friday. By moving these chairs to the side we were able to create an ideal place for dancing, or for Bazaars and Sales of Work. The narthex area at the back of the church housed in their season both a Christmas and an Easter tableau, imaginatively done by Ted and Doreen. On weekdays the narthex was a natural area for coffee and biscuits for all and sundry who popped into church. We hosted many a holiday-maker but we had our regulars. Many of these came to inspect the huge array of good second-hand clothing which was displayed right across the back of the church. An area we called 'the Shop'. Both ventures, the coffee bar and "the Shop," arose out of a need to help those on low incomes. It was sad to see the poverty and plight of many who hunted amongst the clothes racks. Yet there were also many occasions when you had to smile. One bearded man who frequented the Shop a least once a week was hunting through the racks of ladies' clothes.

"What size do you reckon this is?" he inquired, holding a pink nylon slip against himself.

"About a sixteen, I should think," replied one of our church ladies. "What size is your girlfriend?"

"Girlfriend!" he exclaimed. "It's for me!"

Looking eastwards a large window of modern glass was the backdrop to a wide sanctuary with its proportionately long altar. The church had all the Anglo-Catholic appurtenances: crucifixes, a bulbous brass Sanctus bell, the white sanctuary light and the red light over the aumbry which denoted the Holy Presence of the Sacrament reserved for the sick. There were innumerable vestments – albs, chasubles, copes of all the liturgical colours – most neatly and methodically hung in commodious wardrobes in the roomiest of vestries.

With such numinous surroundings the worship of the church just had to be equally exalted. And so it was. We hadn't a large congregation: around sixty. Of these about a dozen adults had various degrees of learning difficulties. I once calculated that only 17% of our faithful were in work and only 15% owned a car. Brian Hick taught a band of altar servers to a very high standard. He trained Stephen, who also had many difficulties, to such a high level, that, despite his problems, he knew the liturgy off by heart. Once, when the curate missed out a chunk of the Eucharist, Stephen interrupted the service by loudly calling out: "Well, yer made a right muck o' that!"

We had three services each Sunday. The early 8.30am Holy Communion used the Book of Common Prayer and attracted only six or seven folk. We had got into the habit of locking the main door as soon as the service started. On several occasions different strangers would attend, always young men. When the ladies went up to the altar rail for Communion, naturally leaving their handbags on the chair, the visitor would grab a handbag and make off. By locking the door and removing the key we effectively locked ourselves in with the thief. But the ploy was successful. The *sounds* of locking the exit was a sufficient deterrent. At Evensong, too, we operated a similar system. We allowed five minutes for latecomers, after which we locked the doors again. The evening service tended to attract the occasional drunkard or petty robber. Several times the men attempted to rive the alms-box from its secure mooring. The ten o'clock Parish Eucharist presented a different picture to those who would do the church harm. There were, at this worship, always more of us than them!

St Barnabas' also had in its congregation a number of young adults from Africa. They were not all from the same country: some from Rwanda, some from Tanzania and a young woman (whom I shall call Maria) with her tiny baby from yet another East African state. She was most beautiful, full of grace and gentleness. I sensed that she was from a royal or aristocratic background. Perhaps on the wrong side of the present political power. Perhaps fortunate to have escaped some unimaginable terror or purge. Her baby was no more than ten weeks old. All these young folk had been granted asylum and were in temporary lodgings in the town until a more permanent home could be found for them in one of our larger conurbations. English was neither their first nor their second language but after a few weeks' attendance at the Eucharist they asked me if they could borrow the service book, in order to learn the Creed and the prayers. Can you imagine *English* congregations doing that?

Sadly for us at church, one by one these admirable young people announced they would be leaving. They were not allowed to say where they were destined for. Perhaps they didn't know. It all had an air of secrecy and danger. Maria was the last one to leave. After the morning service she softly informed me that she would be departing later that day. Ann hastily found her a farewell present and something for her tiny boy. I called round after lunch to say Good-bye. She received me in her sparsely furnished bed-sit. There were two suitcases on the bed, both with their lids turned back. One was barely a third full and contained all her possessions save one. In the other suitcase lay her tiny one, fast asleep. The case was his cot. She was most grateful for the small presents and thanked me for the care which St Barnabas' had shown to her. She directed her large brown eyes towards the suitcases and with utmost sincerity said: "God is good." It was the most humbling experience of my life. Maria and all those lovely African Christians taught us so very much in their short time amongst us.

In all my work over almost forty years the main Sung Parish Eucharist was the highlight of the week. Without wishing my time away, every Monday morning I looked forward to the following Sunday with eager anticipation. St Barnabas' worship was probably the jewel in the crown of all my incumbencies. In my first year we were fortunate to have a brilliant young Roman Catholic organist, who introduced us to the splendid modern liturgical music of his church. Wonderful, sing-able stuff! Far superior to the difficult dirges I come across when doing my locum duties in the villages around Ripon, where tunes are almost impossible for the people to sing, to memorise and to master. Our ordinary (but extraordinary) folk in St Barnabas' took to this music like ducks to water. The mass settings are widely available: why more Anglican congregations don't use them is a mystery. Our talented organist, however, was also somewhat unpredictable and he suddenly resigned, leaving me two years of desperate searching for a replacement I never did find. Organists are rarer than priests.

It was a busy parish. The small Church Council, spearheaded by wardens Betty and Keith, were wisely guided by Sunday, our Nigerian treasurer. There was lots of visiting to be done in the parish. On one occasion I was called to do a funeral visit in the neighbouring parish, where the relatives of the deceased lived. It was a tiny brick terraced house in a tiny street in the town centre. As I approached the door I spotted a plaque fixed to the wall by the door. In this home, it stated, was born Eric Bartholomew, better known as the bespectacled half of the comedians Morecambe and Wise. I sat with the two relatives to discuss the funeral arrangements in a sitting room so small that the three of us filled the entire room. I glanced out into a small backyard which was overlooked by some large warehouse. I thought of Eric Morecambe's career. This humble house was aeons away from his Harpenden home. No doubt as to which milieu had fashioned his humour.

Whilst the face of my parish, its demography if you like, had radically changed in the past twenty years or so, there was still a high proportion of retired people. There were scores of Retirement and Nursing Homes with wonderful names like 'The Haven' (almost 'Heaven'). Was there one in St Peter's Close? These Homes meant a long list of church people who could no longer get to church. So the Church went to them. Alma, Andrew and Brian were licensed by the Bishop to take out the Blessed Sacrament and, with curate Simon and me, 'did' about thirty or forty communions a month.

St Barnabas' had links with both the Royal Air Force Association and the RNLI. Each organisation had an annual service in the presence of 'the chain gang' (the Mayor of Morecambe and entourage) and other officials. We were also the 'Theatre Church'. In those halcyon days of the 1950s, when you could see a different variety show every night of the week, the season always began with an act of worship in St Barnabas', when the front and back stage folk filled the pews to ask God's blessing on their endeavours. With the complete demise of Morecambe's entertainment industry that event no longer took place in my time.

For the first time in my ministry I received spiritual encouragement and financial support from the Church of England. Our parish was an 'urban priority' and we were able to get help from the Church Urban Fund for many of our parish projects. I also received from the Diocese a generous cheque for Ann and me to have a short holiday away from the trials and tribulations. Because there were many. I spent a great deal of time in community regeneration programmes. As a member of the small 'West End Committee' I had suggested we focussed on the renewal of the shopping area around Yorkshire Street, a mere stone's throw from the Promenade. It once had been a vibrant, busy shopping paradise but in recent times it looked as if many a stone had been thrown at it! In its prime the variety and range of Yorkshire Street's energetic tradespeople had been the catalyst for wealth and well-being right across our large parish. So we worked tremendously hard on our project for history to repeat itself. We were shortlisted for a massive National Lottery grant and made our presentation as one of three finalists. Sadly we were not chosen as the winner. Those funds would have meant a real opportunity for our patch. The exercise, however, was not wasted and from it much fruit was borne.

Underlying all this worthwhile work, however, was the abiding fear of the violence that could erupt. The West End's potential for disruption and damage had resulted in the establishment of our own small police unit. Street wardens were appointed to walk and check the area. I suffered an assault at my front door and was threatened very regularly because I refused to dole out money to fuel the habits of dark and dangerous men. I had convinced myself, as I pondered a move to Morecambe, that I had 'another ministry' in me. I had now come to the stark realisation that *physically* I wasn't up to it. Not the priestly work, I hasten to add. But the fact that if I were confronted by violence I was too old and not sufficiently agile *to run away*.

I have another postcard of a 1930s railway poster. It shows a tousled ginger-haired lad playing cricket on the sands. Taking a mighty swipe with his bat, he is clean bowled. His wickets well and truly spread-eagled. The poster exclaims: "Loosen your stumps in Morecambe!" I felt it had loosened more than my stumps. I decided I wasn't up to the job and would retire. Bishop Alan had other ideas. He persuaded me to do my last three years elsewhere. And that's how we came to Sabden for the second time.

CHAPTER FIVE

Parsonages & Other Houses

Parson's Patch

Florence Nightingale, the Bronte sisters, Admiral Lord Nelson, Jane Austen, John and Charles Wesley, Alfred Lord Tennyson, Reginald Heber and Field Marshal Montgomery. What have they in common? They are all sons or daughters of the parsonage. The vicarages and rectories – and manses, of course – were power-houses for future heroes in the literature, armed services, social welfare and Christian mission of this land. The parsonage is something quintessentially very English. The architectural historian Sir Nicholas Pevsner remarked that church and parsonage together make "a feature in the villagescape to which the Continent has no parallel."

In England's history there have been tens of thousands of houses for the parochial clergyman. Today these homes are a diminishing number, perhaps now 20,000 in all. In the Church of England there are at the moment about 7,800 occupied vicarages. Replying to questions in the House of Commons in January 2001, Stuart Bell, the Second Church Estates Commissioner, stated that from 1996 to 2001 *a yearly average* of 97 parsonages had been sold, 42 purchased and 18 built. That's a net loss of 185 rectories and vicarages over the period. In military terminology, that's a retreat. The situation will have undoubtedly worsened since 2001.

At the time of my writing this account, the General Synod of the Church of England is about to debate the proposal for newly-formed Diocesan Parsonages Boards to take control of all the vicarages in England. Synod's initiative is to make the mission of the local church more effective. Moving clergy – and therefore the houses in which they reside – to more central areas of ministry will effect this. Or so it reckons. Those opposed to these proposals argue that the parson should continue to own the freehold, even if his vicarage is inadequately situated. In February 2008, Stuart (now, *Sir* Stuart) Bell again responded to anxious questions in the Commons. MPs were voicing the worries of their constituents up and down the land, who were claiming that these Parsonages Boards were 'stealing' no less than £4 billion worth of clergy homes. "Render unto General Synod the things that are General Synod's" was Sir Stuart's riposte. Will General Synod remember that a large proportion of land for parsonages was given by *local* landowners and that the house itself was invariably paid for by some generous benefactor or by public subscription? I doubt it.

It has always been my contention that the Church Commissioners have erred in selling off their parsonages. Whilst the Church may be experiencing a trough in church-going, who is to say that there will not be revival one day? Another Wilfrid or a Wesley? To have sold the parsonages on a *leasehold* basis – for whatever length of time – would have meant the Church's retaining them and being able to utilise them at some future time. This policy appears a vision too far for the C of E. It quite obviously does not foresee a revival ever again. So as the Church retreats (and regroups?) the vicarages and rectories of our land are for sale at an increasing rate. "They have a wide appeal and make the most sought-after houses of all period properties," said one country estate agent recently.

There is a lovely parsonage story, which I believe is true, that when Walter Frere was Bishop of Truro he went to officiate at a Confirmation service in one of his far-flung rural parishes in deepest Cornwall. The weather apparently was so atrocious that the Bishop could not possibly return home (in the early 1920s he probably still relied on a horse rather than a horseless-carriage). The vicar, whose parish had held the Confirmation, invited His Lordship to stay the night and return in the light of the next day. Bishop Frere kindly accepted. As he was going down the darkened landing to the bathroom – there were no lights – the good Bishop suddenly received a hefty smack around the head, accompanied by the vicar's wife's remark, "That'll teach you to invite the Bishop when we've nothing in the house!"

I have lived in almost a dozen parsonages in my priestly ministry. Some large, some small, some grand, some bland. But never without a landing light. What follows is an account of how we have lived and moved within some of them.

Until her death quite recently my mother-in-law was happily nestled in her Nursing Home. Last Christmas she sent six cards and declared with a sigh of satisfaction "That's it!" Her telephone bill is made up of just three numbers, that of her sister in Uttoxeter and her two daughters. She still possesses, rather than *uses,* her old purple leather-bound Telephone and Address Book, to which she and my late father-in-law referred during their more active life. It is an unusually shaped book, being about fifteen inches long by three inches wide. Presciently she listed her elder daughter's address and phone number under 'V', the initial of her married name, rather than under 'A' for Ann. It was a wise move since there are far fewer names beginning with the twenty second letter of the alphabet than the first. However, a glance at the famous purple book will reveal that the entries under 'V' stretch to almost two feet six inches! Two pages of addresses: superseded and super-superseded: all belonging to us, our changes of address, crossed out and updated. Sixteen homes in all, plus one in Malta.

There are of course, many people who have had many more homes: armed services personnel, missionaries, actors, orphans, and gypsies. Even so, twenty is more than enough! From our first married home to that before Ordination we inhabited three in five years. Then during my ministry we occupied eleven houses, owned by the Church of England. An average of one every three and a half years. During these two periods of time we dabbled in the property market and bought and sold six more. These were partly as a bolt-hole but chiefly as a hedge in case I died. If that had been the case Ann and our children would have been compelled to vacate the vicarage within a few months, unless she married the new incoming vicar. I think, however, that *one* parson was quite sufficient for her.

Our first home

Our first home, however, was quite simply *ours*. We bought it. We borrowed the money at an incredibly low 'staff' rate from the Bank. It cost £1625. We purchased 46 Barrowford Road, Colne, from Mr and Mrs Godby, whose son, then 12 years old, I was to meet again in the Duke of Lancaster's Own Yeomanry. Clifford was the Regiment's Medical Officer to my Chaplain. We were good friends and were often seen together –"body and soul" the troopers called us – making our pastoral visits to the men on exercise.

Ann and I bought the house in early 1964. A large terraced house, situated centrally in a row of about twenty houses. Solidly built in local millstone grit around the end of the nineteenth century, the terrace would have been more imposing then. The row ran alongside a road, originally named Clarendon Drive, presumably after the 14th Duke of Clarendon, who was Chancellor of the Duchy of Lancaster from 1864-5. The house kindly faced south, with an open though somewhat uninteresting vista. Way to the east, high on Colne's steep main street, Albert Road, stood the Town Hall and St Bartholomew's parish church. The road, or rather the 'Drive', to the west led to large houses, less than a quarter of a mile away, including a very large mansion, which had become The Christiana Hartley Maternity Home, where I, and eventually Matthew, were born. There were numerous edifices in the area around Colne built in the name of Hartley. They were jam manufacturers and great benefactors to the town. The Drive also bore right and led to Alkincoats Park and the fine dwellings there. The park, now equipped with recreational facilities such as bowling and putting, was placed behind our terrace, with another terraced row in between. This, then, gave way to a back street, in cobbled stones. Here neighbours would hang out their washing on lines secured to hooks diagonally fixed into the stone walls of their coal-houses. No garden, of course. It was the first time that Ann had not had the luxury of such a thing and I know she missed it terribly. I did make her a window-box as compensation.

Internally the house partially made up for the lack of a garden. A more than adequate kitchen, two spacious reception rooms, both of which had open fireplaces. Our area was a smoke-free zone: we were allowed to use only a certain type of fuel, a hard, nutty anthracite cob. This stuff was extremely difficult to light so almost everyone had invested in a lethal-looking, but very effective, electric poker. It resembled a large toy cannon, which it was. You plugged it in, having first placed the nozzle well into the coals. Switched on, it fired an intense heat which quickly ignited the anthracite. We had roaring fires! I recall having the rector round. He sat on the settee directly in front of the fire but gradually, inch by inch, he moved the seat further and further away!

Our bedroom was a wonderful size, looking out towards the front. The second bedroom was by no means small and our bathroom huge by today's standards. From the landing were steps leading to our roomy attic, easily convertible to a third bedroom. It was here at 46 Barrowford Road that we prepared for our married life together. Throughout the winter and spring of 1964 we would come to clean and paint and plan. One of the young chaps at St James' church in Barnoldswick, John Heaton, had just served his apprenticeship as a painter and decorator. John came over on several occasions to help us with the painting – and, more importantly, to teach me how to paint. I've never forgotten his training.

It was here, too, that our first child was conceived and nurtured. We had a small party on Christmas Eve 1965. Whist we were standing at our front door, waving off the last of our guests, Ann announced that her waters had broken. Carefully, gingerly I got her into the car (we had borrowed my father's) and we made the short journey to the maternity hospital. There I left her, our Christmas plans utterly wrecked. The following day Ann ate a Hospital Christmas Lunch and was visited by the Lady Mayor. I was kindly invited by the Whittams to the rectory for my meal. It was the Nativity of our Lord but not of our child. *That* particular nativity did not occur during the whole of the twelve days of Christmas. Ann was extremely frustrated and not a little upset, since she seemed to be the ever-redundant one in the maternity ward, which saw mothers come and go. Apparently her waters sealed themselves, Ann came home and we waited a further 29 days before it all became real for us. Matthew was born on February 4th.

We had transformed the second bedroom into a most delightful nursery. After some initial fraught moments, entirely owing to our inexperience as parents, we happily and contentedly settled into the routine of feeds, 'winding' and nappy changes. He was a delight.

It was from 46 Barrowford Road that we enjoyed our first holiday: my parents' luxury caravan at Kirkby Lonsdale. We returned home after one week on the Saturday when England won the Word Cup. Glued to the radio during the extra-time being played, I almost left it too late to get the hire car back to the garage!

We had one scary moment at the house. Fifty yards away stood Riddiough's Wood Yard, in which vast amounts of timber were stored for the building industry. No one knows how – presumably arson – but the whole Yard caught fire. It was an incredibly fierce blaze and we and our neighbours were justifiably frightened as the heat became increasingly intense up the road. In fact the glass in our window-panes was very warm and there was a chance they might explode. The fire brigade, however, succeeded in quelling the inferno, though the timber yard was a complete write-off.

It was in 46 Barrowford Road that we were beset by the outrageous behaviour of some members of my family, as it became increasingly clear to us both that GOD was calling us forward. We decided to sell the house (in hindsight we should have let it). I stupidly prophesied that no terraced house would sell for more than £2000. Once I had received the go-ahead for Ordination training, things moved very swiftly. Before we got round to putting the sale into the hands of an estate agent, someone knocked at our door, stated that they wanted to buy the house, did not even wish to look around the property and offered the full asking price of £1875 straight away.

And so it was from 46 Barrowford Road that we set out, all three of us, one late Saturday September afternoon, full of expectancy and excitement for the adventure ahead.

'Vartyville'

Our hired Ford Anglia arrived at number 9 Carline Road in Lincoln well before the removal van. A red-brick semi-detached house, probably

Edwardian, it had been divided into a top and a bottom flat. Ours was the top flat. A spacious open porch led into a large red-tiled hallway. Immediately to the left was a door, through which a steep flight of stairs reached a landing. This was quite wide and from it sprang a kitchen and a second bedroom to the left. A small box room, main bedroom and living room were to the right. From these latter rooms we looked over part of the city and had a wide panoramic view of the Common.

If Barrowford Road was heaven, Carline Road was hell. We didn't realise it at the time through our naiveté, idealism, youth and excitement. After all, we were still a newly-married couple with a wonderful seven month old little son. The hell, I suppose, began on that very first day. The removal men arrived. It was all systems go! The men stopped for a cup of tea during which time the half-full van was left unattended and raided by one of my predecessor's young offenders, who stole several small items, including the Bush radio I had bought Ann for her 21st birthday. Of course, we did not immediately realise the loss of these goods. It is only when you start to sort things out properly in your new home that you start to miss this and that. So it was much later when the theft came to light. The lad was duly apprehended and in court admitted to the theft of our property. Not that we got much in return as compensation. Insurance companies are not the most charitable of organisations.

Carline Road started from the Yarborough road on the west side of the city, adjacent to the heath and the old racecourse of Lincoln Handicap fame. It was common land and many folk used it. Carline Road, lined with trees and very pleasant villa-style dwellings, stretched a quarter of a mile eastwards towards the Cathedral. It became Drury Lane for the last hundred yards or so. A sharp left corner brought you into Castle Square, flanked by picturesque ancient houses and the old Roman Castle, with its imposing gateway to the Law Court, where the Assizes took place at certain times in the year. Opposite the sharp left corner on Drury Lane was the Theological College. A brisk five minutes' walk would get me to Mattins on time.

It was not easy living, especially for Ann, at Carline Road. Did we leave the pram downstairs in the hallway? I cannot see us lugging it up and down those steep stairs every time we used it; then again, I cannot

St John the Baptist parish church, Wolvey.

St George's parish church, Chorley. A splendid Waterloo Church seating almost two thousand when first built.

Grindleton School's 150th Anniversary celebration 'in costume' with Bishop Roy Williamson of Bradford.

The parish church of SS Peter and Paul, Bolton by Bowland:
links with King Henry VI.

The Church of the Risen Christ, Wyken, Coventry, built in the early 1960s
to cater for rapid growth of parish population.

The C12th church of St Mary Magdelene, Wyken,
where I celebrated my first Eucharist.

Morecambe St Barnabas' Vicarage. Or Regent Rest Home?

"Jackanory" House, 4 Wordsworth Street, Lincoln,
directly opposite the college.

Our brand new vicarage in Wolvey.

St Ediths Vicarage, Monks Kirby
which stood in 5 acres of wild garden.

The Vicarage at Sabden in front of St Nicholas' church.

The Rectory at Broughton on a hot day.

see us leaving it at the mercy of the crazy dog of our flat-mates. I really cannot remember.

The downstairs neighbours, Samuel and Mary, were newly-wed. They were both Cornish and married the summer Sam graduated from Cambridge. He was a son of a Cornish vicar, had been to private school, followed by public school (what euphemisms!) and then Cambridge to read theology. They were a happy-go-lucky couple. Samuel, whose ancestor had brought the Gospel to New Zealand, was continually flying off abroad, leaving his wife to her secretarial work in an office in the city. Their lunatic dog *ate* a whole box of precious 35mm slides, which the postman had posted through the letter-box. The slides were of Matthew over the past six months. Because we had little spare money our use of the camera was frugal: those slides were irreplaceable and for a very long time we were inconsolable.

One evening we were anxious about our little son and we called the doctor. He arrived and wanted to examine the little chap who was in his cot in the small box room. He asked if he may put the electric light on to have a closer look. There was no light fitting in the room. He ought to have some heat on, he further advised. We had to admit that the room did not have an electric socket. He was not at all pleased.

However, emboldened by the doctor's comments we decided, along with Sam and Mary, to write to the landlord for a reduction in the rent, pointing out, among other things, the afore-mentioned lack of basic facilities. Naturally Mr Varty was not interested, so we resolved to take our case to the Rent Tribunal. Sam and I informed the College of our intentions but were met with a marked coolness, overridden by a gentle dissuasion from rocking the boat. Had Mr Varty other College students' names on his books? Had the College entered into some sort of deal with him? The older and wiser I become, the more I think it likely. However, it only made us even more determined to seek arbitration: and so we did.

This system of adjudicating a fair rent for tenants had become prominent in this country after a certain notorious landlord, Peter Rachman, was found by the courts to be extracting criminal amounts of rent from his immigrant tenants in North London in the 1950s and 60s. Rachman's name is still associated with bad housing and has even found its way into several English dictionaries. The work of the Tribunals, now labelled Rent Assessment Panels, continues to this day, providing an independent and fair judgement on rents and leases between landlord and tenant. An incredible mythology has developed about Peter Rachman, since his death in 1962. The story has it that he bought a red Jaguar for his wife and a white one for his mistress. He lived sumptuously in Hampstead, wined, dined and partied. He was involved with the Kray twins. When he collected his rent it is said he drove around the capital in a white sharkskin suit, hand-stitched crocodile shoes, smoking a fat cigar.

I don't think Mr Varty was quite so excessive though we did label him 'Rachman'. And the flat disparagingly (but justly) we named "Vartyville". We presented our case to the Tribunal – a comprehensive letter sufficed – and eventually we received adjudication: a reduction of ten shillings a week! There were, however, no material alterations or additions to the flats. And we, Ann and I, had had enough.

At the end of the academic year our friends Bernard and Muriel West were going to East Ham in London, where he was to serve his title. I always remember Muriel's excitement about the parish because "there was a Sainsbury's nearby." Bernard put in a good word on our behalf to the College, who owned the house the Wests had rented for two years. The property was directly opposite the College's main entrance: number 4 Wordsworth Street.

We had a week's wonderful holiday in Pendeen, near Land's End. Mary Marsden's mother owned a small cottage which she let out. I had recently bought a small blue Austin A35 van and in this we set out, following, for a great part of the journey, the old Roman road, the Fosse Way, which linked two of Caesar's important centres, Lincoln and Bath. We clocked over 400 miles and it took us fourteen hours! It was in Land's End that Matthew had his first ice cream!

"Jackanory House"

Refreshed by Cornish air (and ice cream!) we were ready for the move. Bishop's Removals of Lincoln 'removed' us. Their vehicles had a large chess-piece of a bishop painted on both rear and side panels with the clever phrase "Your move. We'll take you." Removal men, as we know from vast experience, enjoy a healthy loading of furniture, interspersed with several tea-breaks, followed by a long journey to the new destination, when the chaps – apart from the driver – can put their feet up (usually on the dashboard), switch off and have a nap. Not so in this particular instance. Carline Road to Wordsworth Street was all of a quarter of a mile. The men were surprisingly cheerful about it, however, and within a day Ann, Matthew and I were ensconced in our new home. Summer 1967.

It was an intriguing house. A cottage, really. It boasted a bright red front door, a mock Tudor black and white overhang, a small yard and pocket handkerchief garden. There were *steps* everywhere: two up to enter, two down to the living room, one slight step to the kitchen and one down to the yard. A narrow twisty staircase reached a narrow landing, at the bottom of which was a dinky bathroom with just sufficient room for the three essentials. Astonishingly the cottage possessed four average-sized bedrooms, with three extra steps to the smallest room and our bedroom, which overlooked Drury Lane and the edges of the castle. To the left of the front door was a delightful 'front' room which we used for special meals and gatherings. Matthew called it 'Jackanory House', a most appropriate name. It was a quirky, cosy, curlicue of a cottage. And quite adorable. We loved it! The rent was £2.10.0d per week, less ten shillings a week for stoking the College Aga morning and night. Easy...

In October of that year I was chosen by the College to join a Student Christian Movement trip to explore and examine the Church in France. Bryan Hackney and Jim Hobbs (both, later, to be Bart's godfathers) were also College emissaries. We were to report back to the assembled College after the ten day exercise by way of an illustrated slide-lecture. I took the 35mm slides and left it to the other two to work out the script. The coach on which we had travelled through Paris, Lyons, Burgundy, Geneva and Rheims finally deposited us at Waterloo Railway station. Meanwhile Ann and Matthew, who was only twenty months old, caught the Inter-City train down to London to meet up with Bernard and Muriel and their family at their home in Aintree Avenue, East Ham. From Waterloo station I joined them. It was there that our second child was conceived.

Philip duly arrived one bright, sunny July morning. I had telephoned Mrs Robinson the midwife who arrived on her bicycle, the machine's pannier full of her essential equipment. "I reckon I'll have time to finish the Daily Telegraph crossword," she surmised, weighing up the situation with all her long midwifery knowledge. Perhaps it was a more difficult crossword that day (the quick or the cryptic?) but Philip beat her to it. Mind you, she would also claim a victory since she delivered him just before Dr. Watson arrived. Apparently midwives like to steal a march on the GPs. I played my small part in it all and Mrs Robinson was wise enough to keep me occupied with little tasks A home delivery was wonderful! The sun poured into our bedroom, the slight breeze wafting the thin delicate voile curtains through the open window. I collected Matthew from the Baddeleys (Martin was College Tutor) and having informed him of the arrival of his new baby brother, he entered the room with a cricket bat and asked if Philip could come and play.

Philip's first visitor was David Lunn, the Sub-Warden. I don't know why he called. It may have been that Martin Baddeley had told him. David was a bachelor, socially shy, in fact rather awkward (though he later made a splendid Bishop of Sheffield). He was genuinely delighted and overwhelmed to see such a newly-born infant, only two hours old. I think Philip had a special place in his heart. Two weeks later, when he wrote to me about my exam results, he made a special mention of Philip.

Life within 4 Wordsworth Street was hectic. By contrast, outside the cottage was quiet. It was summer. The College was on vacation. Margaret Webster, the Warden's wife, offered to be the daily help for the week-end, when Social Services do not operate. College life such a shining example of Christian community life. We would never experience it in all its fullness ever again. Living in 'Jackanory House' was cosy. The cottage was basic. The kitchen, especially, was lacking so many amenities but the gas-fire in the sitting-room, our small TV set and our familiar furniture made it a haven for us and our two little boys. People were always calling in, particularly students, since we were so close to College. During the football season a number of chaps would quietly leave the College chapel after Saturday night Compline and slip into our house, where we would let our hair down with 'Match of the Day.' In my final year I was appointed Hospitality Secretary. The task was simply to arrange accommodation for guests of students – sometimes parents, more often girlfriends. The hosts were married students who had a room to offer. For the arrangement there was a fixed fee which seemed reasonable to both hosts and guests. The system worked very well. Keith Lumsdon was a first year student who asked me to find accommodation for his girlfriend. I suggested she might like to stay with us at number 4, which she did. We were surprised when Keith introduced Anne: the daughter of Canon Hugh Corden, one of my CACTM assessors, who had written to me three years earlier offering me a curacy in his Gateshead parish! Keith and Ann eventually married and returned to serve in the North East.

Whilst we loved entertaining, student grants did not allow much room for splashing out. The Websters had been a wonderful help to us, especially during Philip's early months. We invited them round for an evening meal. Ann liked (still does!) very hot plates and dishes on which to eat our meals. We gathered round the table as she brought on the soup in bowls which had lids. When our guests took off the lids, the bowls were so hot that the soup was still boiling and bubbling! We had to wait and 'chat among ourselves' for several minutes until we dared tackle the first course. My cousin Barbara came to stay with us for a week and we had a thoroughly good time.

The Olympic Games were taking place in Mexico City and the usual wide television coverage meant we were able to keep in touch with events thousands of miles away. What sticks in my mind about those particular games was the extremely high altitude of Mexico City, which helped enormously the sprinters but made life very difficult for the long-distance athletes. The Games were preceded by the now anticipated political demonstrations. They featured Dick Fosbury the high-jumper who approached the bar backwards and leapt towards it head first. He won the gold medal and his technique became known as the Fosbury Flop. The Games, however, were far from a flop.

John and Pauline Newman came to visit us from Rhiwbina and stayed in the Eastgate Hotel. They were Philip's godparents at his Baptism which took place in the College chapel. It was truly a lovely occasion one Sunday afternoon. Alan Webster baptised Philip and in his short homily spoke about biblical and historical Philips – including the father of Alexander the Great and, of course, the disciple.

Towards the end of our residence in Wordsworth Street we exchanged our car. The Austin A35 van had served us very well. Ann had used it to drive herself and three other College wives, all four of them pregnant, to the ante-natal classes. The van had given us some independence and freedom to explore the Lincolnshire Wolds. We especially loved the little villages and would normally stop at Tealby, which had a delightful old fashioned tea room. The van was in need of some repair: it was kept overnight on the free car park of Castle Square and was therefore open to all kinds of weather. One afternoon I went to collect the van only to discover it jacked up on piles of bricks at each corner. Someone had stolen all four wheels. The Vehicle and General Insurance Company, with whom I insured the van, had recently gone bankrupt and I lost my annual premium which had just been paid.

I recalled one of our Skipton customers from my banking days who was a rep. for Preston Farmers, a large agricultural firm supplying animal feeds. He used to tell me that he travelled thousands of miles a year, a fair proportion of which were on rough farm tracks up the Yorkshire Dales. His company always provided Volkswagen Beetles and both the firm and Harry swore by them. With his glowing recommendation in mind we bought one: a pale blue second-hand 1300cc. It made the subsequent journeys to and from Wyken in those last few weeks all the more manageable and easy.

On May 23rd 1969 we all bid a sad farewell to "Jackanory House." In our new VW we drove off down the A46 to the capital of the country's car industry. Apart from our goods and chattels we took one other item from number 4 Wordsworth Street. She would make herself known in seven months' time.

Number Ninety Nine

Several months before we arrived in my first parish an army of church folk had kindly cleaned and decorated our future home, 99, Wyken Croft. The wallpapering group were apparently not very happy with our choice of colour for the main bedroom. The vicar wrote to us to confirm.

Yes: a dark olive green, we affirmed. The men, still somewhat dubious, obliged.

Number 99 was a small three bedroomed house in a terraced block of about thirty houses. Wyken Croft extended for quite some way, the houses ultimately numbering in the 400s. The Croft ran off at right angles to the main A46 trunk road into Coventry. A huge concrete jaguar animal stood guard at this turning, indicating that the famous iconic car manufacturer was a mile ahead, towards the city.

The houses were all very similar down the Croft. Those in our terrace were quite narrow, literally a door and a bay window wide. Neither were they particularly long. Yet somehow they contained a hallway, with stairs leading directly off it, a front sitting room and a dining room. The kitchen was a galley type, a continuation of the hallway and equal in length to the rear reception room. A small porch had been added, convenient for storing boots, shoes and the children's other paraphernalia. At the back there was a pleasant mainly lawned garden, twenty yards long, at the bottom of which stood a wooden garage. This opened into an unmade narrow back lane but beyond was the vast expanse of sports fields and play areas of Saints Fisher More Roman Catholic School.

Everything and everywhere was tiny. Upstairs, Matthew had the back bedroom, Philip slept in his cot in the small box room, whilst Ann and I shared the (dark green wallpapered) front bedroom. We overlooked the road but beyond were fields and heath, enclosed a long distance away by the boundary walls of a housing estate, hence the word 'croft', I suppose.

Our arrival was quite daunting. We had moved house before but this was something different. There was both a sense of excitement and foreboding about it. Ann said, years afterwards, that she uttered an arrow prayer, "Please God, help me to get through it!" as we turned the corner into Wyken Croft. She did not know how on earth we were going to face three years in such cramped conditions. Matthew, three and a quarters years old, was certainly going to make his mark on the area immediately. There were several children playing in neighbouring gardens. Unabashed and in his usual extrovert character he loudly announced to the world that he was Matthew Vaughan and he had come to stay!

Our home was indeed very restricting. The previous curate was a bachelor and therefore occupied a lot less space than we would. I had, for example, no study, which meant that every morning the breakfast pots were cleared from the table and we transformed the dining room into a work place with desk. The only phone, however, was permanently situated in the hallway. But because of the cramped conditions we received a visit from Coventry Social Services. The result of that visit was a place for Matthew at the local Nursery School at the top of Wyken Croft. There was – 'officially' – not enough space for him to play at home. It was a godsend. Not because of the space but because he was a clever boy and was certainly ready for some appropriate 'education'.

His teacher was a young lady, Mrs Khalia. He had not been at Nursery very long when he complained that she had insisted that leopards had *stripes,* whereas he had, very politely, informed her that leopards had *spots.* Mrs Khalia was an Indian. "Just because your father is a priest," she told Matthew, "does not mean you know everything!" Ann complained to the Head teacher about her attitude. He simply replied that she came from a rather aristocratic Indian family. It was to be hoped they lived in a city and not in some remote rural area of the sub-continent, since she obviously did not know her leopards from her tigers.

The walls of the houses in the Croft were paper-thin. The front bay window was almost the entire width of the house. The back was very similar. In other words, there was very little privacy to be had. The neighbours, fortunately, were grand: salt of the earth. One evening Ann and I had some friends round for a candle-lit dinner. The neighbours could obviously see in and came knocking at the door, to ask if we were in the middle of a power-cut! I might have replied that we were in the middle of a *meal* but it would have been unkind.

The craze in the Croft was to knock down the downstairs dividing wall and install in its place a small bar area. The basic, popular plan was to build a hemispherical counter between the site of the two doors (front and back reception rooms). Behind this counter mirrored shelves would be erected, to which was added an array of upturned bottles of spirits, complete with optics. It is hard to believe how neighbour imitated neighbour, like a line of falling dominoes, each succumbing to this strange obsession. Our immediate neighbours poured scorn on our suggestion that two separate downstairs rooms afforded space and quiet for the children to get on with their homework. But they were generous folk for all that. I recall one Christmas morning. We were returning with the family from church when we were spotted and called in for a Christmas drink. Being mid-morning we were more ready for a tea or coffee than alcohol. Thanks to their bar facilities I was proffered a cup of whisky with a splash or two of hot tea.

Towards the end of 1969 our daughter was born in the then very modern Walsgrave Hospital, a couple of miles north of Wyken. Poor Ann: she, amongst many, was suffering from Asian flu. Our baby was overdue, December 15th was the given date, but staff Christmas holidays meant a shortage of nurses over the festive period. Many confinements were thus given a prod. And in that context I drove Ann into 'the Walsgrave' in the afternoon of the 18th. I returned, fed the boys, organised the baby-sitter and charged back to the Maternity wing. Rebecca was born about one o'clock in the morning of December 19th. I witnessed her birth but it was a completely different kettle of fish to Philip's cosy home birth. Ann struggled with the wretched flu all the time and to make matters worse I was ordered to wear a surgical gown and face mask, which prompted me to pass out! Kenneth, my vicar, allowed me *two* whole days off and I had to be back at full-time work for the Christmas build-up. No part-time duties: back to the usual 12 to 14 hours shift. I don't know how we coped, especially Ann. To compound the whole episode, Kenneth was somewhat miffed that Ann declined to be 'churched'. She was recovering from the flu, it was a darned cold December, and she had three children under four years to care for. I don't think he ever really understood.

Paradoxically Kenneth was most sensitive and caring over my father's illness. When it became certain that Dad would die, he was extremely accommodating. The parish, under his leadership, was wonderful to me and Ann and we felt enormously strengthened by the prayers and thoughts of our parishioners. Unlike at Rebecca's birth, I was given an extended leave of absence to help arrange and attend the funeral when Dad eventually passed away on December 9th 1971.

Towards the end of our three years' stay in Wyken, Ann attended, as she always did, the monthly meeting of our local Mothers' Union branch. We are both great supporters of the organisation and our admiration for it derives from our experience of the Wyken branch. It had a large membership but, unlike many of its sister branches, it was energetic and busy in the right spheres of parish life. The branch was like an extra curate. At one particular meeting a lady from the Church of England Children's Society spoke about adoption. Typically, Ann left her name with the speaker, to whom we then wrote for further information on adoption. We received a reply that a Society Social Worker would get in touch once we had moved to our new parish.

Old Town, Stratford upon Avon

33, College Street Stratford upon Avon was situated in a short road of semi-detached houses, built in the 1930s in an area called Old Town. The houses were built identically: small front gardens with a few bushes, a single tree and a border of plants around a pocket handkerchief lawn. To the side of this was a short tarmac drive and a garage, at the far side of which lay a path around the side of the house to a much larger garden.

The Parochial Church Council had spent a substantial sum of money on the house. Before we arrived a new downstairs extension had been added to the rear, doubling, if not trebling, the area. It was ostensibly planned for a play area for the children of curates. The space meant that we enjoyed not only a children's 'patch' but a combined dining and sitting room too. This arrangement meant that the front reception room could be my much-desired study. And it fitted the bill perfectly. It had a separate phone plug, bookcases and room for a table-cum-desk. It also possessed the added advantage of looking out onto the drive so that I was able to have a moment's warning of any parishioner who might be about to ring the door bell. I only once hid under the desk to avoid such a person – and it wasn't at Stratford!

Upstairs, our College Street home was smaller and much more traditional in design. The boys shared the front bedroom, Rebecca in her cot in the smallest room, overlooking the back garden and – beyond – the spire of Holy Trinity parish church, from which rang each Sunday and Wednesday a magnificent peal of bells. Rebecca, however, was frightened by them and even to this day *abhors* the sound of church bells. Our bedroom, too, overlooked this aspect. It was a delightful room, reasonably spacious and letting in a pleasing amount of light.

It is an all too obvious statement to say that Stratford is a magical town in which to live. Ann adored it. It was speckled with historic buildings. At the top of *our* street was Hall's Croft, a sensitively restored and elegant early seventeenth century house, where William Shakespeare's daughter Susannah lived with her wealthy doctor husband. Dr Hall could be famous for simply being the bard's son-in-law but he was an important gentleman in his own right in the 1600s. As a physician he was renowned for his medical cures, especially that for scurvy, which he made up from herbs. His treatment of this particular ailment predated the use of lime – as used to treat scurvied sailors of the British Navy a century later. Today, the public can visit the house and grounds and discover the herbs mentioned in Dr Hall's case notes.

The town always had a number of famous actors and actresses going about their daily business like everyone else. When the Royal Shakespeare Company was performing at the Memorial Theatre, not too far down the river from Old Town, it was possible to be mesmerised by the abundance of these famous people, queuing in shops, taking a stroll, seated in some café. Ann, whose main subject at College was English and who *delighted* in the plays of Shakespeare, would return from a trip down town all excited, having bumped into Richard Pascoe at the grocer's or spoke to Brenda Bruce at the end of the street. (both true episodes!)

As this was my second curacy it was always understood that it would be a shorter one than my first. For reasons explained later our stay was a mere 18 months. The most notable event during our residence at number 33 was our eventual adoption of a hard-to-place child through the Church of England Children's Society.

Miss Burman, the Society's Social Worker, contacted us after her initial encounter with Ann at the Wyken Mothers' Union meeting. She came to visit us regularly at Stratford until we reached a point when we both felt we wanted to adopt and the Society was happy that we should. That was late November 1972. Being accepted as adoptive parents was no pushover! The fact that I was a priest was an obstacle in the eyes of the Society. So many clergy, we were informed, felt it the "right and proper" thing to do. A good- example-to-the-parish gesture. Whereas, of course, the real issue was whether the priest would be a good father and that the child would be loved and wanted for its own sake. Having been accepted, Miss Burman's visits became more serious and formal. She was a lovely lady, in her early forties I would think, extremely quietly spoken and totally unflappable. In the midst of our visits there was a lengthy absence. She had become ill. She resumed and saw our process to its completion. But with a year or so of this we heard that she had died of cancer.

We had intimated that we were ambivalent as to the sex of our adopted child. We did, however, stipulate that we wanted as young a baby as possible but were happy to have whomsoever we were given. The child would be a 'hard-to-place child'. There were three categories of this awful title, in reality meaning three 'handicaps'. The child would either be physically handicapped, mentally handicapped or one of mixed race. With the energy and exuberance of our three children, now almost six, four and two, we felt the former two options would not be for us. A healthy child of whatever colour, however, would fit the bill much better. The Children's Society's policy in those days was always to place a child of the opposite sex to the youngest member of the family. In our case, then, it would mean a boy. Miss Burman visited us once again to announce that an Anglo-Caribbean boy had been born, some weeks ago, on July 3rd. He was all set to go to his adoptive parents when suddenly they pulled out of the arrangement. Were we happy to have him? We had time to consider since his foster parents were doing a great job with him in the north of England. But rather than being a few weeks old, because of the tiresome bureaucracy that would have to be undone and then re-done, he would be several months old when we could collect him.

Excitement seized us all, even the children. What should we call him? He had been given a name by his biological mother but as adoptive parents we were free to give him a new start with a new name. Something that would fit in happily with those of his brothers and sister. A biblical name, therefore, would be odds-on favourite. A glance at the Gospels, say St Matthew chapter 10, might give us a clue as the Evangelist lists the twelve disciples. There, tucked in between Philip and Matthew, was Bartholomew. *Bartholomew?* We knew no one with that mouthful of a name, though since that time we have come to learn of a handful of Bartholomews. It was an inspiration: apostolic, highly uncommon and slightly flamboyant...but he was, after all, half West Indian. Ann's grandmother never got his name right. She always called him 'Barnoldswick'! A few years later, in another parish, a lady from church sympathised with us over his name. "It's a pity" she said "that you couldn't have chosen your own name for him." We kept silent.

We were given the green light to collect him from his Cheshire foster home on December 12th. A priest friend and his wife looked after our other three whilst we journeyed northwards. We loaded the car with our carry-cot, baby paraphernalia and gifts for his foster parents. It was early evening when we returned to College Street to introduce our latest – and last – child.

Bartholomew was a lively, bouncing five months old baby. His foster mum had indulged him. She was terribly upset to see him go, since she had had him from being a few days' old. Normally her charges left her for adoption after about six weeks but because of the 'rejection', time had dragged out. Along with our baby we carried his favourite toy and presents for our three children from their new baby brother – a delightful thought from his foster parents. What did surprise us was the reaction of the townspeople. Our new son was totally accepted within our family (the five of us), though there were some reservations from the wider family.

On the street, however, it was often a very different picture. Bartholomew had typical Caribbean features: a flat nose, big lips, tight jet-black frizzy hair and coloured skin. "You are lucky", confided one of our church ladies, a prominent member of the local branch of the Children's Society, "he's very *pale!*" Another member asked Ann what sort of food would he eat! Had she bananas and mangoes in mind? Yet another member of our church's Children's Society enquired as to the *language* he would speak when he grew up! And all these ladies were respectable, upright, church-attending figures of Stratford-upon-Avon. There was much worse for Ann to face. On several occasions she was harassed by people who shouted at her and in one particularly torrid episode a member of the public loudly insinuated that she had been 'carrying on' with a black man. Despite this rather unexpected antipathy we were a very happy six-some. We had a most delightful family of four children in just over six years, though this fact prompted yet another parishioner (they feel they can say *anything* to their clergy!) to berate me with the words, "It's disgusting – and you, a man of the cloth!"

Bartholomew wasn't entirely ours however. Not yet. We would have to go to Court and appear before a judge to have it all completely finalised. This eventually took place in September 1973. By that time we had moved to Monks Kirby and my first parish of real responsibility.

The back garden at 33 College Street provided a wonderful play area for our children. The new rear extension had French windows which opened directly onto a patio, big enough for the largest of toys. The rest of the sizeable garden was 'laid to lawn' as the estate agents eulogise. There were some tired borders containing old and woody shrubs but there existed no paths by which to reach these areas. A couple of paths would also bring some pattern and shape to the lawn and garden. With this in mind we decided to lay a concrete path running down the length of one side, with a smaller pathway branching out at right-angles somewhere in the middle. Peter Healey, a very keen DIY handyman and friend from Wyken offered his help. On Peter's instruction I procured yards and yards of wood planks for shuttering. And I ordered a ton of concrete to be delivered on Saturday, September 30th. Peter and his wife Peggy arrived in good time and we awaited the cement wagon. When it came, the vehicle took up a large part of the street, began to lower its long trough and proceeded to spew out the wet mix into the middle of our driveway. Out and out and out...As the mountain of cement grew Peter commented that there looked a lot more than a ton of the stuff. But he was not certain and we would, in any case, have to play it by ear – or rather, by shovel!

I paid the driver and we began the task of loading the wheelbarrow, trundling it to the furthest point of the path and depositing it between the shuttering, which was already in place. It soon became apparent that the wagon driver had given us the remainder of his Saturday 'mix'. We were obviously the last of his week-end calls and he was not going to return to base with what was left on board. The long pathway was full of cement, tamped down and levelled. So, too, was the central pathway. There was, however, as much cement still standing – and *setting!* – on the drive as we had put down. I envisaged a solid concrete carbuncle, several feet high, obstructing both garage doors and preventing the car ever entering the drive again. There was nothing else for it but to create more paths. Hastily, other spare pieces of wood were deployed as shuttering and barrow-loads of concrete poured into these new and makeshift channels. It was mad! We were constructing a Spaghetti Junction in our own back garden. Paths were springing up everywhere. At last the pile at the front diminished and we were able to hose down the remaining few inches into the gutter and clean up. All's well that ends well – even in Shakespeare's town!

Monks Kirby Vicarage

For reasons outlined elsewhere, our stay in Stratford ought to have been longer. Sadly, it wasn't. Having privately seen the Archdeacon of Warwick, a lovely, wise and elderly priest, I was offered the post of priest-in-charge of a multiple of parishes in the very north of both county and diocese. The parish eventually became known as The Wolvey Group of Parishes. Coventry Diocese explained that we were to live for the first six months in the Vicarage at Monks Kirby. After that period the new Vicarage at Wolvey would be complete and we would move there.

Ann and I visited St Edith's Vicarage in late August of 1973. It was a colossal building, red-brick, early Victorian, decorated externally by the occasional pattern of black brick. Everything about it was huge! It was set in five acres of grounds, mostly rough land, with an acre of lawn at the front, which was always kept tidy and mown by Mike, one of the young church chaps, who was an agricultural mechanic and brought his own sit-on mower to tackle the job. This front lawn was delightfully framed by mature trees, hiding both the road and the driveway. In its hey-day this would have been one glorious edifice set in magnificent environs. There were still vestiges of that halcyon day: for example, a gorgeous gingko tree. This mature tree must have been over a hundred years old and over a hundred feet tall, standing majestically at the edge of the lawn, extending a leafy welcome to visitors to the parsonage. Still a rarity in this country, the Japanese gingko possessed three-in-one leaves, not dissimilar to the Irish shamrock. The gingko's alternative name is 'maidenhair', since the strange-shaped leaves resemble the hairstyle of Oriental girls. Beyond the lawn and to the east of it was a copse. Matthew later wrote in a school composition, "we have a forest at the bottom of our garden." In this wooded area were all kinds of wild creatures. On more than one occasion Ann borrowed a neighbour's shotgun in the hope of bagging a couple of pheasants who frequented the wood.

The house itself was in a serious state of dilapidation. In all truth no one should have been allowed to reside there. Idris Davis, the local Church Primary School Head teacher, showed us round. From the large tiled hallway in grand proportions ran the main staircase, broad and impressive. To the left of the main door was a vast sitting-room, looking out onto the front lawn. At the top end a dais had been constructed, large enough for a grand piano or even a quartet. Clockwise, next door was another big room by today's standards, though perhaps only a third of the size of the former room. Here I planned to have my study. After the staircase a door leading into the domestic quarters: kitchen, larder, scullery and the back door opening onto outhouses surrounding a spacious courtyard. On the right of the main door, off the hallway, was another enormous room. It became the children's play room, where they could race around on their tricycles and bicycles, push a pram or build a towering tent.

It was in this room that the previous incumbent, the Reverend Arthur Fagg, used to sit for the best part of the day, wrapped in a shawl in front of an old electric fire. He was in his eighties. In those days most clergy did not retire but died in their cassocks. The stipends were so poor that the majority could not afford to retire. It had to be admitted that Mr Fagg rarely attended divine service for which he was paid his small stipend. He had so arranged the monthly time-table of services that Mattins featured three times out of four, when a Lay Reader officiated. On the fourth remaining Sabbath Holy Communion was indeed scheduled for him to celebrate. However, he was always unwell a day or so before and managed to obtain a locum priest to stand in for him. "The parish don't like me and I don't like them!" he once barked at a priest friend of mine who happened to drop by to see how he was. He was an eccentric of the highest order. Parishioners told me how he used to drive his car on the opposite side of the road, as if on the continent, because, he claimed, the camber of the road was wearing down the tyres on the passenger side of his motor. He was also wont to saw the bottom few feet off telegraph poles in order to keep his home fires burning!

The home fires were chiefly a boiler in the spacious cellar which ran almost the whole length and breadth of the house. When Mr Davis gave us the guided tour he indicated the outside door which led to the cellar. He marched into the courtyard, unlocked the sturdy door, descended the three steps into the basement – and found himself standing waist-high in black, still waters! Fortunately one of my ten churchwardens was a Royal Navy Commander (the other nine were farmers!). Commander Mike Cooper was seconded on a tour of duty to Rolls Royce in neighbouring Ansty. He was able to obtain from his place of work an efficient pump which cleared out the water in record time. It took slightly longer for the cellar to dry out but eventually it did and we were able to re-employ this ship's engine of a vicarage boiler, which did indeed provide us with adequate heat to the ancient radiators within.

The vicarage lacked several basic amenities. It is, not for the first time, a sad indictment on the Church that it will somehow turn a blind eye to the safety and wellbeing of its priests. Before we moved in I requested a visit on site from the Archdeacon. What I wanted primarily was a couple of electric sockets in the kitchen and scullery. There was nowhere to plug in the washing-machine. "Why on earth do you want a washing-machine?" asked the bachelor Archdeacon, "my housekeeper manages quite well without one." He was an oily, rather touchy-feely sort of cleric, one whom I would not and could not trust. But he was powerful. Powerful in the Church.

Commander Cooper, a man of the world, was, however, an excellent ally and one who would not be bullied by any Church hierarchy. He insisted that some sockets were installed and the Church – if they wanted us to live there – had to accede. Of course, as the Diocesan authorities knew only too well, the electrician examined the existing wiring and discovered that it was in a most dangerous state. The house, therefore, was unfit for habitation. Yellow and black striped stickers were posted on several sockets and mains fuse cupboard, warning of the perilous condition. The vicarage had to be rewired. The Archdeacon would be well aware of this all along but would not wish to cause further expenditure for the Diocesan Board of Finance. To hell with the new incumbent and his young family!

In addition, the Diocese had promised that we would move from this minefield in six months when the new vicarage at Wolvey was built. I suppose we were naïve but the Archdeacon and his Committee were at best foolish or at worst downright deceitful. On the day we moved in, despite the promise, the glebe land at Wolvey had not even been sold. So naturally not one single spadeful of footing had been dug. It was fourteen months before we finally made the move.

The splendid staircase led to two landings. To the right were situated the incumbent's five family bedrooms. To the left, behind another door, emphasising further the difference in class between Vicarage family and servants, to say nothing of added privacy, were three small bedrooms for domestic staff. From the main landing was an attic which extended the whole length of the house. Here, we discovered, stood a tiny iron stove. It was the smallest available, I imagine, because it had moulded into its base the simple cipher "No. 1" within an oval. From this stove ran a long metal pipe reaching and piercing the slates of the roof above. This contraption, together with three simple wooden pegs, were the only evidence of sleeping quarters for three (I presume) very junior domestics. It was strange that they would, of necessity, have to descend the attic stairs and walk a few paces on the *master* landing before disappearing through the door and down the servants' stairs. My only answer is that they probably rose from their beds so early that there was very little chance of meeting the Vicar or his wife in their night attire on the landing. The master bedroom had two enormous windows complete with wooden shutters. The windows looked out onto two aspects of the lawn. We had no bedside lamp and with the shutters closed the last one into bed had to turn the light out at the switch by the door and wander over to where you thought the bed might be. It was rather like walking across the Mecca ballroom blindfolded! In winter it was so cold that ice would cover the wooden floor boards near the windows. We regularly moved the bed around (which made the blindfold Mecca ballroom act even more complicated!) in order to find the warmest spot. I don't think there was one. Again, when we first moved in the children chose their own bedrooms but warmth in numbers was the key strategy. We soon learnt that we were warmer when together. The children finished up sleeping in one room.

Despite the fact that the house was literally crumbling around us, we thoroughly enjoyed our time at St Edith's Vicarage. The first family duty, however, was to return to Stratford upon Avon. We had been bidden by the County Court to present ourselves at the Town Hall in Stratford on Thursday September 20th at 10 a.m. and to produce the Plaint Note. This legal notice cited Ann and me as the "applicants" and our adoptive son, in his birth name, as "respondent." This important Plaint Note stated that "at Court the Registrar will consider giving directions for securing the just, expeditious and economical disposal of the proceedings." The very wording was enough to give you the shivers but we were very tense because, even at this late stage, there could be a hitch. Perhaps Bartholomew's mother had had second thoughts and now wanted to keep him? Our Court appearance, however, was a very relaxed affair. The Judge, his red robes fascinating our children, asked Ann and me a few formal questions. He then leaned over his bench, smiled warmly at Matthew, Philip and Rebecca, and asked *them,* "Do you want a new baby brother?" "Yes!" they chorused. And that seemed to be it. It was all done. The adoption became legal. We were told that there are only two acts in the British judicial system which cannot be revoked. One is hanging; the other, adoption. Our adoption had become law. We had become Mum and Dad once again.

Like most small villages, the community at Monks Kirby was very gregarious. We loved our socials and dances and merry-making. So much so that getting a baby-sitter became a problem. There were simply not enough teenagers to go round. Families who lived near each other arranged for one set of children to sleep at the other's, thus eliminating the need for two baby-sitters. And whilst no child under legal age was ever left alone, or unattended, on the evenings of social occasions, the village policeman exercised a remarkable ministry. He was informed as to where the 'sitters' were operating and he made sure, by a series of pastoral visits throughout the evening, that everything was well in all these houses. If anything were amiss he could easily report to the village hall and tell the relevant parents. It was a wonderful system. We up at the Vicarage had more difficulties than most to recruit a baby-sitter.

Nothing to do with the remoteness of the house – we were only two hundred yards up the hill from the village centre – nor with the enormous size of the house. It was a matter of *television*. We only possessed a very humble black and white set. The 'sitters' made it absolutely clear that *colour TV* was de rigueur (though they didn't put it quite like that!) Not even Ann's appetising suppers were sufficient to tip the scales in our favour. We had no option but to invest in a colour television set. We went to nearby Bedworth to shop around for good deal.

Bedworth, by the way, was one of the first places in Britain (certainly the first I had come across) to have a *hyper*market, as opposed to a *super*market. 'Hyper', by inference, was bigger than 'super'. But whether Greek or Latin, the words mean exactly the same. It was, however, a cathedral of a store! The marriage of Princess Anne to Captain Mark Phillips was imminent. Electrical shops all over were cashing in on the occasion and some were offering reasonable bargains. We bought one and it was installed, up and running in time for the Wedding. Thrilled with our acquisition we invited an elderly lady from the almshouses to watch it with us. I settled her down in front of the screen, turned on the set in time for the introductory sequence. "What!" she exclaimed in puzzlement, "can't you get *black and white* up here?"

The following New Year's Eve celebrations took place in a very hot, steamy Village Hall. Just before midnight we trooped out to the centre of the village, opposite our parish church, to see the New Year in with more revelry and song. Unknown to us – until the morning – was a band of thieves working silently on the church roof stripping its precious lead. Their lorry, apparently, parked in the graveyard on the rear side of the church. Where were the police? Well, one, I suppose, was doing his nightly rounds checking on the baby-sitters!

Monks Kirby Vicarage was a fine example of what clerical life was like certainly before the Great War. There was bedroom accommodation for at least six servants, more if they shared. The back staircase was very much a separate entity. The enormous kitchen still possessed its long line of bells, fixed high on the wall, all numbered so that the vigilant staff could ascertain the correct location from which the call had been made and to which they must now report. Through the kitchen was the larder connected to the servants 'stairs. From the larder was a large wash-house, what we would today call a 'utility room', though in 1973 there was not much of the 'utility' about it. Its only facility was a large stone sink, though even this had hardly any sides. Leaving this room, via a stout back door with heavy bolt, you entered a pleasant, airy courtyard.

To the right were old stables. These were converted by Ann and two ladies from the village into pig-sties. Three piglets were purchased from a local pig-breeder and were to be intensively fed by Ann or me. As these horrors grew in size – at an incredibly rapid rate – they became quite ferocious. It was a matter of wearing high Wellington boots and protective clothing when you went in to feed them. Usually I entered the sty kicking out, so as to get the first punch in! Valerie and Brenda's job was to clean out the sties. There was one remarkable thing about our three creatures. They were easily identifiable because one had a curly tail, the second a straight tail and the third no tail at all. When they were duly fattened, about twenty weeks if I remember aright, the pigs were driven into Valerie's horse-box and delivered to a specialist "Farm to Freezer" establishment. Two days later we received our pigs back in three heavy packages. Every part of a pig, from its head to its trotters, can be eaten. In each package were cellophane-wrapped joints, chops, cuts and portions of pork. One package per one pig. On the top of each of the three packages the butcher had placed one joint with the tail still attached. It was better than any label: one package contained Curly, one Straight and the other No-Tail. The late 1970s were an uneconomic time for the professional pig-breeder but we managed a small profit and enjoyed excellent meat in the many months ahead.

The pig venture was certainly more successful than my vegetable growing one. A farmer friend brought his rotavator and we turned over a sizeable area of ground in which to grow potatoes. Potatoes, he said, would break the soil up nicely for future years when we could expand our repertoire. Atrocious wet weather, rabbits by the score – and no doubt my lack of time and energy in the project – contributed to a complete failure. I didn't try next season.

One of our abiding memories of Monks Kirby was the sound of the wood pigeon. We were deep in North Warwickshire countryside. The county was always dubbed, and not without good reason, "leafy Warwickshire." Is this still true? Or has creeping urbanisation erased the term from modern man's mind? Perhaps regionalisation has not helped: "leafy West Midlands" hasn't the same ring. But without its trees, Shakespeare's County just wouldn't be Warwickshire and I prefer to remember it as 'leafy', from which the wood pigeon happily carolled its throaty 'chr-coo'. Whenever we hear the sound of the wood pigeon we are fondly reminded of our time at St Edith's Vicarage. *Outside* was far superior to inside. So much so that in the summer of '74 we decided to have a caravan holiday on our front lawn. Peter Wilson, whom we knew at Lincoln, was working in a parish in nearby Rugby. We had allowed him to winter his caravan on the far side of our lawn, some 60 or 70 yards from our house. Peter offered us the use of his 'van and we were determined to holiday in it for two whole weeks without even setting foot in our home. Since we had an outside stand-pipe – and even a toilet – we succeeded in our aim. It was a super holiday –and the site fees were so cheap!

When we considered our house in the cold light of day, we had to admit that it was a minefield – and the fact we were living there was actually a serious and damning slur on the Coventry Diocese. It would not have happened in the Diocese of Blackburn. The Vicarage at Monks Kirby was a lethal concoction of disasters all waiting to happen. And they did.

A very tall elm at the far end of the courtyard was dead and leaning precariously towards the house. I asked one of our farmers, young John, son of old John, to cut it down. He had all the right tree-felling equipment. Whether he got his angles all wrong or he simply did not know the first thing about bringing down a tree, the upshot was that the huge elm crashed diagonally across the yard, its upper branches packing against the back door so that we could not possibly get out. If the tree had been another ten feet higher it would have caused severe damage to the house. The strange thing was that young John thought it a great joke that he had landed his elm so expertly on the back doorstep of our home. Rather like delivering a sack of firewood and leaving it on the step.

On another occasion, high wintry winds blew out our bathroom window. This was no lightweight object but a heavy iron-framed article with lattice-shaped diagonals manufactured into the frame mould. We had gone shopping and left Nana, Ann's grandmother, alone in the house. As we approached the front of the house we could not believe our eyes: there, where we would normally park the car, was this weighty window deeply embedded in the gravel, like an enormous arrow, outside the front door. It would without doubt have killed anyone who happened to be there – or done untold damage to our car. Since our move to the new Vicarage at Wolvey was imminent, we knew it would be fruitless to ask the Diocese to replace the window. A large piece of thick plastic taped to the bathroom's inside walls had to suffice. There were gaps around the edges and it was darned cold having a bath...

Ann and I had found a good friend in Pat Huxter. Pat was a member of Holy Cross choir, one of the three churches in the parish of Wyken, where she sometimes played the organ. She was a committed Christian, unmarried, in her early-thirties when we first got to know her and taught at a Primary School in a nearby parish. Pat was very generous to our children and most kind to us when we lived at Wyken. Our friendship continued and grew during our time at Stratford and when we settled in to Monks Kirby. She was an obvious choice to be a godmother to Bart, which she became. We saw her quite regularly at St Edith's Vicarage. She and I ran a day course for my Confirmation candidates in and around the vicarage. Teaching about the Eucharist we involved the fifteen or so young people in preparing – and eating – a Passover meal. Outside activities were also in the programme as we took advantage of the vast area of vicarage grounds. The Leicester Mercury even came and took some photographs for their local paper!

Pat was not only generous and kind, sociable and helpful, she was also incredibly brave! Like a real Primary school teacher, she encouraged Ann and me to have a couple of days away to celebrate our tenth Wedding Anniversary, whilst she looked after our brood. On July 25th, therefore, Ann and I set off to explore the Long Mynd, Shrewsbury and many stations in between. We decided to follow one of the recommended tours in Egon Ronay's *Pub and Tourist Guide* of 1974. We departed early that afternoon. Literally within minutes of our departure disaster struck. They heard a rumbling within the chimney, followed by a sudden thud. A search through the house led them to discover a solid mass of bees on the hearth in the main bedroom. Along with their nest, the insects had tumbled from the chimney-pot, down the stack and had been rudely awakened by their sudden impact in the fireplace. Immediately they began to swarm all around the large room. They were angry, frenzied and very sooty. Pat managed to persuade the younger children to remain in another room whilst she battled with the bees. Windows were opened and with the aid of rolled up newspaper she succeeded in driving the confused and crazed insects out of the window. It was a tremendously brave effort. Pat could have been very badly stung. She, however, remained unharmed, if somewhat breathless by her exertions. As to the bees, they were never seen again in the vicinity of the vicarage. I trust they didn't come to a sticky end.

Poor Pat seemed to attract calamity in that house. On another occasion she had come to share an evening meal with us. Sitting in the lounge we began to smell burning. The radiators were all hot, as I had stoked up the boiler before Pat arrived. The whiff of burning increased in intensity but it wasn't until we saw smoke drifting up through the cracks in the floor-boards that we realised something critical was afoot. I raced downstairs into the cellar and discovered the source of the smoking and smell: I had previously stacked up quite mathematically on the boiler a great cube of damp logs in order to dry them out for future fires. The fire in the old boiler, however, was so furious and raging that the logs were not only dried out but actually *on fire*! Ten minutes of frenetic *re-dampening* the logs and removing them to a safe part of the cellar saved the day. Another ten minutes and the sitting-room, in fact the whole house, could have gone up in smoke. The danger averted, we returned to our drinks and our supper, being both astounded and astonished at yet another near miss.

Was our house – or its occupants – jinxed? Matthew broke his arm playing on the lawn (a 'green stick fracture'); we had a burst pipe which put the hallway under two inches of water and our mail floated across the tiles – 'by sea-mail'! Taking the children to school in the car one morning, I ran over and killed our lovely kitten, Philip's pride and joy; slates fell off the roof unaccountably; trees suddenly crashed down. Someone in the parish was not joking when he suggested that Mr Fagge was not resting in peace but was still up to his old tricks. I would normally have scorned such a suggestion but a series of ultra-strange episodes made me change my mind.

One winter's evening I was out at a meeting. Ann, having put the children to bed, was relaxing in the sitting-room, the door closed, the house locked, and a good fire in the grate. Matthew, who was then eight, for some reason awoke and came out of his bedroom onto the landing at the top of the main staircase. From this vantage point he could look down onto the hallway below. There he saw an old man trying the handle of the door to the sitting-room. He watched for several minutes as the man lingered outside the door, then disappeared. Matthew thought that the old chap had entered the sitting-room, thought no more about it since we were always having visitors, and returned to his bed. He could not sleep, however, and within an hour he was up again. He asked Ann about the old man. What did he want? Ann replied that no one had entered all evening. Matthew was insistent about the elderly visitor and described the gentleman in fullest detail. As only a mother can, Ann appeased our son and he went off to bed once again. But next morning Ann enquired of some villagers who this old man might be. From our son's description it was undoubtedly the ghost of the Reverend Arthur Fagge. None of our family had ever met my priestly predecessor and certainly our children, as far as we were aware, had ever heard anyone describe him.

That was not the end of the evening's action, however. Later, after Matthew had returned to bed, Rebecca awoke, quite frightened. She complained that 'an old man was pressing on her tummy.' Later still, Bartholomew, who *never* awoke at night once bedded down in his cot, suddenly began to cry and cry uncontrollably. Something – or someone – had obviously greatly disturbed him. Being a one year old he could not, of course, explain. Had the 'old man' aroused our baby as well?

Several months later I accompanied our church organist's husband, John Higley, to Highfield Road, the ground of Coventry City Football Club. Coventry were back in the 'top flight' of the Football League, as the old Division One was called. The team had risen rapidly from the Third Division under the charismatic management of Jimmy Hill, who was to become a renowned television presenter. The city seemed to be able to do no wrong: whether in religion or football (which is many people's religion), things were hunky-dory. These two great spheres of human interest were united in our city since our diocesan bishop, Cuthbert Bardsley was also President of the Football Club.

Cuthbert was another charismatic leader. Well over six feet tall he was a splendid orator and communicator. He related to men; not many bishops do. He was an active chairman of the Church of England's Men's Society. And he ordained me! There was, however, one short episode when Bishop Cuthbert was not too popular with the people. He had written of his total support for Sunday football, when the idea was only just being mooted. By so doing he incurred the outrage of all the residents of the small terraced houses which tightly surrounded the City's football ground. Saturdays and the occasional day during the week were quite sufficient to stage their matches, they protested. They were quite right, of course. It was quite some time – and well after the Bishop's retirement – before a game took place on the Sabbath.

I had been to the ground a few times before – it was in the next -door-but-one parish to Wyken and quite walkable from there. I had seen the Sky Blues, as Coventry were called, take on Manchester Utd., who then (surprisingly) were in the Second Division. The day in question was an important sporting day because Coventry City were playing my team Burnley. It was New Year's Day 1974 and I took Matthew and Philip along with me. They too were Burnley supporters... they had no choice in the matter! It was an uneventful match, only exciting because I was actually seeing my claret and blue heroes, a rarity since we have moved down to the Midlands. The match ended in a one-all draw. I entered the name of the goal-scorer, Nulty, in my News of the World Football Annual. What is more important to my story is the episode which occurred at the Vicarage that afternoon.

We had arranged that John's wife Julia would come to the Vicarage in the early afternoon to stay and chat with Ann and that we men would join them for a family meal when we returned from the game. Before Julia arrived, Ann was busy in the kitchen preparing food and making some seasonal mince pies. Suddenly, in the study of all places, Ann heard the sound of a piano, which we did not possess. Confirming the tinkling sound, Rebecca appeared and asked "Mummy, what is that noise?" Ann, hesitant to say what she really perceived it to be, tried to satisfy our inquisitive daughter by explaining that it would be the 'tinny' sound of the mobile ice-cream van which often toured the village in its enticement of customers. Or perhaps it was the convent bell? Rebecca accepted the two possible explanations and resumed her play. When Julia arrived, Ann mentioned the experience to her. Julia was not only the church organist but the primary school's music teacher and a very able pianist. She was astonished at Ann's story. She had bought a piano from Mr Fagge, himself an accomplished player, two years previously. And today, of all days, was the anniversary of its removal to her house down the village! "But the noise did not come from the sitting-room," said Ann, "but from the smaller room, Trevor's study." "Yes," Julia replied, "that's where he kept and played the piano!"

By the autumn of 1974 our new house in Wolvey was almost complete. Over the past few months we had made numerous inspection visits to mark the progress – and to add our own preferences, where possible. The Diocesan architect, Mr Fedeski, was tremendously helpful and allowed us to have some input. After all, we were the ones who were going to live in the house. He was a small man, Eastern European in appearance, who knew his mind as to what sort of materials he wanted for his creation. We were fortunate to have him as architect and lucky with the timing. Within a very short time of our new parsonage being built, dioceses were cutting back on expenditure, thus reducing the size and amenities of clergy houses.

We planned our removal for the week which began with Remembrance Day. They were dull but dry mid-November days. But the ghost of my predecessor – or was it the house itself that protested at its imminent demise? – had one last tactical strike. It was almost tea-time and the three younger children were letting off steam in the playroom, racing round the enormous room on their bikes. They were called for tea and it was a blessing that they were obedient and came into the kitchen. For within minutes of their being seated at the table we heard an ominous creaking followed by a series of hefty crashes. We leapt to our feet to trace the source of the commotion. Not this time the flooded hallway, nor the reeking drawing-room; neither the smoking cellar nor the gusty bathroom. To our horror we discovered that a gigantic piece of cornicing, probably ten feet long, a thick and ornate berg of plasterwork had broken away from the ceiling and left its heavy debris scattered all over the floor of the children's playroom. Undoubtedly the children would have been seriously maimed if they had ignored their summons to eat. The weirdest thing was that *that* room was where the Reverend Mr Fagge spent most of his clerical days: sitting stooped over his small electric fire draped in his woollen cape. That appeared to be his last salvo. Not a little relieved, we finally moved out four miles to the other side of the parish, to our brand-new Wolvey Vicarage. The parsonage at Monks Kirby was eventually sold by the Diocese to a local sports entrepreneur from nearby Rugby. We heard on the parish grapevine that within weeks of his purchase a towering, healthy pine tree had inexplicably crashed onto his finely manicured side-lawn...

A brand-new Vicarage

The village of Wolvey had a population of eleven hundred in the mid-1970s. I believe it has almost doubled now. It had a splendid selection of facilities which would be the envy of most villages in the early years of the 21st century: two public houses, two garages, both supplying petrol and one selling cars, a police house, a splendid playing-field with a well-kept cricket square and a loyal enthusiastic set of cricketers to match. The village also boasted a flat green Bowling Club, one of the finest in Warwickshire, where players were obliged to wear whites on match days. Wolvey had a large primary school, taking in pupils from neighbouring Ansty, Shilton, Burton Hastings, plus the (mainly Glaswegian) kids from the Army Camp at Bramcote. The Infants section was housed in the 'old school', the former Church School, directly opposite our new vicarage. The larger, modern site was a few hundred yards away on the Bulkington Road. It was a Church of England Controlled School and I was a member of the Governing Body, eventually becoming Chairman. The village also possessed a tiny Roman Catholic chapel, a large Baptist chapel and the parish church of St John the Baptist, seated on a hillock, a welcoming sight for travellers approaching the village from Leicester.

Our new home was completed in November 1974, replacing a Victorian parsonage which was demolished. The land on which this stood, less a fraction for the new vicarage, was sold for a ridiculously low sum to a builder who subsequently erected four 'superior dwellings'. Why the Church could not have retained the land and done likewise beats me. The profits from this sole venture would have been enormous. In every diocese up and down the land it was a similar tale of the Church selling the family silver. Nevertheless our new home was wonderful! We chose the bright yellow front door which was under an open porch at the end of a short curving drive. The house was faced in the mellow creamy Cotswold stone. A magnificent, if rather extravagant, wall of the same material divided the house from the small lane and the old school. Immediately to the left of the front door was my study, separated, quite rightly, by another door which led into the 'house' part of the domestic arrangements, as distinct from the 'work' bit. A small hallway had stairs leading off it. Straight ahead was a delightful sitting-room with Cotswold stone fireplace, tapering to the ceiling. French windows opened up onto a patio, beyond which a fairly rough garden. Builders today lay the most basic of lawns. However, many mature trees had been preserved and they formed a natural frame and gave us total privacy. To the right of the hallway was a corridor from which ran a dining room, downstairs toilet and a bright roomy kitchen which in turn led to a utility room and then outside. A sizeable brick garage had been built at the end of the drive, nearest to the utility area.

Upstairs were four bedrooms, a spacious bathroom and, amazingly, a shower room, as big as most people's bathrooms. The larger bathroom was the venue for our children's board games. Every school holiday Matthew, Philip and Rebecca (and sometimes Bart) with a few friends would spread out the Monopoly board for a mammoth game which would last for days. Each night the board, red houses, green hotels, tokens (remember the top hat, old boot and racing car?) and the paper money, of course, would be gently, gingerly stashed away to a safe place until the next day. Vicarages technically are to house incumbents or, since the increasing elimination of the freehold, priests-in-charge – and their families. That is, those who *run* the parish, who are responsible for its day to day existence. It seems to be the case, if not the law, that these houses contain a minimum of four bedrooms. Three for the family and one for the visiting Bishop. Though, unlike Bishop Frere in Truro in the early part of the last century, bishops can usually get home after a visit to the parish. Much to the relief of both parties.

It didn't take us long to become very settled in our new home. It was everything Monks Kirby wasn't: warm, cosy, manageable and safe. And because it was a completely new building it came with no malevolent clerical ghost. The walls of every room were painted in colours of our choice: mainly pastel hues of green, blue, primrose. The garden required more than a 'makeover'. When 1974 gave way to 1975 I set to work on a rockery. Our house was adequately screened off from the rest of the old vicarage land, which was still awaiting development. In this rough area were vestiges of the demolished parsonage and outhouses: an old lintel, a door-post or two, differently- shaped steps, some broken, some intact. These and a host of other large stones were ideal material for my rock garden. As spring passed to summer my labours began to reveal a very fine rockery. I was never a gardener but I felt proud of that achievement. The basic lawn, too, was worked upon. Regular cutting of the grass improved both its texture and colour.

It was during the early spring of that year when the chimney caught fire. Our four children were asleep in their beds; I, as usual, was out – either visiting or at a meeting – and Ann had settled down to a cosy night in with a roaring fire, which she continued to feed. So enthusiastic was her piling on the logs that, when I arrived home, I saw sparks and a few flames belching out of the chimney. The roaring fire had ignited the soot both on the fire-back and inside the chimney lining. It was lucky I spotted it from outside. I burst in shouting the fact of our sparking chimney. Ann suggested sand to extinguish it. I rushed to the French windows, knowing full well we had no sand. But we had *soil*. Plenty of soil around my rockery work. A shovel, too. I raced out, piled a huge load of soil onto the shovel, dashed back in – and tripped over the small step, spilling the entire earthy contents all over our *brown* carpet! Everywhere but on the fire! It was like some frenzied round of "It's a Knockout!" My second attempt at fire-dousing was more successful and eventually we succeeded in extinguishing it. Outside, we examined the chimney which was now spewing out only thick black smoke. The soil had done its job. Back inside, however, the commotion had awakened Matthew, who in turn had aroused his siblings, as trained by his prep. school. "Fire drill! Fire drill!" he shouted. Ann discovered all four children, neatly marshalled in line at the foot of the stairs. Matthew was in position, ready to lead the evacuation of the building. Fortunately that was not to be the case. Having laughed about our antics – and congratulated the children on the orderly and calm way in which they had behaved – we quickly resumed 'normal service'.

Wolvey Vicarage also had a lawn and border to the front, on the right of the drive. Intent on developing the potential of the rear garden, so that we could enjoy some relaxation and privacy, we neglected the front. The grass was regularly cut but the borders needed digging over. The addition of shrubs and ornamental trees wouldn't go amiss. Some unexpected help came from a succession of 'gentlemen of the road'. First one tramp called at our door: a genuine chap who had fallen on very hard times. He came from Leicester and repeatedly walked the A46 via Coventry to Birmingham, where he collected his accumulated State Benefit. And then did the journey in reverse. For some food and drink (a very strong cup of tea with three or four sugars) he would do a job. And so the front garden began to get some attention. As he was about to leave us on his southbound trek he asked if we had some gloves for him. We hadn't but Ann suggested an old pair of my woollen socks, which he eagerly accepted. The weird thing was that from that day onwards every 'gentleman' who visited us worked on the front garden in exchange for tea and a sandwich and asked if we had a pair of socks which he could use as gloves! It is a known fact that true men of the road leave markers on pillars, posts or milestones for their fellow travellers. I wonder what the sign is for "Vicarage ahead: good for socks as gloves"?

The mention of tramps reminds me of the account a priest-friend of mine tells against himself. Another 'gentleman of the road' called at his vicarage in a large housing estate of Derby. He asked for the usual mug of tea and a bite to eat. As he sat down relishing his food, he complained that his feet were terribly sore from all his trudging and tramping. He, too, no doubt was on some long journey before returning the same way. It happened to be Maundy Thursday, the night Jesus washed His disciples' feet. Bryan offered to wash the tramp's tired and tender feet: surely *the* appropriate gesture on the Thursday of Holy Week. To the loudly expressed bliss of the poor chap, his feet were duly bathed. It was not a pleasant task but Bryan completed his Maundy ministration. But before he reached for his socks the tramp, wiggling his calloused toes, at the end of which were long, brown horny talons, turned to the priest and pleaded "You couldn't cut my toe nails as well, could you, Father?" The priest, as his Lord would have done, obliged.

Ann succeeded in getting the post of Infants' Teacher at Wolvey Old School. Yes! Literally ten yards away from our vicarage front door. It was a tremendous boon: not only for Ann to resume her career *and* to supplement my meagre church stipend but not to have to travel to and from work. The whole question of schooling had been a priority for us throughout our children's educational years. When we arrived at Monks Kirby we realised that they would go to the nearest secondary school, a large Comprehensive in Bedworth. At that time the Headmaster was a renowned atheist with particularly pronounced anti-Christian views. We would not, could not, send our brood there. The alternative was private education, at which we originally baulked. It was a heart-rending dilemma. Matthew was an exceptionally bright boy who would thrive on academia. We therefore, after careful thought and much prayer, decided to look at Emscote Lawn Preparatory School in Warwick. We made arrangements for the three of us to meet Mr Riley the Headmaster. He, with his brother, ran the school, as had their father before them. He was a man in his mid-thirties, energetic, business-like and visionary. We warmed to him immediately.

After an informal chat with Matthew, and then with us, he set Matthew some tests in our presence. The tests were mainly Maths and English. I recall that our seven year old son was presented with the Schonell reading list, a guide to establishing a child's reading age. Matthew romped through the list impressively – with just one error. Instead of the word 'social', he uttered 'socialist'. Mr Riley laughed. Not many seven year olds would know that word. Matthew, always on the Left of politics, was something of a Red even then. Not wanting the Headmaster to think that we were Labour voters, I stammered some sort of apology about our son 'not getting the word from us'. Mr Riley laughed even more heartily at our embarrassment.

There was certainly a place for Matthew and he would start the following term. He did, thanks to a generous financial grant from The Sons of the Clergy Corporation. He was, technically, a weekly border but the week-end activities at school were every lad's dream: sport, more sport and time for a myriad of hobbies. He naturally wanted to stay on and so it was we five who went to see him, usually on Saturdays when he was playing football or cricket for his School Year. Emscote was a wonderful place. It had playing fields, gardens and even a small farm. The other three children loved it as much as Matthew.

Before Philip was to join Matthew at Emscote, however, our school timetable was like a football pools plan. To visit Matthew involved at least one 50 mile round trip (on Sundays it generally meant racing back home at break-neck speed to be in time for Evensong!); Philip was enjoying life at the new Wolvey School building, to which he could walk; Rebecca thrived on the quiet teaching technique of her convent Montessori school in Rugby, involving a twice daily 16 miles return journey, when invariably a very cross Reverend Mother would reprimand me for being late (despite my dog-collar – she obviously was not too concerned about Anglican-Roman Catholic relations!); meanwhile our three year old toddler Bart attended Nursery School for half a day each day at Bulkington, four miles away in the exact opposite direction to Rebecca's Rugby. Our stubborn principles regarding our children's education was reducing us to a school taxi service. We consoled ourselves in the knowledge that so many other parents were doing exactly the same thing.

Having sent Matthew to boarding school, for which, sadly, in his adult life he castigates us, we had to do likewise for Philip when he reached seven years of age. Philip, bless him, was so different to his elder brother. Not academic at all: but of good practical common sense. He learnt little from his lessons but was chiefly occupied and happiest with the Rileys' hens and chicks.

Prep. School fees were not cheap and the annual increases were rising faster than those of Ann's and my salaries. With Rebecca and Bart on the educational conveyor-belt we could not keep pace. We were being out-priced, despite the generous pro-rata grants from Church bodies.

Early in 1975 my mother became ill. She was in and out of Burnley Hospital and it became obvious that her condition was serious. My two brothers were on hand to tend to her. Edward lived a few hundred yards away in the same village, Kelbrook, and Stephen, whose young marriage had failed, was living with Mum. The demands of my five churches and eight villages meant that it was never easy to travel the 150 miles to visit my mother. Sundays, of course, were out of the question for obvious reasons. We did go to visit her but I regret that I did not go as frequently as I ought to have done. During Holy Week Mum deteriorated in Burnley Victoria Hospital. Very early in the morning of Maundy Thursday

Edward telephoned to say she had died. We would come at once. Of course. Three services had been planned for that holy day. I cancelled the two morning ones and promised the churchwardens I would be back for the 8 o'clock service of the Commemoration of the Last Supper at Wolvey parish church.

Ann and I made the journey, saw my mother in the chapel-of-rest at Windles' undertakers, made several arrangements with my brothers and set off on our homeward drive. Traffic conditions were bad. The first stirrings of an Easter holiday had brought out the inevitable cars and caravans. We pulled up at the vicarage at almost 8.30pm., half an hour late in what had been a most exhausting day, physically and emotionally. But the day wasn't over yet. I raced into the church certain that the congregation would have gone home. Not a bit of it. No one had left: everyone had remained quietly in their pews, knowing that I *would* appear. It was the kindest corporate act of any congregation in my entire ministry. It was a *very special service* that followed.

Despite the school transport nightmare (which was entirely of our own making) and the sorrow surrounding my mother's death, our new vicarage was a comfortable and comforting haven. Life was indeed hectic but we were young and fit enough to combat the stress. Social life in the parish did make its demands: there was *always* some dance, disco or dinner to attend. It was 'work' of course, in the strictest sense, but we thoroughly enjoyed ourselves – and why shouldn't the vicar and his wife have fun?! Each year a farmer parishioner organised a Salmon and Champagne Dance in his enormous potato hangar, appropriately decorated to the evening's theme. And it came with a live band. Village Hall dances were by comparison much smaller affairs. The energy expounded in the Barn Dances rendered such do's hot, steamy and much more intimate. Ann, a far better dancer than I, delighted in being swirled and spun around by many of the local farmers whose strong arms and sturdy bodies belied the lightness of their nimble feet. Most farmers, especially in Wolvey and Burton Hastings seemed to be good dancers. Products, no doubt, of a lively Young Farmers' Club.

Dances and socials were not the forte of the Wolvey Baptists. The chapel-goers, however, were excellent at Bring and Buy sales and Afternoon Teas. The Christmas Fair by tradition was always held in the

Chapel School room. This was an acknowledged permanent fixture in the village social calendar. Our postman, Roy, was a faithful member of the chapel, whilst his wife was a regular, faithful communicant at the church. Roy loved children. Over the years Roy had obtained the undisputed claim to be Santa Claus at the Christmas Fair. The trouble was he sometimes forgot his role. Our six year old daughter returned from Santa's Grotto somewhat perplexed. "That's funny," she said thoughtfully, "Father Christmas said 'Hello, Rebecca, and what's *your* name?' Why would he ask me if he already knew?" Out of the mouths of babes...

By the turn of the New Year, 1976, our house was really home. We experienced an incredibly long, hot summer; one of the hottest on record. The vicarage curtains were almost permanently drawn to keep out both the incredible light and the intense heat. The garden came into its own for the children, though water was becoming a scarce commodity as summer stretched its warm limbs into a late autumn. The thick stone walls of our mediaeval churches retained the summer's heat and one could still feel the residual warmth well into October. It was central heating, a gift from Nature, and it certainly helped to keep down the heating bills for the last two quarters of the year. 7/6/76 was my 35th birthday and we celebrated *en famille* the day (and the special number) by a simple party in the garden. I cannot recall anything momentous happening, except the sun continued to shine powerfully but, for some reason, all our children remember the day.

It was during this extended sweltering summer that we received a young guest to stay with us for a week. Ann had read about a WRVS scheme, whereby children of very poor inner-city families would be able to have a country holiday through the kind invitation of hosts. We decided to volunteer and in August Katy arrived with the tiniest of suitcases. She was almost seven years old, our Rebecca's age, but she was so doll-like and undernourished she could have been mistaken for a five year-old. My cousin Barbara was a children's clothes designer for the celebrated Viyella House. Periodically she would send some fabulous dresses for Rebecca to wear. Since she had outgrown them, Ann offered them to Katy, whom they would perfectly fit. "No, it's no good havin' 'em," our little guest commented in her old fashioned way, "my Mam won't want to iron 'em!"

The pattern of Katy's home life became increasingly clear to us as the week passed. She would not and could not eat at the table. Her Mam, Dad and big brothers, she explained, just sat around on the settee with their meals, watching television. Knives and forks proved difficult also. Katy resorted to a spoon, though we did eventually make progress in the cutlery stakes. It was a trying week. Having only elder brothers she wasn't interested in playing *girl's* games or with *girl's* toys: she much preferred to follow Philip and his pals. All that she did and all that she said left us with the impression that her family were extremely hard up. And that money was scarce. Until, that is, towards the end of her holiday. She noticed some £5 notes I had received for doing a funeral. "I've seen lots of *them*!" she exclaimed, "my Mam takes them to the bookies when she puts bets on for my Dad." It was a trying, tiring week for Ann and me. It was for our children, too, who were their usual generous selves. We satisfied ourselves with the knowledge that the week was, as they say in the trade, "a work of supererogation".

It was partly the widening gap of expenditure over income concerning school fees and partly having been home for Mother's funeral that we began to consider about returning to where we had come from. We had, after all, originally moved to the Midlands on the (correct) advice of the Diocese of Blackburn – that in the light of my family's opposition to my vocation, and that of my father's especially, my priestly work might be hindered. He was no longer alive and the rest of the family who had previously shown opposition had gone rather silent on the subject. We made a few subsequent visits to our home area, combining a camping holiday at Cracoe, near Skipton, whilst attending the auction sale of my mother's possessions. I lost the battle in attempting to share out her private things without incurring the cost of an auctioneer's commission but to no avail. I did give my mother's engagement ring to Barbara, as it was her expressed wish that she should have it. However, this simple act caused bitter resentment. Consequently I had to undergo the humiliation of bidding for my mother's personal effects, using the fairly obvious pseudonym "Mr Trevor". I purchased for Ann my mother's cameo brooch which Dad had bought her all those years ago in Kendal Milne's, Manchester, some other jewellery and a set of crockery pieces, called 'Princess', which always adorned our Christmas dinner table at Park Avenue.

Whilst still a curate in Stratford I met Laurence Jackson. I knew him slightly when I was a curate in Coventry and he was the Vicar of Holy Trinity, in the city centre, next door to the cathedral complex. He had become Provost of Blackburn but was in the town for the Shakespeare celebrations. He often stayed with a prominent wine merchant friend in Stratford. Laurence had asked me if I ever wanted to return 'up north' he would look out for a suitable parish. I indicated that one day we would probably return. In the late autumn of 1976 I received a letter from him. The parish of St Nicholas, Heyhouses, Sabden was vacant and the patron was looking for a priest. Was I interested? In his description the parish was traditional Catholic, an industrial village of 1600 people, situated in a valley on Pendle Hill, where the Quaker George Fox had gazed down on the likes of industrial Burnley, ripe for evangelisation. And though it was not there in Fox's time, 20th century Burnley comprised of Turf Moor, the home of my favourite football club, a mere *four* miles away.

Excitedly we thought about it; continuously talked about it; fervently prayed about it. "It seemed good to the Holy Spirit and to us", St Luke records in his book of the Acts of the Apostles: and it began to seem good for us too. I replied to Provost Jackson and eventually a date was arranged for me to meet the patron of the living, Mr Guy le Gendre Starkie of Huntroyde Hall, near Padiham.

On a grey mid-December day I drove to meet Mr Starkie. I first called in at Clitheroe Royal Grammar School, where I was able to meet Mr Gerald Hood the Headmaster. He was a jovial, kindly man and a practising Christian. Many years later he was to be a member of my congregation at Grindleton. I explained the purpose of my journey to Sabden but wanted to know something of the area's secondary schools. He graciously took time to tell me about his school. It was so similar to my own Grammar school at Skipton that I was more than satisfied.

From Clitheroe I proceeded over Pendle Hill down into Sabden, up again over White Hill and descended yet again to the Huntroyde estate. When I drew up outside the Hall Mr Starkie appeared more nervous than I. He really did not know much about the parish he was possibly going to offer me. An hour of polite, not-very-useful conversation passed before it was time to return to Sabden and meet the churchwardens. I followed the large Volvo estate car of the patron of the living and duly arrived at the complex of buildings, known in church circles as the 'plant' – church, vicarage and hall. Tom and John were grand Lancashire, down-to-earth men. We talked briefly about the needs of the parish and I outlined my priorities, my 'style' of doing things. "You come from round here, don't you?" one warden remarked. "Yes," I replied "from Barnoldswick." "Right," said the other, "does that make you a Burnley or a Blackburn supporter?" *"Burnley"* I emphasised. "That'll do," they said with a smile. And so it seemed. I'd got the job. Unless Mr Starkie supported Blackburn Rovers...

Shortly after my return home to Wolvey the Bishop of Burnley wrote to me, confirming my appointment and setting a date for my Induction: Tuesday, March 15th at 7.30pm. It was necessary in those days to give three months' notice to my current parishioners. So, rather than be able to wait until the jollifications of Christmas were over, I had to break the news to them in mid-December. It is still customary to announce one's departure from the pulpit at all the Sunday services held on that particular day. And because I wanted all the churchwardens to receive the news *before* the general pulpit announcement, there was nothing else for it but to get up very early on Sunday December 12th and deliver a letter to each warden's house. It was a dark, bitterly cold morning at 6am as I set out in my car to deliver these very short formal notes of resignation. The journey embraced a visit to six houses, three of which were farmsteads and in five different villages. The Diocese had transferred Monks Kirby and Pailton to Brinklow, Withybrook to Ansty, otherwise my trek would have meant twelve calls in all – and a *five* o'clock start! It took well over an hour as it was. Of course the news travelled fast, so that by the time I was due to appear at my second and third services of the day, the congregation already knew! Nevertheless it was an emotional time and I did not relish it one bit. There was much gloom that we were leaving. We ourselves had very mixed feelings: Sabden vicarage was nowhere near as splendid as our home in School Lane, Wolvey. It was Bill Thorpe, a born and bred Wolveyite, chorister for 70 years, pillar of the church, whose philosophy hit the nail on the head: "The lad's going back home," he said, " which is only natural." Good old Bill.

The united parish laid on a most fantastic Farewell Dance and Buffet Supper for us in Wolvey Village Hall on the eve of my last Eucharist.

There were laughs and a few tears. Strong farmhands whirled and twirled Ann, David Eglin, my younger churchwarden gave a speech and presented us with gifts. The following day's Eucharist was a united act of worship for all the villages. Like the Dance the night before, it was emotional and affectionate. We had three days to complete our packing. With the removal van gone we spent half an hour searching for Tammy, Philip's cat, who had other ideas about moving. We eventually found her and placed the reluctant, complaining creature in her cage. We were Lancashire bound!

The Bungalow – in *Wesley* Street!

An imposing cube of an edifice, Sabden's Vicarage. Large reception rooms, vast kitchen, umpteen bedrooms and set in spacious grounds backing on to the wonderful Sabden valley, where there is nothing but fields and a couple of lodges, the local name for areas of water which fed the flow to power the cotton mills downstream. And sheep, of course. Plenty of them. Sadly, this splendid parsonage ceased to be the Vicarage in the late 1960's. The then incumbent lived in temporary accommodation until 1971 when his new house was ready. This was built in the old parsonage's neighbouring field but carried with it the proviso that a long, high stone wall would be erected in order that up against it farmer Gill's sheep could safely lamb in spring.

Dropping steeply down into Sabden from either Clitheroe or Padiham, the road crosses the Whalley road, a continuation of which is hilly Wesley Street. The name gives the game away: here once stood the Methodist chapel. No longer. On that hallowed ground now stand four houses called *St Nicholas'* Mews, would you believe! Wesley Street's tiny, pretty cottages flanked the left hand side. At the top stood the church gates and the long drive to the parish church. Before reaching the church you could enter "the School". Despite its name it was never a Day School, apart from a brief spell when the local Primary School was hors de combat in the early part of last century. It was the home of St Nicholas' Sunday School and inside was a huge hall and well equipped stage. Tacked on behind the stage was the Institute, which in better days had witnessed many fierce rivalries over the two Riley's billiard tables.

Opposite the Institute door stood the new Vicarage. At first sight it looked like an overgrown bungalow. People used to ask me, "Is that where you live, in that *bungalow*?" Like the surrounding hills, it had steeply sloping roofs, out of which poked two large dormer windows with breath-taking views down the valley. The vicarage was deceptively large. In the living-room to the front you looked westward through immense plate-glass windows, which measured at least twelve feet wide and six feet high. On the south side of this room was another window of similar size overlooking the valley. Magnificent light and awesome views but in the high winds the windows shuddered and shivered in an alarming fashion. The house had better than average rooms everywhere and each came with majestic panoramas of the Sabden valley.

It could be very wild and windy, as I said. The oil-fired central heating system was indispensable, though costly. I bought 500 gallons of oil at the cheaper summer price ready for the winter onslaught. When October arrived I smugly congratulated myself on my thrift and preparation and fired up the boiler. Except it did not fire. Would not fire. There was no oil. The contents of the whole tank had leaked away in the corroded pipes under the back lawn. The Parsonages Board paid for a new oil tank and pipes but was less impressed by my request for a shower over the bath. Despite the old argument that one bath equals eight showers, the Board declined, intimating that showers were too much of a luxury for parsons. When we arrived for our second stint at the house in 2003 a shower had been installed, though the white accoutrements were still the original ones of over thirty years. Even the wallpapers were the ones we had chosen in 1977. The living-room windows, however, had been thankfully double-glazed, thus eliminating the unnerving rattle of their predecessors.

Yet we loved Sabden Vicarage. It was the scene of a myriad of memories: buffet suppers, coffee mornings, sherry evenings, children's parties with Uncle Pye the magician – and, to mark my 39th birthday, a 'do' when the ladies wore stockings and suspenders! Outside, the front lawn was the 'hallowed' area for the crowning of the Rose Queen which heralded the start of the annual Church Garden party.

When we left in 1980 Bishop Robert quickly filled the post: a friend of his, one of his children's godfather. His wife was a masseuse who practised her profession, it is said, in the living room with the large windows – for all to see! My churchwardens, Bert and Leonard, continued in office for the first part of my successor's incumbency. They told me of a strange episode which occurred one night at the Vicarage. Round about midnight Leonard received a telephone call from the Vicar's wife. She could hear water running somewhere in the house. Could the wardens investigate? Leonard got dressed, phoned Bert who had also been asleep, and they both duly arrived at the Vicarage. They, too, could hear water. After a preliminary check of the boiler and taps, the men decided to examine each radiator. All in order downstairs. The wardens, followed by the Vicar's wife, climbed the stairs. One by one the bedrooms were inspected. When they entered the master bedroom they switched on the light to discover the Vicar fast asleep in bed! "I didn't want to disturb him on such a small matter" she explained to the two astonished and rather miffed gentlemen. 'The Churchwardens Handbook' does not deal with such eventualities. And they never did discover the source of the running water...

It was an odd feeling to move back into a house where you had lived almost a quarter of a century before. It was equally odd, as I said, that so little of the interior decoration had changed. Apart from the shower over the bath and the new windows, the only addition appeared to be a shaver-point in the downstairs cloakroom! By contrast, the garden and its borders were very much improved. The wife of the previous incumbent (not the somnolent one) had lovingly created and cared for it.

In our second stint at the Vicarage we had our own 'Exodus plague'. Late one evening, as we got ready for bed, we discovered a huge swarm of large bluebottles on our bedroom ceiling. Unable to persuade them to leave via the window, I set about exterminating them all. Standing in my pyjamas very unsteadily on our squashy mattress I brandished the extended vacuum hose (on full power) across the ceiling: my action being a cross between a very amateur painter and a Star Wars combatant. Within a week the flies' cousins arrived and the exercise was repeated. It was time to contact the Parsonages Board. The Pest Control officer duly arrived to take notes "The trouble is" he said, shaking his head in a most serious matter, "the flies have laid their eggs here and they and their offspring will keep coming back. It might be years before we're finally shut of them." There were no flies on him. But we'd make a start and he arranged to return in a few days hence to destroy the eggs and any would-be latecomers. Harry our eight year old grandson was staying with us and was excited at the prospect of a battle. The Pest man appeared in full combats: white overalls from top to toe, helmet and face-mask. Onto his back was strapped a bulky cylinder of the latest DichloroDiphanylTrichloroethane that science could concoct. Leading from this vessel of deadly insecticide was a sprayer. Thus clad, the controller entered the space under the eaves. Before the Lord of the Flies could press his trigger, young Harry spotted a solitary fly. Armed with a red plastic fly-swatter he swiped out with great verve and vigour. So loud was the smack on the bluebottle that the officer visibly jumped, his gun leaping from his hand. "All right, son," he grimaced, "I'll take over now." Fortunately the plague passed over. The exodus complete.

Country comes to town

St George's Vicarage in Chorley was a brisk seven minutes' walk from the centre of town where stood the church. Built in the garden of the old vicarage in Letchworth Place, the new parsonage was a brick four-bedroomed house. I followed a priest who had lived there from new, though he left after only one year. When Ann and I looked around at our interview, we were amazed at the number of rooms painted or wallpapered in tones of tangerine. "He was a Blackpool Football Club supporter," confided the churchwarden who recognised our obvious astonishment. The parish's very able 'working team' of men included a retired painter and decorator, so the décor could easily be de-'Blackpooled.' The garden, on the other hand, could have done with some bright colour. It was a large bland and blank square, surrounded on all sides by a white concrete 'fence' – one of those pseudo-interwoven look-alikes, each pair of concrete posts supporting three horizontal concrete slats. It possessed the appearance of an animal enclosure at some second-rate zoo. Of course, the land had great potential and we – Ann especially – set about installing borders, planting bushes and trees. I particularly liked a young Chinese willow tree we planted in the centre of the lawn. Its corkscrew curly branches looking like an old gnarled man well before his time. It was here in this garden that I discovered several empty Durex packets.

Ann and I had one of our very rare week-ends away. Rebecca and Bart stayed with friends; Matthew and Philip were old enough to stay at home and hold the fort. For most teenagers, I assume, the absence of parents is a signal to invite pals round for a party. Which is what they did. On our return we did not suspect any such goings on. The house was clean and tidy: all traces had been meticulously expunged. Except for the aforementioned *'lettres'* in the garden. "You'll have to have a word with Matthew," Ann said with a worried voice. I suppose I had known for a while that a facts-of-life heart-to-heart with our eldest son was overdue. I invited him into the study and closed the door. I began my chat about boys and girls fancying each other; moved on to sexual urges, which in turn led to contraceptives. I added that his mother and I were disappointed that we had found several in the garden on our return home. Whereupon he burst out laughing. "For goodness' sake, Dad," he chuckled, "we bought the rubbers for a game. We filled them full of water and threw them around the garden as water bombs!" As for the birds and bees stuff, he advised, he knew it already. To my great relief it all appeared to be harmless fun. Though I did wonder what the neighbours thought when they spotted over the vicarage fence several squishy multi-coloured 'Slim Sensations' tossed in the air to the undoubted howls of delight from a group of exuberant lads.

We looked out onto the garden from the wide French windows of a very pleasant living-room. My only real recollection of time spent in that room was our constant attention to the events in the Falklands via our television set.

It was a well-planned Vicarage with double gates leading from the pavement to a spacious tarmacadamed drive, sufficient for half a dozen cars for members of this or that committee meeting at the Vicarage. The side facing this area had windows to kitchen, front door and study. It was to the kitchen window that the tramps would come. They were not the sort of tramps – 'gentlemen of the road' – as we encountered in Warwickshire, but ex-prisoners who were finding life extra tough and rough on the outside. Ann had taught English to a group of men in nearby Wymott Prison. So successful was she in teaching one inmate to read and write that he was soon back in prison after his release – this time for forging cheques!

One of our regulars at the kitchen window was one she recognised (though had not taught) from the prison. One afternoon when we were both out he called. Philip our second son answered his tap on the window but was wise enough not to open it. "Yer Mam makes me a brew," he called through the window, "it's the yeller tin mug down under t'sink. Milk and three sugars." Philip duly obliged, carefully passing the mug through the narrow gap made when the front door was opened but still on the chain. This Vicarage front door was made of good solid wood, stained light brown. Towards the top, at head height, was a small window about a foot square. Its glass was very thick, formed into a swirl, resembling a large clear marble, the sort we kids played with on the cracked kerbs and pavements of our back streets. "Pop-olleys" my mother used to call such windows, since we had six set into our front door at home. Our Chorley front door window was as clear as our marbles but, of course, its shape produced an indistinct view from either side. It gave both visitor and visited a chance, albeit somewhat distortedly, to see who was at the other side.

We had another regular visitor, an ex-convict, who always did some gardening in exchange for a meal. He had been in some road accident or terrible fight, I can't remember which. The upshot was that his face was horrendously disfigured and contorted. He called one day and rang the front door bell. Our daughter Rebecca answered it. Her glance through the window met the close-up of the man's dreadfully misshapen face. The distortion of the glass had doubled the poor chap's disfigurement. Rebecca was petrified, screamed and fled to her room.

To the right of this door was my study window. From which I could be forewarned (and forearmed) on the approach of visitors. It gave me a few vital seconds to be prepared.

Our move to an urban parish was not the most popular thing I instigated as far as the family members were concerned. Our three younger children in particular missed the country life. Philip especially. So much so that we decided to compensate him. He loved animals and had always wanted a few chickens. We saw an advert in the local paper: a night ark for sale at a farm at Bashall Eaves in the Ribble Valley. The farmer's wife was a staunch church lady and Mothers Union member and she took a shine to us. We bought it there and then, though how we transported it back to Chorley, heaven knows! We installed it in the far corner of the Vicarage garden, along with six Rhode Island Reds, who despite their attempts to fly the ark, provided us with an adequate supply of eggs. Philip, more than the hens I reckon, was in his element.

Two elderly sisters, Louie and Eleanor, often came round to look after the younger two children if we were out. Eleanor had once worked in a Home for Retired Clergy and would regale us with lurid stories of ancient clergymen and their unseemly habits. Our children used to say that *they* baby-sat the ladies, as they were continually plying the 'sitters' with tea and cakes. One midweek spring morning the sisters called at the Vicarage. "One of Philip's hens is in Pall Mall," they breathlessly informed us. "It's strutting around Kentucky Fried Chicken!" Philip sped off in his Wellingtons to the shop. Needless to say the scene was a cause for much jocularity. A chicken offering itself to KFC! There was a small crowd of amused pedestrians, some of whom helped to corner the creature and allow Philip to gather it up tightly in his arms. It was the last act of "Chicken Run" – the six birds literally had their wings clipped when Philip got home.

These creatures were to feature again when we heeded the call to the country and moved to Grindleton.

From Vicarage to Rectory

July 8th was sweltering hot when we moved to the parsonage at Grindleton. Over ninety degrees. We had arrived well ahead of the removal van, looking like the Swiss Family Robinson. Six of us in the car, behind which was attached our camping trailer with six hens in cages. Whether it was the intense heat of the day or the slipstream from the M61, we discovered to our horror that all the fowl had died *en voyage*. It was a sorry start. To add to our woes, when the Pickford's van arrived the driver managed to veer off the rough earthen drive and become completely stuck in the paddock. No amount of revving or pushing would remove it. It was then that Ann remembered Karl Simpson, one of the village 'characters', who was at school when she taught there and now ran his own tree-felling business. Luckily we were able to contact him and he appeared at great speed up the drive. Hitching the removal van to his tractor, a sudden savage surge freed the vehicle. A David and Goliath or nut and sledgehammer metaphor springs to mind. The violent jolt of liberation, of course, did nothing to improve our furniture inside the van but at least we could proceed. Aided by copious cups of strong tea, the removers completed the task in good time and received a well-earned tip. Matthew and Philip had a tremendous fight in our newly-decorated bedroom, damaging the wallpaper. Perhaps it was all down to the heat...

* * * * *

Once my appointment to the living had become public I had been able to visit the Vicarage on a number of occasions to inspect the major internal works being carried out. I was particularly concerned with the installation of the central heating. The Archdeacon had informed me that it was to be fixed on the ground floor only. His reason was that clergy never use heating upstairs! I told him that that was a very short-sighted policy. If ever the house were to be sold to a private buyer, the lack of an upstairs heating system would lower the potential value. In any case, I argued, we had four children who would require some degree of warmth whilst they did their homework in their bedrooms. "It's the boiler, you see," explained the Archdeacon, "its output is only sufficient for downstairs radiators." I urged him to recommend a bigger boiler. "That's too expensive," he went on, "unless *you* can contribute several hundred pounds." It was bloody mean and typical of the C of E, spoiling the ship for a ha'p'orth of tar. But I agreed to pay for upstairs central heating. I had no idea where I'd get the money from but if it were installed we'd cross that bridge when we came to it. There was always a bank loan.

My next visit to Grindleton was a month later. To my great dismay – and anger – the plumbers had finished their work and had not incorporated any heating in the upstairs rooms. Not for the first time, nor for the last, would I encounter such shameful and shoddy practice from the Church.

The Vicarage was now to be called 'The Rectory'. The parish of Grindleton was to be amalgamated with the ancient parish of Bolton by

Bowland, whose incumbent possessed the original rights to the Church land, or glebe, and was consequently known as 'rector'. It really made no odds. The stipend was the same.

The Rectory was a solid stone edifice constructed, I suspect, in the early nineteenth century. It stood in two paddocks adjacent to a sizeable graveyard on the south side with the little church of St Ambrose at the bottom of the garden. The Primary School and playground, where Ann had taught three years before, wrapped itself partly round its parish church. We both adored the sounds of children's voices at School playtime.

The old coach-house-cum-stable, with its stone arched front and side stable-door, had been converted into a large garage. It still contained its original hay-loft. A pleasant reminder of times before the horseless carriage. A covered open veranda led to the main door. Study immediately to the left and a glass partition wisely separating official from domestic areas. Two very large reception rooms looked out southwards to magnificent Pendle Hill and Chatburn village below it. Kitchen and utility room behind the study, leading to a good-sized gravelled courtyard, a small lawn and a wilder area. Four large bedrooms, bathroom and separate w.c. made up the complement of rooms. The latter was a weird room: windowless and four feet wide by twelve feet long. The toilet-roll was *not* fixed to the inside of the door! Over six happy years we decorated most rooms. William Morris-designed wallpapers on the main reception rooms – wonderful! Philip in his vegan days slept first in the cellar, then in a most dilapidated caravan in the courtyard, where he grew his own pulses and mung beans. Bart had a stint of deliberately sleeping rough in the playing field's hut, whilst Matthew and Rebecca revised for their 'A' and 'O' levels respectively in a long spring and early summer of 1984. A fraught time, which included one knife-throwing incident!

The rectory at Grindleton was an idyllic place. I recall being ambushed with a hail of snowballs by our children one dark winter evening as we returned from 'The Duke of York'. At the rear of the house we kept two Chinese geese – better guards than dogs! We had hens, plus two vicious White Suffolk cocks, and of course, our lovely Swaledale sheep.

So many glorious, merry times we had in that house. The boys' bedroom (the largest) became the base for an unofficial Youth Club. Its ceiling was decorated like some Victorian church chancel by Butterfield, blue and white like the stars of heaven. Except the décor was accidental: the blue being the chalk marks from the snooker cues wielded carelessly by the lads. It was also the era of 'punk'. On one occasion, neither Ann nor I could gain access to our bathroom, as Youth Club member Michael was 'soaping up' his hair. A performance he was forbidden to do at home.

We hoped The Rectory would be home to both sets of parishes. It was certainly the venue for a medley of parish activities and private parties.

July 25ᵗʰ 1989 was our Silver Wedding Anniversary. Bishop Roy Williamson had just offered me the living of Holy Ascension, Settle. Ann did not want to leave her beloved Grindleton home, nor did she relish the difficult journey from Settle to her work in East Lancashire, especially in the winter. Unknown to her I had engaged an ex-teacher of pottery to make a clay model of our rectory. He spent a whole morning taking careful measurements of every aspect of the building. The result was a superb scale model, down to every fine detail, including the half-open cellar window. It was my Anniversary present to her and it has now become a family treasure. It is true to say that wherever we have lived since, Grindleton Rectory has always gone with us. Physically and emotionally.

Sleepless in Settle

In the past few years there has been a worrying increase in the incidence of bullying in the Church. The Archbishop of Canterbury has recently admitted that this has become a serious problem. Some of the bullying is subtle, some more obvious. It exists in all religions and in all Christian denominations. It is perpetrated both by clergy upon clergy and by laity upon clergy. There is also, unquestionably, some bullying of lay folk by the clergy. Whilst this latter circumstance is blatantly wrong, the former do have the option of abandoning ship or taking one's bat home and going elsewhere Not so those ordained and whose very livelihood is at stake. I recall one Rural Dean who, terrier-like, attacked all clergy who were new arrivals in his Deanery with a ferocity most unbecoming. After a handful of encounters his vitriol would subside and he would even become quite friendly. But his initial caustic comments would have done the trick: the rules were laid down; you knew who was boss. You behaved accordingly from that day on.

I was on the receiving end of a small number of bullying episodes, I suppose, though none ever intimidated me. Over the years some Archdeacons made me angry with the way my family were treated concerning our home (*their* Diocesan buildings!). In my final parish I would meet the Archdeacon from time to time. Without fail his first broadside was always "When is it you retire, Trevor?" Apparently the Bishop had scuppered his plans for the parish by appointing me as priest-in-charge and the Archdeacon could not get over it. A solicitor friend, as well as my doctor, pointed out that his comment was tantamount to constructive dismissal and that I would have a strong case in law. Since "the Arch-demon's" remarks only irritated rather than depressed me, I shrugged them off. Besides the Church gets into enough mire without my adding to it.

What is equally a cause for concern is the bullying of clergy which is perpetrated by a few but powerful members of the laity. Powerful in the sense of church politics – elected officers – rather than those with authority and standing in a civic or a national context. In one of my small villages there existed a small band of 'mafia'. Under the rules of my 'Baptism policy', I pointed out to a family who applied to have their baby baptised, that I could not perform the rite unless they attended church and carry out the promises made at the christening. The father refused to make any such commitment but insisted on the service. Now this family was exceedingly rich. They carried a lot of clout in the district. To many people money is a god and a number of the villagers regarded this moneyed family in awe and disproportionate esteem. I was therefore put under great pressure to succumb and relax my rules. The episode began to gnaw at the church community. At every service I was harried and hounded to give in. After several weeks their bluster turned into browbeating. The issue had grown out of all proportion. To my mind the unity of the local church was at risk. Open criticism of its clergyman was bad publicity for God's Church. I decided to yield. I visited the family and agreed to conduct the baptism. The news quickly spread around the village. Were my detractors overjoyed? Not likely. They continued their criticism of me because, *now*, I had shown weakness. They were indulging in a spot of clergy-baiting. In a word, bullying.

The only other case of my being bullied by parishioners was some twenty years later. I suggested to one of my churchwardens that he stand down, since his work commitments, even on a Sunday, meant he had little or no time for the work of the Church. He strongly objected, took umbrage and with a small *clique des nouveaux riches* reported me to both the Bishop and the Archdeacon, both of whom, mindful of the *riches,* were as inert as argon. The churchwarden's supporters would repeatedly address me with shouts of "Resign!" during Church Council meetings. They generally made life quite hellish for me and the rest of the flock. The disgruntled gentleman even threatened to "mow [me] down" with one of his vehicles. A ministry of nothing? Was it all for 'nowt'? It made you think.

This lengthy preamble about bullying is a result of my thinking about the Vicarage at Settle, our next home. I am told that the door of this house was always locked and that visitors could never gain access, despite the Vicar's presence. The wardens, I believe, communicated with him through the letter-box. He had become a prisoner in his own house, performing the bare minimum of his outside duties. He had lived in the former large Vicarage in the town for over twenty years. With a couple of years left before retirement, however, he had to undergo the stress of packing and unpacking his furniture and belongings to another residence no further than four hundred yards away. No sooner would he have completely unpacked when he would have to pack it all over again as he moved into his Harrogate retirement. His self-imposed house-arrest, however, was much more than the consequence of moving house. There was undoubtedly an element of manipulation and controlling – some would say bullying – of this poor elderly bachelor. His past tribulation became increasingly apparent to me as I moved about the parish and listened to the townsfolk. And it explained why I, too, had become the new target.

The new mid-1980s Vicarage stood proudly at the top of the rise in Town Head, opposite an equally splendid-looking doctors' surgery. The parish church, 150 yards at the bottom of the hill, was sited at the corner of the main street, once the A65 trunk road from Bradford to

Morecambe and the Lake District. An easy few minutes' walk from the Vicarage for Sunday worship and the Daily Offices.

Our house was built of local stone. From the front it had the appearance of a bungalow, with a study to the left of the main door and the large window of the lounge to the right. A connected garage had been constructed onto the study. These two, though joined to the rest of the house, were separate. The 'living' quarters were all situated to the right of the house, which proved most manageable and comfortable in its design. It commanded wonderful views over Giggleswick, the dome of its famous School chapel and the hills beyond. On special days a chartered steam train from Preston or Blackburn would pull packed carriages of loco-enthusiasts up the Settle-Carlisle line. These trains normally stopped at Settle to take on water and we often felt the droplets of sooty steam as it began to pull away again and plough on northwards. Always, of course, to the utter rapture of hordes of camera-laden train-spotters.

Looking up from the main road one could see the limestone hills of Malham. The Union Jack was often flying from Castleburg, a small ledge up the steep climb of the hill above the town. The small new estate which included our home was in the foreground of all this delightful scenery. On June 24th 1991 – St John the Baptist's Day – we hung a huge bed sheet from the house, legible from the main road. In large letters we had simply painted "Welcome Home, Gulf War Hero!" Our youngest son Bart had served with the Royal Artillery there. He arrived home on that day for a well-earned rest of three weeks.

It was from Castleburg that Ann and I sat that Sunday morning before the Induction. We watched from our high and distant vantage point tiny figures, ant-like, scurrying about their duties. A group of hikers, a steady stream for the Sunday papers outside the Naked Man Café and a smaller trickle of mainly elderly ladies heading for the parish church and morning worship. As is my wont I began to count them. When the solitary bell ceased its tolling the count was less than thirty. It could only get better I told myself.

The house in the fields

My brother Edward was best man at our Wedding. In his speech at the reception he proposed a toast to Ann and me, couching our names in the phrase "an Ezra Laycock bus romance." Ezra Laycock was the name of the Barnoldswick bus company which ran the school transport service to and from the secondary schools in Skipton, nine miles away. Ann and I started our long and lasting romance on those school buses way back in 1956. If, then, we had cared to look out of the bus window on the Broughton road, towards Elslack Moor, we would have spotted across the fields the small ancient parish church of Broughton and next to it a large barn-looking building, which was the rectory. I suppose we did see it from time to time but took it for granted. Familiarity breeds inattention and forgetfulness. Furthermore, I had never been on that road on which the buildings stood: Primrose Lane. I didn't even consider the lane's existence. Even years later when I borrowed my father's Hillman bread van for a spot of courting with Ann on Elslack Moor, I never once ventured down that lane. In retrospect, it might have been more private than the Moor. When you are canoodling in a van with words painted on both sides, "Vaughan's the Bakers~ Beef at its best in a golden crust," there's not much privacy about it!

It was to be almost thirty years later when I first set foot in Primrose Lane. Ann and I met churchwarden Mr David Nelson who was to show us around the rectory prior to my interview in Oxford for the living. The setting of that interview, at Christ Church College, was quite surreal. Almost out of a Harry Potter movie. Amongst Oxford's spires and towers sits the College and the Cathedral. It was a Thursday, April 19th 1991, when I arrived at the main gate where a porter led me through a cloistered walkway to a waiting room. From there I eventually entered the dark panelled interview room and saw the six eminent sages who were my interviewers. One of them I knew about: Dr Eric Heaton, a Professor of Old Testament and an Old Boy of Ermysted's Grammar School in Skipton. He actually made reference to our common educational ancestry. They were seated at the largest table I have ever seen. It must have been at least thirty feet in length. My inquisitors were seated in equal spaces along the board's entire length. So much so that when I was receiving a question from the extremities I was compelled to move my chair to face them. It was impossible to hold all six in my vision at any one time.

I learnt two days later that the interview was successful. I was to give the statutory three months' notice by announcing it from the Settle pulpit in three weeks' time. The new job would commence some time in September.

Broughton's rectory housed the incumbent of the villages of Thornton-in-Craven, East and West Marton, Elslack and Broughton. By that I mean there was *one* priest for the five villages. Once upon a time – in relatively recent days – three parsons had served these villages. The Rectory was really a 1795 barn conversion, having been given to the Church by the Tempest family of nearby Broughton Hall who were Roman Catholics. A twelve feet wide double gate, painted white, opened into a spacious driveway The parsonage stood in its own grounds, with a large L-shaped lawn, borders of shrubs and several trees, the finest of which was a 200 year old copper beech. The porch's stout main door led into a pleasant hallway, whose floor was decorated in maroon and yellow Victorian tiles. A study to the left, big enough for all my books and the ubiquitous parish photocopier. To the right a small cloakroom, under which was a damp cellar kitted out with pits for salting pigs. Across the hallway were two doors leading into two delightful and large reception rooms, separated by panelled double doors, which when folded back revealed a most commodious room suitable for sizeable parish gatherings. Each reception room had wide bay windows added in Victorian times and looked out across the fields, the A59 in the far distance. Each bay was probably nine feet high, possessed shutters and were castellated. From the corresponding bedroom windows you could climb out onto the bays. The hallway led down to the kitchen then into a garage (formerly the maid's kitchen) behind which was a pantry with a stone slab. Butcher's hooks pierced the ceiling. Under this pantry was yet another – drier – cellar. From the hallway rose a splendid staircase. At the turn in the stairs was a tall narrow window, its three panes forming an outward semi-hexagonal shape. Its wide window-ledge enabled you to perch there and gaze out on the distant farms and the ever-changing hues of the moorland's heather.

At the top of the stairs, just to the left, was a tiny room, accessed by three wooden steps. The space – it really was too minute to be called a room – was four feet square, though high enough for an adult to stand. This was 'the Lamp Room', where the most junior maid would prepare the lamps for the Rector and his household. There were three bedrooms, the master being of a most generous size, with shutters at its expansive windows. Further down the landing were two more bedrooms, one of which at least would be occupied by a maid. Clergy in those days were possessors of a much higher status and income than today. Separating these two bedrooms from the other three was a door, on which a hasp-and-staple lock device was fixed. But fixed to the *other* (the *wrong?*) side. Was this to keep the rector away from the maids? A disproportionately small bathroom was to be found at the end of the landing. Next door was an extra room, plumbed in with another lavatory and washbasin, and used by my predecessor's wife as a laundry.

Looking back on that summer of 1991 I can only recall warm days and bright blue skies. I'm sure it wasn't all like that but I took the opportunity of travelling over to Broughton a couple of days a week to do some interior decorating. Philip and I set about painting the two enormous reception rooms. We prepared, primed and painted about forty five yards of skirting board, between which we had 'working' lunches and teas lying on the rectory grass. There was quite a lot of basic work for the Diocese to carry out but we decided to get on with the cosmetics.

August 21st was Removal Day: a mere half hour's journey from Settle. It was another fine warm day. To our utter dismay, however, we discovered that the Diocesan Parsonages Board had done almost nothing to the house. The kitchen was still bereft of a sink, draining board and cupboard top. The small courtyard on the east end of the house was covered in healthy weeds well over a foot high, their remarkable stature enhanced by the effluence from a leak in one of the upstairs toilets. Thornton's churchwardens, Robert and Eugene, had paid us a visit quite early in the day and were as angry and frustrated as we were. They set off at once and returned by mid-afternoon with all three items – and a plumber booked to fit it! The faulty waste pipe would have to be dealt with the following day. I phoned the Diocesan Architect and asked him to explain why the outstanding jobs were still outstanding. He agreed to come round. Before his arrival Ann and I devised a cunning plan. I would take the architect into the courtyard, ostensibly to show him the open soil-pipe, and 'manoeuvre' him under the offending outlet. Meanwhile Ann would dash upstairs to the bathroom and flush the lavatory, thereby giving our man from the Diocese a much deserved dousing for all his dilly-dallying. Unfortunately Ann flushed the wrong 'loo': the *laundry* had the faulty spout, not the bathroom! Our man was spared a second baptism.

The rectory was everything Ann and I could wish for: lots of space for family, friends and parishioners, some elegant internal fixtures and green sheep-filled fields all around. Here was the venue for parties, parish socials and gatherings. Even the Mothers Union Annual General Meetings took place here. Discussion groups, Confirmation classes, lunches, dinners and afternoon teas, when sometimes ramblers and cyclists would stop for a cup of tea. (I recall reading in the *Craven Herald* the obituary of a lady who owned a local café, which stated "she did a lot for cyclists"). Of course, our large parsonage was not without its faults. To do justice to such a fine house repairs and maintenance would require its resident to be earning several times the stipend of its clerical incumbent. Its sandstone west wall, opposite our squat parish church, always took the full force of the prevailing west winds straight from the Atlantic. Consequently damp was a bit of a problem. The top layers of the porous sandstone had over the years slightly crumbled like burnt toast. To rectify the matter a builder was called in to spray the entire massive wall with a silicon shield. The gormless operator, oblivious of a north-westerly wind, managed to include our car into the bargain! On the following Christmas Eve mighty gale-force winds hurled the weighty Yorkshire flagstones off the roof. Wet-rotted wood of several window-frames had to be removed and replaced and, like the Forth Bridge, painting the outside was almost a continuous task. For all that, we considered it a fabulous house and delighted in residing there.

The garden was, in estate agent-speak, "mainly laid to lawn," the mowing of which took me well over two hours and a mile of walking in ever-decreasing L-shapes. The borders were full of bushes, hydrangea, laurel, rudbeckia; bright yellow aconites preceded the snowdrops which heralded the spring and its banks of daffodils. And then there were the trees: sycamore and ash and that glorious copper beech. Experts estimated the beech was two hundred years old. I reckon it was planted when the old barn first became the parsonage in the middle of George III's reign.

In season the beech's leaves were a vibrant dark red. Its huge branches presented both a welcome shade to part of the rectory garden and a possible hazard to traffic on the lane. One summer's day a gigantic hay-wagon motored past the rectory. It ought not to have been there: perhaps the driver had been an innocent victim of his impish sat-nav. With a thundering bang the high vehicle struck some of the beech's thicker branches. The curved windscreen splintered into a myriad of fragments. Some of the boughs were forced into the cab, whose driver, miraculously, was unhurt. It was almost dark when the last bits of the wreckage were cleared from the lane: glass and metal oddments from the wagon, branches, twigs and, of course, much hay. I reported the incident to the Parsonages Committee who sent round the Diocesan Arboriculturist. It's surprising what experts the Church of England has up its sleeve! And he *was* an expert. Our beech was sadly showing signs of old age. He reckoned, however, that she could be saved and recommended some sensitive surgery befitting an elderly lady: some crowning and thinning. She appeared to be no worse for her head-on collision and continued, post-operatively, to flaunt her leafy flames every summer.

From a hook on the west gable end to a metal pole on the edge of the lawn we fixed a washing-line. Ann would organise the week's washing before departing for work and instruct me to peg it out when the washer's cycle was complete. One week, however, I was in sole charge. I filled the machine with my white underwear and a handful of those bright yellow dusters which housewives buy from the catalogues of Betterware or Kleen-Eze. The result – naturally – was catastrophic. All my whites were now non-whites. Members of the Liberal Party. A second washing made not a scrap of difference. Resigned to the fact that underneath I would resemble a banana for months ahead, I hung out the eight pants and four dusters on the line. Debbie, our young neighbour across the lane, immediately telephoned. "The sun has got his hat on," she said enigmatically.

"Pardon?" I asked.

"I see you've brought out the sunshine!" she teased.

"Oh," I sighed, "yes: sunshine...yellow."

It was not the first time I had been confronted, affronted and Y-fronted all at the same time.

Broughton Rectory holds indelible memories for us. Matthew in 1995 and Rebecca in 2000 were both married from there, in the church across the lawn. Each time we travel on the A59 through Broughton, the old school-run, we glance through the car window across the fields to 'our' rectory. It no longer serves the people of the parish. My successor has moved to an eco-home in West Marton and the parsonage is 'Under Offer' – at a *mere* £550,000. Will the C of E ever learn?

Numbered

By contrast the Vicarage in the parish of St Barnabas Morecambe was under fifty years old, having undergone an extension in the 1970s. It was the only parsonage we inhabited which was known by its number and street rather than its name. Like the hairs of our head, all the dwellings in Regent Road were numbered. Our new abode was 101, Regent Road. Morecambe. Of course, it made more sense to have a number. It made life easier for the Royal Mail Sorting Office and the postman could deliver straight down the road, without the distraction of looking for a name on a gate. It was also a good thing in that it probably saved the house from random and malicious damage by the wild characters who roamed Regent Road. So serious was this scenario that my predecessor, a young and well-built man, refused to wear his dog-collar whilst walking about in the streets of the parish. He was genuinely afraid of some random and malicious damage to his person. Contrarily I opted for the dog-collar and allowed it to be extremely visible at all times, purely as a protection. Either way, I'm sure you get the picture. The parish was, at times and in parts, a somewhat scary place. Those who really wanted to know where the Vicar lived, of course, could easily track me down. My name and address were painted in large letters on the notice board affixed to the church wall further up Regent Road. And it was there for all to see in the parish magazine.

Number 101 was a large L-shaped building. A small front garden had a central path to the main door. On our arrival this garden was something of a jumble. Or should I say 'jungle.' It had been deliberately 'cultivated' by the previous occupant to have that 'tropical rainforest' look. "The last chap liked to grow nettles," an old parishioner informed me. There was a small side lawn and a delightful lawn and borders at the rear. It was in this garden area – pint-sized compared to Broughton rectory – that we held a Church Garden Party one summer. We had a variety of stalls, a few games and afternoon cream teas, served from the kitchen which fortuitously led straight out into the garden. Previous experience told Ann and me that the whole affair could be done and dusted in two hours. The tickets, therefore, stated quite categorically "From 2pm to 4pm." It was a bright, warm Saturday afternoon. Ann had enlisted a few helpers for the catering. The lawns were cut, edges trimmed, chairs and tables casually placed amongst the sideshows. At *one* o'clock the first few folk turned up. Not the helpers. The 'public.'

"It doesn't start till two o'clock," said Ann in desperation.

"Aye, we're a bit early," they replied, "but there's no point in going home now."

So we sat them down in chairs in the garden. By half past one a good crowd had arrived and found the few unoccupied seats. Which is where these early birds remained for the entirety of the afternoon.

"Not long to go," I whispered encouragingly to Ann at quarter to four.

"Good," she murmured, "because it's going to *pour down*!"

The weather had suddenly taken a turn for the worse. It can do that on the coast, as the west winds blow clouds towards us from the Atlantic. Then the heavens opened. And it rained with a ferocity and velocity not often seen in those parts. Within minutes our lawn was a quagmire. It was just four o'clock and the rain was a miraculous sign for the public to make their way home after a very pleasant afternoon. But did they? They did not. They all traipsed into the kitchen, which couldn't contain fifty bodies. The overspill spilled over into the living room, bearing their cream teas with them and depositing wet soil on the floors. The last of our visitors left just after six o'clock. It was very late in the evening when we finally de-soiled and un-creamed the carpets.

* * * * *

The study was to the left of the main door, wisely sectioned off from the rest of the living area by a glass screen. One dreadful evening there I thought my number was 'up'. A rough character had hoodwinked his way into the study and began to behave erratically and oddly. At one time he fell on his knees in prayer, which quickly turned into threats. I feared for my life. I suggested he leave. He refused. I ordered him to leave. He still refused. I threatened him with the police. He continued to refuse. In sheer desperation I made an excuse to leave the study and sharply told Ann to phone the police. Whether my visitor got wind of my ploy, I don't know, but within a few minutes he suddenly shot to his feet and left. The sergeant arrived a few moments after and rightly reprimanded me for inviting the chap into our home.

The Vicarage was extremely vulnerable from this kind of visitor. These episodes were not rare. The Blackburn Diocese, aware of the defencelessness of its clergy in their homes, decided to act after this particular event. What brought such concerted action was the case of the young Liverpool vicar who was stabbed to death at his front door. A sturdy double-glazed uPVC porch was constructed in front of the main door. The porch door was purposely positioned at right-angles to the main door for obvious defensive reasons. Both sets of doors were fitted with solid locks and strong chains. I was instructed, when answering the door bell, always to close the main door behind me -and lock it if I did not know the person standing outside. Only then was I to open the porch door, and then on the chain. It was such a rigmarole: but both a necessary and reassuring one.

No sooner had the amendments been made to the front door of 101 Regent Road than the Disability Discrimination Act loomed into focus. It goes without saying that disabled people should have access to all that the able-bodied have. Dioceses up and down the land, however, applied a knee-jerk reaction to the situation. More men were dispatched to our home, armed with plans for ramps and rails. The upshot was the laying of a long concrete ramp, taking up much of the garden path. The ramp turned a sharp left to reach the porch door. Alongside this slope strong metal hand-rails were securely fixed. Not only were the rails painted white, there were sufficient white lines on the ramp and path to give it the appearance of an athletics track. One morning a large white pharmaceuticals delivery van pulled up outside number 101. The driver staggered up the path, carefully negotiating the slope, with a huge armful of incontinence pads.

"Is this Regent Rest Home?" he wheezed under the strain.

"No. This is St Barnabas' Vicarage," I replied.

"Sorry," he muttered, nodding his head to the white hand-rails and ramp, "but it looks more like an old folks' home."

He was right. Noting the contents of his packages I was reminded of the joke about the Essex signpost which directed travellers to the port for Europe. "Harwich for the continent" it said. Underneath, some wit had scribbled "Frinton-on-Sea for the incontinent."

I don't suppose Howard was incontinent but he consumed a great deal of alcohol all the same. He was the most regular of our regulars. A man who wanted a cup of strong tea ("four sugars, love") and a sandwich or two. We always kept an extra loaf in the bread bin especially for Howard. We had a soft spot for him. He called occasionally when he was sober and we fed him then, too. His wife had gone a long time ago but he had a daughter in the next parish. One dark Saturday evening, when he was worse for wear, I manoeuvred his sagging body into my car and drove him to her, as he requested. I dropped him off at the door, saw they were in conversation over the threshold and returned home. I learned later that she didn't want to know him and closed the door on him. Consequently he spent most of the darker hours staggering back home. Often Ann would give him a hot meal. He was always happy to eat outside; never once did he ask to come inside. "That's just put me on fine, love," he would say to Ann, "I'll be set up now till morning." But come morning, we'd find Howard slumped in a paralytic state up against the porch.

It was a spacious home. Its many windows let in the brilliance of the coastal light. Garden Parties apart, the weather was invariably fine in Morecambe. Any rain was swiftly sent speeding westwards towards the Pennines to drop its load there. It could be stair-rods in Sabden or a cloudburst in Broughton but Morecambe would remain bright and sunny. Our home was venue to many kinds of gatherings. One of the first things we ever organised was a Buffet Supper for members of the Church Council and their spouses. Since it was autumn Ann prepared a choice of two hot meals: a curry with rice or a Lancashire hotpot. It went down a treat. People had seconds and a couple of chaps tried both choices. One man, however, looked glum. Ann overheard him murmuring to his wife, "That were all right but where's the pudding? I don't reckon they've done one. Last vicar's wife served some grand puddings." When everyone had had their fill of the first course, we brought out a wide selection of desserts, including Ann's family-famous chestnut torte. Trying to please the P.C.C. really was a piece of cake...

The frontage of our house looked out onto Regent Park. Towards the latter end of the nineteenth century the land had been used for horse-racing. Later, it had become the Summer Gardens with a boating lake. Lake Road, at right-angles to the Vicarage, still bears witness to this past attraction. Now, all signs of water have disappeared. Tennis courts and bowling greens provide facilities for the energetic; park benches and café for the sluggish. There is also one fairly new innovation to the Park's activities. Most Sunday mornings, as I returned from the early morning Communion, I would see bent figures raking or tamping down rectangles of powdery clay. These 'courts' were too small for tennis and too large for marbles. Those stooped men and women were preparing the terrain (I think that's the correct name) for pétanque. It's a sort of French bowls-cum-curling and played on a surface about fifteen yards by four. They take it very seriously in Morecambe. Regent Park hosts several regional pétanque tournaments in the season, when coach-loads from all parts of Britain descend to toss their heavy metal *boules* towards the jack (should that be '*jacques*'?) It was always good to see such enthusiastic crowds in our part of the town. Even if their vehicles blocked the very pleasant view of the Park from number 101 Regent Road.

Unless the Lord build the house...

I'm not bad at reading upside down. When the *print* is that way, not me. I was once being interviewed for a post and could read some of the lines which one of my referees had written about me. Her testimonial was lying on the desk in front of the chairman of the Trustees. The gist of those few lines was that I had had far too many career moves. She was quite right. The 'tour' of the parsonages I have just described involved ten 'clergy houses' plus two during my training at Lincoln. Of the ten church residences I am sad to record that no less than seven are no longer used or owned by the Church of England. 70% is a huge proportion. It represents a major retreat by the Church at grass roots. Fewer clergy means fewer parsonages. Fewer worshippers mean fewer finances. Fewer finances and fewer clergy lead to parish amalgamations. More amalgamations inevitably mean less worshippers. Less worshippers mean less finances means less parsonages. Ad infinitum. It's simply human mathematics.

Has it all been closures? Or has the Church exchanged one old parsonage for a brand new one, more central to the parish mission? Yes, sometimes. But seldom rather than often. This retreat – the wholesale selling off of vicarages is an example of bad management. A lack of foresight. The spacious rectories and vicarages up and down the land provided a much needed practical place for parish activities, especially in rural areas. Even folk who do not attend church or are not in sympathy with its aims see the value of a large parsonage for the community. I have never met anyone who was envious of or complained about the size or status of our church house. Some clergy, it has to be said, do not like living in the traditional clergy home. They argue that it makes them 'different' from the rest of the parish. Other clergy, it has to be said, insist that their parsonage is for the sole and private use of its resident. That has been proved in law not to be the case. Besides, there are more clergy who relish the space provided by the old parsonage. Two parishes in which I served have both lost their Vicarage at give-away, knock-down prices. In both instances the houses were allowed to deteriorate. Despite the architects' recommendations in the five yearly inspection – the dreaded 'Quinquennial' – maintenance was not always carried out. That updating, together with ongoing repairs and modernising prior to the sale, could have produced much greater profits for the Church. It is almost sacrilege that the Church Commissioners actually *lose* so much on its sales of parsonages. Where they did replace old for new, and larger for smaller, it often resulted in the costs of purchase outweighing the proceeds of sale. Hardly good stewardship.

The National Housing Federation is an organisation representing over a thousand independent housing associations across England. Its aim is to campaign for better housing and neighbourhoods and through its member associations are responsible for two and a half million affordable homes. The Federation has entered the dangerous waters of faith, advocating the need for urban religious communities, or 'faith groups', to find appropriate buildings for worship. Very commendable. The flip side of this, however, is their call to the Established Church to release land for new homes in the countryside. With over nine thousand rural churches and 129,000 acres of land the Church Commissioners are urged to turn over some of their assets into new housing. It would dramatically ease the rural housing crisis, the Federation says, and boost church congregations into the bargain. If the Church did act upon this suggestion and create a host of Glebe Corners, Rectory Places and Church Closes, both village and church populations would grow. And we'd need the parsonages for all those communal activities and for promoting the Christian message...

On several occasions I have argued that the Church should let, or better still, lease out its redundant parsonages. In the former case there would be money for repairs and maintenance – and perhaps even for mission! In the latter case, on a 99-year lease, say, the house could be available once more as a significant tool in the Church's pastoral ministry. That this just does not happen points sadly to the fact that the Church of England does not anticipate a future revival of faith. As the C of E stands today, it is not difficult to see why.

CHAPTER SIX

Pastoralia

"The Rector's sheep"

On every occasion I have been admitted to a parish post, either as rector, vicar or priest-in-charge, what is termed in the trade as 'The Induction," the Bishop has handed me a scroll of parchment-like paper. In some legal ecclesiastical jargon, typically unpunctuated, is written a message from the Bishop to me, whom he calls his 'beloved in Christ'. Affixed to this letter is the seal of the diocese. I have had them in wax, though recent ones are usually on stiff red paper embossed with the arms of the See. What the scroll says, in fact, is simply written evidence: proof of what the Bishop says to me at the Induction. I kneel before him and he presents me with this paper, the Licence, and he addresses me with these words: "Receive this cure which is both yours and mine."

'Cure' is the correct word. It is more to do with healing or reconciliation than 'care'. Unless you are a pig, of course.

The secular priest represents God to mankind, and mankind to God. He is a mediator between heaven and earth, set firmly in society to bring home eternal values, healing and a taste of heaven on earth. Such a tall order cannot possibly be straightforward: a cure of souls will necessarily involve heartache and disappointment, friction and fury. But Christianity is the religion of love and there is also an intimate relationship between love and laughter. The pastoral ministry is a cocktail of all these elements and I hope that in the following snippets that will become apparent. They are all true tales of just a fraction of my work of the cure of souls – what we at Theological College glibly, unknowingly, labelled as 'Pastoralia'.

'Pastoralia' is another good word. It is to do with sheep and shepherding. In the Church of England Ordinal, the service for making deacons, ordaining priests and consecrating bishops, there is frequent allusion to the aspect of shepherding. In the ordination of a bishop the Gospel reading is from St John chapter 21, where Jesus tells Peter to "feed my sheep". At the ordination of priests the bishop addresses those to be ordained. A priest, he states, must "set the Good Shepherd always before him as the pattern of his calling, caring for the people committed to his charge, and joining with them in a common witness to the world."

I kept a few Swaledale sheep in the two small paddocks at Grindleton rectory. What a happy time! I learnt that a good shepherd must look at his sheep often, very often. At least twice a day. Sheep are queer creatures and can quickly become unwell. If one falls on its back it has difficulty in righting itself and will quickly die. Humans, like sheep, require regular inspection. I am astonished that so many clergy today no longer carry out routine pastoral visits. One of my successors announced to his Parochial Church Council members that he "did not do cold calling." He only visited *church* folk: how he thought he would ever increase his flock by that method, God only knows. It is bad and it is sad. As a well-trained curate I was handed out at each Monday morning's Staff Meeting a list of people on whom I had to call in that week. And report back the following Monday. Of course, the list is longer when one hasn't the weighty burden of responsibility for running the parish but my vicar, Kenneth, was a fine example for any pastoral clergyman. Despite his TB arm, he was out every afternoon, come hail, snow, wind or rain, calling on the flock – and the 'other sheep' of which the Lord also spoke.

As I said, tending the flock – the woolly sort – was an inspiration and an aid to my care of the human flock. The first couple of sheep I bought were Teeswaters. They had stylish curly coats – or should that be 'jumpers' because they could leap over any wall or fence! It was a difficult task trying to keep them in the paddock, though at least they ensured that I sealed all the gaps in the fences or hedges. The Teeswaters were eventually replaced by Swaledale sheep. Lovely creatures: shaggy coats, wise heads with a black muzzle, horned and indigenous to our part of England. My next door neighbour John was our milkman as well as a farmer. As he delivered the morning's milk he cast an eye on my sheep, an expert eye. It was he who took the ewes to be tupped and, when the time came for them to deliver their lambs, he placed them once again in his 'maternity pens' in order to watch over them. Pastoralia at its best! When the lambs were fat enough I took them to the local auction marts, either Gisburn or Clitheroe. One season I presented four splendid fat lambs for sale.

"Nah then, rector, what are you doin' here?" asked Bill, whose omnipresence at the local Marts was well known. I'm not sure what actual job Bill had at the auctions. Nothing official, I'm certain, but he was always there and acting in a very official manner. I told him that I had four lambs for sale. "Pens 82 and 83" I added. I followed the auction of the lambs from Pen 1 onwards. The auctioneer walked across planks laid over the whole grid of pens, as with great dexterity, both of tongue and limb, he rattled through the sale. "Pens 82 and 83," he yelled to a healthy number of farmers. Before he could continue, however, Bill suddenly reappeared like some elf in a pantomime. "Nah then," he addressed the buyers in a loud authoritative voice, "these are t'rector's sheep and if tha wants to go to heaven, tha'll give him a good price!" The crowd was suitably tickled by Bill's endorsement, if not by his theology, and I did get a good price for my four. Another parishioner, a cattle and sheep dealer by occupation, met me later on that afternoon. "By gum, rector, tha's got best bloody price of the day!" I later learnt that the local imam had bought my lambs. It was a quietly satisfying feeling to think that our Muslim neighbours in Nelson were being sustained by Christian lambs fed on good Christian rectory grass. When we moved from Grindleton rectory to a modern, smaller vicarage in Settle with a pocket handkerchief garden, an elderly lady in the parish wrote to me and asked if I would be keeping sheep in the garden at Settle. Well, no...

I recall visiting a young farming family, rough and ready but equally helpful and friendly. "Come on in, Vicar," the husband said, "sit yersel' down." I sat down on the proffered settee. "I got a rat out o' that settee last week," he boasted.

Mention of settees reminds me of the true story of our local vicar who married Ann and me. He was a skilful 'extractor' of gifts for the church and he badly needed tens of thousands of pounds for a new parish church. He went to 'chat up' a rich elderly lady in the hope of a generous donation to the New Church Building Fund. She plied him with a cup of tea and a piece of her home-made cake. One bite was sufficient to tell him that he could not stomach it. As his hostess left the room he deftly placed the cake in his coat pocket. On her return with more tea she saw that he had finished the cake. "Do have another slice," she urged. Not wanting to hurt her feelings, and ever mindful of the possible donation, he acquiesced. Again, she left for the kitchen and again he stuffed the cake into his coat pocket. At last he was able to make his leave. Breathing a great sigh of relief he reached into his pocket to retrieve the offending confectionery, only to discover that his pocket was empty. He quickly realised what he had done. He had thrust the cake, not into his pocket, but down into the side of the settee! I reckon the Building Fund missed out on a sizeable contribution.

In the main, most pastoral visits I made were of the 'keeping an eye on the flock' variety. Encouraging newcomers to church, supporting older, more established members. I visited a house in a rather affluent suburb of Stratford upon Avon, the home of a young couple and their two children, who had started attending the Family Service. It was a gloriously hot afternoon. I rang the front doorbell and the attractive young lady of the house appeared from the side of the house. "Oh, do come round the back!" she invited, "we're all there!" I imagined she meant the family. Instead I saw half a dozen bikini-clad young ladies lounging by the swimming pool. They were obviously delighted to see me put on the spot. Reminiscent of Father Ted and his clergy friends 'trapped' in the Lingerie Department of a big store! I reckoned, however, that I handled it very well, like a professional cleric! Not all visits are so pleasant. I had to break the news to a church man that his father had died. It was a 'first' for me and I remember rehearsing over and over again how I was to deliver the solemn message.

I had been in the job exactly one week when I received a call from the Samaritans in Coventry. They had phoned the Vicar but being Saturday afternoon he was watching Coventry Rugby Club at their nearby Coundon ground. Would I go and talk to a young man on the top floor of one of the parish's high block of flats? He was threatening to throw himself fourteen floors overboard. My knees were literally knocking as I ascended in the lift, which was putrid and covered in graffiti. He let me in and for a couple of hours poured out his misery that his partner had left him. There was nothing else for him but to jump. It transpired that his partner had gone back to her mother in Blackpool. As good luck would have it, I knew a priest who had just taken a curacy there. He had been at Theological College with me. I managed to calm down the young chap with the promise that my clergy friend would visit her and attempt to talk her round. With that vague promise I left, descended in the elevator, arrived home and fainted on the doorstep.

Sometimes one can stay in one place and make numerous 'visits' to parishioners. A sister of a famous Coventry car manufacturer had died. The ensuing sale of many of the contents of her large house, on the edge of my parish, took place over three days. I initially went on the first day to bid for (and bought) some delightful cane chairs.

I was fascinated by it – rich carpets and rugs, furniture both antique and modern, standard lamps, table lamps, pottery and cutlery, water-colours and pictures in oils. Table linen, bed linen, kitchen gadgets by the score. And outside, everything to amaze the gardener and plantsman. It was such an exciting event for the onlooker. Very different for the family, of course. People were milling about, eyeing a particular piece, noting the lot number of a certain article. And if you were not there to bid or even view the lots, there were friends to meet, farming to discuss, and tea and sandwiches to be quaffed at the mobile snack bar, wisely laid on by the astute estate agents. Over the entire period of the sale I met and chatted to more parishioners than I ever could by more traditional means. By the way, some thirty four years on, we still possess those cane chairs.

* * * * *

Ted was an amorous 80 year-old. "Don't visit me on Tuesday afternoons, Vicar," he cautioned, "me and the missus go to bed for a little bit of you-know-what". I promised I would make a note not to disturb him on Tuesdays. Not many 80 year-olds are so active.

Lizzie had had a very hard life, brought up in near poverty in the South Wales coal-mining valleys. She was a most faithful, religious lady and very near to death. My vicar suggested I prepare her, and give her the Last Rites. It was, after all, a necessary part of my training. I visited Lizzie and ministered to her.She devoutly received the Blessed Sacrament. A few days later she revived, much to my consternation! Kenneth humorously suggested I had done too good a job. Lizzie deteriorated again. And again I gave her the Last Rites. Lizzie recovered once more. The third time, however, the Lord was ready to receive her and I had had some good training in that particular department.

In the good old days it was always stressed that parsons should go about their parish on foot, so as to be seen by and among his flock. If the parish were too large, then horseback; and if not *à cheval* then on his bicycle. Motor cars on the other hand were anti-social, anti-pastoral. With a geographically vast area of pastoral responsibility in North Warwickshire, I opted for a moped. A 50cc. Puch, made in Austria, built for the twisty roads of the Tyrol and, I hoped, for the winding ways of Warwickshire. On its pannier I carried all sorts of items – vegetables given to me by parishioners, my clerical robes, service books and often the Marriage registers. By moped-ing *al fresco* I was able to speak to villagers as I passed by and catch up with the latest news in that particular corner of my empire. The downside to all this was riding back home on the A46 trunk road from Coventry to Leicester. A straight stretch of about a mile in length meant traffic raced by at tremendous speed. I always felt I was being pulled in towards these passing vehicles, particularly if the Puch was unequally balanced with a load of cabbages and a box of carrots.

Visits were sometimes on the other foot – no pun intended. We always had a succession of 'regular' non-parishioners who called on us. We were regularly visited by a pair of Jehovah's Witnesses. They always come in braces – and not just to hold their trousers up. They even called at the Vicarage on two consecutive Christmas Days, which said a lot for their zeal and little for their sensitivity. It was sad sometimes to see the junior struggling to remember his or her lines whilst the other sternly looked on. The spiel was always the same. If I interjected by asking a question or disputing a point, they were completely put off their stride. I fixed a crucifix to the door and we never saw them again!

Another frequent visitor to our home was B, a rather tragic unmarried woman in her early forties. Even in her adulthood she had been physically beaten by her father. She had a "thing" about me (or rather, the dog-collar). About 9 o'clock one evening I returned home to discover B's moped outside. I just could not face her and cowardly left Ann to cope with her. I went off to do some more visits but there's a limit to how long you can make night-time pastoral calls on parishioners. I returned home to find, to my dismay, the moped still there. There was no way I could put off meeting her. "I'm so glad you've come," said Ann, "B has been preparing some supper for you." I recognised the warning in my wife's voice. B proudly presented her tripe and onions, boiled in milk, which of course I had to eat. I heaved at every mouthful. It was my penance for being such a coward.

Two church stalwarts from another of my parishes visited me whilst I was in hospital. I was an orthopaedic patient undergoing traction. The treatment entailed having my feet attached to weights which hung down over the bottom of the bed. A late twentieth century torture version of the mediaeval rack. The chaps who had come to cheer me up outstayed Ann and our daughter Rebecca, and continued to stay and stay. All they talked about was "church": It was sheer purgatory. Well, torture...

Visitors also came in their droves to many of the churches where I served. Holy Trinity, Stratford-upon-Avon had coach-loads of tourists all the year round to gaze on Shakespeare's grave inside the chancel. You can spot the Russians, I was told: they always look grim and grey and come in November. Have they lightened up, post-perestroika? On the Bard's birthday, April 23rd, Stratford holds a great celebration. Representatives from almost every nation on earth are invited to come and unfurl their national flag which, with all the others, line the streets to the church. Some countries do not, or cannot, send a representative so someone is seconded to do the unfurling. In 1973 I performed the act on behalf of the Peruvian ambassador!

Japanese tourists are among the wealthiest whatever the season. They are always polite and attentive, fingering their expensive cameras. They stayed at the best hotels and, naturally, had Stratford's parish church high on their itinerary. The Japanese also travel to the English Lake District. Many express coaches have a short 20 minutes "toilets" stop in Settle on the A65. The buses pull up on the coach park opposite the church of The Holy Ascension, where I was Vicar. Foregoing the toilets many of these Japanese visitors find their way into the church. One Sunday morning, minutes before the main Parish Eucharist of the day, a group of them were reverently looking at the various artefacts in our side chapel. My churchwardens and sidesmen simply pretended they were not there. Ann recognised the impending disaster of these people if they were not told. Their humiliation and embarrassment would be immeasurable. Indeed, they would probably 'freeze' and wait courteously until the end of the service, thereby missing their coach. She told me where they were. Apparently they knew no English and I no Japanese, save one six-syllable phrase. I approached our tourists in my Eucharistic vestments. They were probably delighted to see a kimono-clad figure. "Nippon Sei Ko Kai," I uttered as diplomatically as I could, remembering that the 'pp' is silent. "Ah!" they chorused, their eyes opening wide in realisation. They all bowed graciously and left the church to continue their excursion. What had I said to initiate their immediate exit? Four words from the Anglican Communion Calendar of Intercessions: the words simply mean 'The Holy Catholic Church of Japan'.

Christian Aid Week was a good opportunity to visit many parishioners whom you never saw from one May to the next. It was good, systematic visiting with lots of surprises! To knock at a door and ask for the envelope was a chance to re-introduce myself. I always made sure my dog-collar was very visible. Christian Aid Week was a good test of the generosity of my wider flock. Some gave their widow's mite and I was deeply touched by their obvious sacrifice. Most of the time I left a door dismayed and disappointed at people's meanness. "Hello!" I'd say. "It's the Vicar. I've just called for your Christian Aid envelope." "I'm sorry but the dog ate it." "Well, here's another one!" "It's no good, he'd just eat that as well!" These types would say anything to get out of contributing: "It's the Government's job," "Let their Governments sort it out" and "Charity begins at home," which always makes my blood boil, as my father was always using the adage. The language we collectors endured on those thresholds was horrendous: often obscene, sometimes blasphemous.

This reminds me of a similar response I got when making a parish call one evening at dusk. Arthur ran his own garage business, specialising in towing back broken-down cars with his old breakdown vehicle. He lived with his cantankerous invalid wife in a tiny bungalow to one side of his petrol pumps. As I knocked at his door I saw the curtains twitch. "Who is it?" yelled Mrs Arthur. "It's the bloody vicar!" Arthur shouted back. He opened the door to me. "Good evening, Arthur," I began "it's only the bloody vicar." He mumbled and stumbled over some half-hearted apology. It didn't really matter: he was always like that. He was just being himself.

I was asked to make an even later call in another of my patches. It was after 11pm when she phoned: a middle-aged lady, one of my regular congregation, whose husband was away, working overseas. Could I possibly call with a few of my back-pain tablets? She had run out of her own medication and her back was really playing her up. I said I'd call straight away, even though it was very late. But Ann smelled a rat. "I'll take them," she ordered, "you stay here!" Ann took our car and arrived at the house to find her in a black negligee. Just as she thought! Next day another church lady saw Ann in the village. "And what was Trevor doing at So-and-so's at midnight?" she enquired teasingly. "I saw his car." We clergy are often too innocent as doves and not sufficiently serpent-wise.

It has always amazed me that most *men* think religion is a *woman's* matter. I would ring a doorbell and be greeted by the man of the house. "Hello, Vicar," he'd say "I'm sorry but the wife is out shopping." "Well, I've called to see you as well," I would reply. To which he would reluctantly show me in. Where husbands and wives were *both* committed Christians it was always a pleasure to visit, though I was ever conscious to give both of them equal time and opportunity in our conversation. Not always easy. A husband and wife, not church-goers, lived next door to us in one parish. They were, sadly, having some serious matrimonial problems. It was Christmas time and my mother had come to stay. First, the husband

Our Pilgrimage Eucharist among the ruins of Sawley Abbey.

Celebrating at the altar at All Saints', Broughton.

Signing the legal documents at my induction at Settle Parish Church.

Cartoons by t REV

SABDEN vicar the Rev. Trevor Vaughan seldom has any trouble getting his ideas across to the children he teaches. He just reaches for a sketchpad and a pen and sets to work on a cartoon illustrating his point!

For years he has found great pleasure in drawing cartoons, and in the 10 months he has been at St Nicholas's Church, Sabden, he has made his presence felt with cartoons for the parish newsletter and illustrated lessons at school.

Said Mr Vaughan: "I have always been very fond of drawing. My father was very good at it and wanted to be a professional cartoonist, and I suppose I just followed in his footsteps.

"I often use the sketches to get a point over in school assembly, lessons and at confirmation classes, too. I also draw for my own and my four children's amusement."

Mr Vaughan recently taught a class at St Mary's RC School in the village using his cartoon technique to put across the message that the church is made up of all sorts of people.

Using an age-old rhyme, Mr Vaughan drew cartoons of people of varying size, race and statute, illustrating the point that everyone and anyone can be considered God's children.

Personalities

In his own time, however, he relaxes with caricatures of various personalities . . . among his favourites are Harold MacMillan and Harold Wilson, and as well as politicians he revels in cartoons of sportsmen.

"In my last diocese in Coventry, I made a contribution to an annual carnival magazine, and since I have been in Sabden I have also done several sketches for the parish newsletter."

Mr Vaughan, whose interests also include cricket, takes a lot of pleasure in drawing for his four children as well.

"I am settling down very well in Sabden," he added, "and I hope my cartoons are going down well, too."

THE Rev. Trevor Vaughan, who fittingly signs his work "t REV."

The Burnley Express article about my drawings.

236

Harvest Festival
with Trev

"It must be the holy water, Father: you know, 'It refreshes the parts...'"

"To thee, O Lord, our h-a-ts we raise."

"Name this child."

"Only last week you preached about 'entering by the narrow gate' . . . and now look what you've done!"

Some of my cartoons for the
Blackburn Diocesan magazine.

Father Dogsbody
by Trev.

We're ringing in the New Year, Father, not the Ascension!

Some of the post-confirmation 'Magnificats' at Broughton Rectory with Bp
and Mrs Evans.

Rogationtide Procession down Primrose Lane in Broughton!

Mothers Union Deanery Day with members from Bolton by Bowland, Martons Both and Thornton-in-Craven.

Our family at St George's Chorley in 1982

My Farewell Eucharist at St Nicholas' Sabden, 30th April 2006

came round to open his heart. I went next door to chat to them both. Then the wife popped round to tell me her side of the story. I called round once again. And, like the star in the east in 'The First Nowell', so the Pastoralia "continued both day and night" all over the seasonal period. What with the plethora of Christmas services and all the pastoral work, I hardly saw Mum, who commented to Ann that "curates should have Christmas off!" A lovely but rather impossible thought.

Morecambe in the latter years of the twentieth century was a dangerous place. The smarter sides of the town, in Heysham and Hest Bank, were safe and serene by comparison. The central area, however, part of which comprised my parish, was fraught with tension and not a little fear. Whether by accident or design, no agency of care existed *both* day and night in the parish, except me. Good old Church of England! There were no other churches in the parish; more importantly no manses or presbyteries; there were no doctors, no police station, though no less than three officers were designated to the area. There was no social work centre, save 'Signpost' which did a marvellous job until 5pm, when its social worker-trained staff left for home – well outside the parish.

A Morecambe 'son', Roger Bingham, had written a book about his town, entitled *A Lost Resort, The Flow and Ebb of Morecambe*. In it he describes the demise from a wealthy, healthy, lively seaside town to one with little hope for the future. Drugs and drink had damaged many aspects of community life. The former substantial boarding-houses of the pre-package holiday era (one of which was owned by my grandparents) had been converted to hundreds of bed-sits. Their occupants were those who had heeded the adverts in our northern prisons, which asked inmates who were about to be released, "Why live in East Lancashire when you can live by the seaside in Morecambe?" Many such residents were unemployed but needed money for their habit. Invariably after the main Sunday Eucharist some such person would be hassling me for money at the church door. One character was more persistent – and dangerous – than the rest. I could not get rid of him until I promised to discuss his request (for money) with my churchwardens. I said I would call round to his flat with their decision after Evensong. I had no intention of giving him money. It was pretty obvious what he would spend it on. I had heard a catalogue of 'plights' from his likes: "Ten pounds, Vicar, to phone my mother who is ill in Latvia," "Twenty quid, Father, to bring my grandma's body down from Scotland" and one who quite pathetically said he had to feed his dog! My Lay Reader, Andrew, was six feet six inches tall, broad and outwardly fit. He accompanied me to the man's flat after Evensong. I nervously rang the bell and waited. As we heard him approach we changed places and Andrew stood in the doorway. And literally *filled* it! I told the man the PCC did not give money. He took one look at Andrew's towering figure framed by the door posts, grunted and shuffled off upstairs. Josephine, Andrew's wife, laughed when we told her of our 'victory'. "Andrew is as soft as butter," she said, "he couldn't hurt a fly!" The con. man didn't know that. It was a case of 'size matters'!

Another con. man, recently released from Armley Gaol called at our vicarage. He boasted that he could climb into our smallest window of the house. If that threat was unnerving his next move was frightening. He put out his hand for me to shake and like a fool I responded. Whereupon he twisted his hand in such a way as to place my hand in an inescapable thumb-screw. Highly painful. He finally released me and I threatened to inform the police. He returned just before dusk: we saw him crawling on all fours around the garden. Quickly, but (again) foolishly, I sprung open the door and he sped off but not before deflating all four tyres on our car. I phoned the police who arrived *24 hours* later. "Would you say the gentleman [sic] had learning difficulties?" enquired the policewoman. "How about common assault, trespass and criminal damage?" I suggested. She recommended us to Victim Support.

* * * * *

Headgear has always been a problem for me. What to wear? Cicely, a lovely, elderly parishioner from Settle once knitted me a bobble hat – in claret and blue, Burnley's colours. It was ideal for home matches but not around the parish. I would probably have been beaten up by local Leeds United fans. In warm weather I was happy to be hatless. Those days are in a minority, however, especially 'up north', and a house-going parson requires an appropriate piece for his pate. I fancied a boxy biretta with a pom-pom. Too Catholic for my parishes! A beret would be a good compromise, churchmanship-wise, though I wore a beret in the T.A. and it just would not feel the same treading the streets of the parish. A country Barbour is weatherproof but too prone to flight in gusty weather. A flat cap identifies too closely with the working-class, whilst a deer-stalker with the landed gentry. And clergy must be neutral at all times in these affairs. A sou'wester is too pessimistic and a floppy sun-hat over-optimistic. I wouldn't entertain a baseball cap, not even with an embroidered cross over the neb (a good northern word!).

So I purchased a Breton fisherman's cap. It proved to be an excellent happy medium. It was black (and therefore clerical), it was warm, it was secure about my head and it was a trilby and flat cap rolled into one. Since I was called to be a *fisher* of men, the fisherman's cap was absolutely ideal for parish visiting... except on one occasion. I knocked on the door of a lady who was just on her way home. She spotted me some way off and realised that I was standing at her house. "Are you gas or electricity?" she called out. From a distance, my Breton cap could easily be mistaken for that of a NORWEB or British Gas meter reader. As she approached she repeated her question. "Is it gas or electric?" Amused, I touched my cap and replied, "I am sent from a much higher power!"

I have done lots of knocking on doors. I have always found it to be true that 'a house-going parson means a church-going people'. The following story has never featured in my experience but it's a splendid tail-piece to this topic. A little girl was desperately trying to reach the door-knocker of a house but could not quite get there. The Vicar was passing by. "Here, let me do it" he kindly offered and knocked loudly on the door. "*Now run like hell!*" cried the little girl.

An extension of house-visiting for the priest is his calls on the sick and infirm and on the housebound. The great thing about the churches of Catholic Christendom is that they can bring the Church to the people if the people cannot bring themselves to the Church. Especially is this beneficial in the taking of the Blessed Sacrament of Holy Communion. Bread and wine, having been consecrated at an earlier service, can be brought to the faithful in their homes, to their bed-sides. The sense that the house-communicant is joining with the more able-bodied worshipper at church is here strongly reinforced. Whilst most house-communions take place without incident, just now and then something comic happens. It is made all the more funny because, of course, the context is sacred. Undoubtedly the Lord will smile, too.

"Come in, my duck!" Mrs M called as I visited her with Communion, "I've just finished on the commode." And so she had. The smell was terrible.

I used to take the Sacrament to an old lady in Pall Mall – not in London, so not the Queen. She was very worried about the cost of living. "The Body of Christ," I said. "And the price of coal's gone up!" she responded.

In the same town I had to cancel a House Communion at the last moment owing to an emergency. I phoned Mrs T to say we would have to postpone it. "Don't worry, my dear," she said "I'll do it with the radio," meaning that she would listen to the Morning Service.

Often house-communicants would attempt to transform their living room into a church nave. A delightful and faithful couple always prepared for my coming by placing two chairs at one end of their long room and a small altar/table yards away at the other. Two elderly sisters did likewise. As I entered their home one of them would shout to her sibling who was always upstairs. "Ethel!" she would call in a shrill voice, "Church!"

Taking the Sacrament into hospital is a great privilege for the priest. It is likewise for the patient. When I was in hospital myself in 2008, old John in the next bed heard the bells of the adjacent parish church. He asked what the 'noise' was. The parish church calling folk to Evensong, I explained. "Nah, that's not for me," he said, shaking his head disparagingly, "I'm one for the wild life." He had no sooner uttered it than into the ward walked the Dean of Ripon, resplendent in his brand new black cassock with red piping, carrying the Reserved Sacrament for me. The look on the old man's face was a picture: had the Grim Reaper come for him as a result of his comment?

Acting as Hospital Chaplain myself at the Walsgrave Hospital, I had visited the wards some days earlier and arranged times with those who desired to have Holy Communion in or at the side of their beds. The communicants were all informed that the service would be relayed by the hospital radio and that they were only to tune in to channel 5, follow the service and then be ready to make their communion when I duly appeared on the ward. The Sunday morning Eucharist in the hospital chapel was rather eerie since all my congregation were *in bed* and, hopefully, wired for sound. As I arrived I got the impression that not *everyone* had listened: some were still asleep, some completely forgot and some couldn't find the right radio channel. The Church Somnolent! I approached one would-be communicant: "Your Communion," I said. "Well, all right," came the sleepy reply, "but I had ordered cereal and toast."

Of wheelchairs...and hearses

Taking the Sacrament to Homes for the Elderly proved difficult on many occasions. Either the staff forgot I was coming or the communicants had gone to have their hair done or to Blackpool on a day trip. "This bread is foisty!" one irreverent lady remarked as I went round the small room with the wine-intincted bread. The rules of most Homes for the Elderly stipulate that at least one member of staff is present wherever there is some extra-curricular activity taking place. This, naturally, includes the service of Holy Communion. Invariably, however, I performed the whole operation without the presence of any staff member. On one occasion I recall getting eight old ladies, *all* wheelchair –bound, organised around the room. Half-way through the service the fire alarm sounded. What was I to do? I could ignore it and continue with the holy mysteries, thereby achieving martyrdom. I could rush out and leave the tethered octet to their own devices. Or perhaps push one – the youngest? – out into safety, whilst the others perished. I had a sudden vision of lining up all eight wheelchairs and pushing them, like a crocodile of supermarket trolleys, through the door to freedom. But there wouldn't be time. I reluctantly broke off the liturgy, found a nurse, who explained it was a false alarm. At least I was spared a flurry of funerals!

Visits to the bereaved take up a sizeable proportion of any parson's ministry. Normally there is at least one visit before the funeral, sometimes two. This is when the service is arranged and for the clergyman to learn a little of the person who has just died. Facts which form some part of the funeral address. Today most Christian clergy appear to have got it all wrong. Current emphasis is on 'giving thanks for John's life,' or 'a celebration of the life of Mary.' Hardly anything is said of our need to ask for divine forgiveness for the times when the deceased – and we ourselves – have fallen short of God's will. The funeral rite explicitly reminds us that we are all sinners. We recognise this and in the knowledge of God's grace and pardon we go on to commit the body of our departed loved one to its final resting-place and to pray for his or her soul in the faith of Jesus Christ who died and rose again from the dead. We pray, I used to tell the bereaved, that the deceased may find eternal rest in the presence of Almighty God. Serious stuff. By contrast, it appears to me, the tenor of present day funeral sermons, especially those delivered by Church of England clergy, is one of light-hearted comedy. Do they have to include jokes? Do they have to induce laughter at every line? Isn't it the case that this approach simply *hides* the reality of the occasion and bottles up the grief, instead of releasing it? I am not a kill-joy and often incorporate one or two humorous aspects of the deceased's life; yet the overall aim of the homily must be to underline the *seriousness* of what has taken place (i.e. the death) and the gravity of all that we pray and say and do at the service. And, of course, to emphasise that "as in Adam all die, so also in Christ shall all be made alive."

The truth is that because we clergy perform in this context of solemnity, any accidental (as opposed to contrived) deviation from the norm produces the comic. It is the *unintentional* act which amuses and delights us.

I reckon I have taken about a thousand funerals and, on that reckoning, made two or three thousand funeral visits. Most of these pastoral chats and the ensuing committing and commending of the departed go like clockwork, hopefully bringing some measure of comfort and consolation and the good news of resurrection. Among the occasions there have been, of course, some silly episodes. Scary ones, too. The bereaved relations' choice of funeral music has sometimes proved to be one or the other of those adjectives. For most of my years as a parish priest the organist played some appropriate music: Radio 3 material, or at least Classic FM. Music such as Elgar's 'Nimrod' or Handel's 'Largo'. And no one ever objected or desired to change it. In my latter years, however, post-modernism's 'pick 'n' mix' theology has given the right to every grieving party to have whatever music they want. I generally succeeded in dissuading funeral congregations to have to sit through CDs of Frank

Sinatra's "I did it my way," but sometimes the pressure of resisting grief-stricken spouses did not seem worth it. Peter, a priest friend, had to suffer Elvis Presley's "Great balls of fire" at the crematorium. And even normally-accepted hymns can be inappropriate, especially at a cremation. At first glance "Colours of day" seems totally inoffensive until you come to the chorus "So light up the fire and let the flames burn". Even traditional, ancient hymns are not immune: I took the funeral of an old man who had been a constant trouble to his family. They were so relieved at his passing that they all wanted "Now thank we all our God"! At a Scoutmaster's funeral the assembled gathering was asked to render the scouting song "Tiddley winkey, winkey, winkey, Tiddley winkey woo" – together with the hand actions.

Most funeral services end up at the crematorium today. City and town cemeteries are all but full and it is a fact, when space is such a priority, that you can inter 20 caskets of ashes in a burial plot for one.

> *"There once was a milkman of Cheam,*
> *who had a most horrible dream*
> *that he'd called his emporium*
> *'Smith's Crematorium',*
> *supposing that 'crema' meant cream!"*

When I was a curate I was occasionally 'volunteered' by my Vicar to do a locum duty at the crematorium. The sermon, of course, was devoid of any personal reference, since you had no idea whose body you were committing to the flames. At these times I always endeavoured to discover the name and the sex of the deceased, since this small point of reference made the sermon and the service more personal. You could at least substitute a name for 'N' in the Funeral booklet and confidently announce 'he' or 'she' where the rite had printed the awful 's/he'. My method did not work on one occasion. The undertaker had forgotten to pass on any information about the departed. So as we sang the opening hymn I quietly approached one of the chief mourners to verify the name of the deceased. A clever ruse, since it would give me *both* the name and the sex for the price of one question. "Leslie," she whispered. Or was that "Lesley"? I asked myself. Too late: the hymn finished and I was no nearer in my quest. I had, therefore, to stick to the safe, non-committal phrases "this your servant" for the name, and simply "your servant" for the 'he' or 'she' bit.

Jim, another priest colleague, was financially hard up. To help him pay the bills he volunteered to do *all* the crematorium's locum duties for the entire day. His wife even packed him *roast* ham sandwiches for his lunch! It was a taxing day for him in more ways than one. He pocketed a substantial amount of fees for his work but the Church Commissioners deducted the amount from his monthly stipend.

I once had to perform the funeral service of a little girl who had died tragically. The pre-funeral visits were traumatic enough, with both mother and grandmother in a constant state of hysteria. The whole service was to be at Canley, the crematorium for the whole city of Coventry and thus serving a population of well over a third of a million. And it was to be on a Friday afternoon. The journey from our parish on the N E edge of the city would normally take 20 minutes to reach our destination on the opposite S W rim. But on Fridays the car factories finish early. In the 1960s Coventry boasted half a dozen major motor manufacturing plants – Humber, Hillman, Morris, Triumph, Jaguar, Alvis – and may be more.

The hearse and following limousines, plus family cars, crawled through an almost gridlocked city centre. We missed our 20 minutes' slot (a ridiculously short time at any part of day) and two other funerals, scheduled after us, had taken place before our arrival.

As we drove up, the superintendent stormed out of his little office and lambasted, in turn, the funeral director, the hearse driver and me with the most foul language. His outburst would have been unacceptable in any situation but in the context of the present circumstance – a dead little girl, hysterical relatives – it was highly unprofessional. He was, I'm glad to say, severely reprimanded but he kept his job. Once inside the building there was even more pandemonium. Grandma rushed out of her pew and attempted to open up the small coffin. It took relatives and the undertaker all their time to restrain the poor lady. Cremations always seem more final than burials, though I don't know why. On a brighter note, the *Accrington Observer* reported the retirement of Joe Burns, the local crematorium superintendent. If his surname wasn't appropriate enough, "Joe," the column ran "aged 60 years, was presented with a barbecue set".

Whilst most urban churchyards are now full, their village counterparts still offer ample room for burial. Funerals, however 'difficult' they may be, are much more pleasant when they are held in your 'home' church. Though that does not mean they were without their surprises. I recall a funeral in our village church. The coffin bearers had placed their charge on its bier in the chancel, bowed low to the altar and made their way to the rear of the church. I had only uttered a few words when everyone heard the most mournful and loud groan emanating, most definitely, from the coffin. Was it the start of the General Resurrection? It startled the entire congregation. Happily the lid was not prized open from the inside and no more was heard from the deceased. The only explanation was that some air had become trapped inside the body. The sudden movement of lowering the box onto its stand had caused the air to filter up the windpipe and out of the mouth.

I went to visit an elderly lady whose husband had died some days ago. "How are you?" I asked her. "I'm fine," she replied, "and Harry's looking grand, isn't he?" pointing her head to behind the sofa. There he was, lying in state for family, friends and neighbours. A visual aid for folk to pop in and pay their last respects. This practice of the departed lying in an open coffin in the house has sadly all but disappeared. We have become too clinical. Our lives too sanitized. This present generation wants no 'unsightly' scenes. Yet what could be more natural than the body of a departed loved one, duly washed and made presentable, to remain within his family until the day of the funeral? This was certainly the case in past centuries: a necessary reminder that "in the midst of life we are in death," as the Book of Common Prayer puts it.

Arnold had suffered long and terribly with his cancer. Again, there was no question about his being shipped off to the funeral director's chapel of rest. Arnold was to remain in the small front room in his open coffin. Around his coffin, like six funeral candles, were six bottles of Airwick disinfectant, each with their pads fully extended to counteract the odour of his awful death. Why not? It meant that people – and priest – could quietly enter the room, say a short silent prayer and bid farewell to a brave man. These two episodes were in Lancashire: perhaps our land's last bastion of this gentle – and instructive – practice.

It is still customary, I'm pleased to report, that the cortège normally leaves the home of the deceased as it makes its way to the church or cemetery or crematorium. I always travelled in the hearse from church to the place of burial. I was anxious that if I travelled in my car and it broke down I would miss the 'committal' bit. It would look rather unprofessional, if not careless. However, on my first trip to the Oakley Wood Crematorium outside Stratford upon Avon, the *hearse* broke down. Driver, funeral director, priest and deceased were utterly stranded. A mobile phone message to the undertaker's office met with failure. Passers-by stared at us as if we were having a relaxing lunch-break on the roadside but like the Levite and the Pharisee did not stop to help. After one hour we were rescued. To my surprise the mourners were all there, waiting patiently.

Another time I was conducting a funeral at Coventry's enormous cemetery. You enter it up a steep incline and through high, imposing iron gates. I was riding in the limousine following the hearse, which, half way up the slope unaccountably stopped. And remained so. My driver got out, chatted solemnly to his colleague in the hearse, returned to his car and set off steadily. Very steadily until our bumper touched the rear end of the hearse. The hearse then moved forwards and I realised that we were *pushing* the vehicle up the hill and along the narrow road which led to the grave-side. The hearse's engine had stopped and could not be restarted. One slightly heavier push sent the hearse a few yards ahead of us in order that the back hatch could be opened. The drivers behaved in such a way that the mourners were none the wiser for the mishap. Perhaps the drivers did that sort of thing regularly.

Another incident at the same cemetery could have resulted in a pastorally parlous predicament. The grieving family gathered around the open grave as the coffin bearers lowered the box into the hole. Unfortunately the grave had been dug slightly too short. Only a matter of two or three inches but every inch counts in these serious situations. No way would the coffin go in horizontally. It certainly could not descend diagonally or vertically. The funeral conductor took matters into his own hands, or rather feet. With the coffin balanced level but protruding over the hole, he stamped hard on the top end... and gradually the box squeezed itself down and landed safely six feet under the soil. After the short words of committal the conductor approached the widow to offer his sincerest apologies for the unseemly, unsightly episode. "It's all right," she replied positively, "he was an awkward old bugger when he was alive and he's still an awkward one now he's dead!" Relieved smiles all around. All was forgiven, if not quite forgotten.

Not many farmers are regular church-goers. Like Jewish shepherds who watched their flocks by night, our farmers are occupied almost every hour of every day of every week, day and night. But come a farmer's funeral and they are all there! Country churches are invariably bursting at the seams with a congregation when one of the farming fraternity is laid to rest. Land Rovers and other 4x4s block the lanes for hundreds of yards. Extra chairs from the church hall are brought into church, filling every available nook and cranny. Often the nearby church hall acts as an extra chapel, and a tannoy system installed so that the overspill can hear what is said and sung, though I'm told they rarely sing, despite the music over the loudspeaker. It seems that without the *visible* means of musical support, singing is difficult. Very odd. At one farmer's funeral the church was typically overflowing. I solemnly led in the procession of coffin, undertaker and chief mourners. "I am the resurrection and the life," I intoned and continued with the rest of the Sentences. I turned automatically to go into my stall, only to find it firmly filled by a large, burly farmer. I gestured to him that that was *my* place but he made no effort to shift. There was nowhere else he could go, I had to admit. I gathered up my sermon notes, hymn book and other relevant papers and performed the entire service (appropriately for a farmer) "on the hoof" somewhere round the chancel step.

We came out of church to head for the burial plot in another of my parishes. The funeral of an 84 year old village lady. As I passed through the church porch an old resident hissed at me, "She was not a villager, you know, Vicar. She came here when she were two!" Part of the churchyard of that particular parish is built on very sandy soil. It also has a steep slope and it is not uncommon for coffins to mysteriously move from one grave to another. The fine sandy soil allows weighty coffins to slide – sometimes with disastrous and embarrassing results. By contrast another of my graveyards was situated on rock. Most graves, consequently, were single ones. It was impossible to dig down more than a couple of feet. To my horror, the sexton and I were investigating a grave of a young man whose widow had just died, some sixty years or more later. We removed the horizontal headstone, thinking that after all that time it would be feasible to bury his wife in the same plot. But no! On removal of the slab we discovered, a mere six inches from the surface, the skeleton of her husband. He had been buried in his morning dress, most of which was incredibly intact. I whispered a prayer and we replaced the tombstone. Luckily there was a space next door and she was eventually reunited by her husband's side.

Sandy graves; rocky graves. I have also had my fair share of watery ones, especially in the rainy North West of England. On several occasions water pumps have been deployed to draw water away from the grave, continually being filled from the rain-sodden land. At the last minute the grave-digger would hurriedly remove his water pump and spread branches of nearby conifers to conceal the watery bottom of the grave. Many a time it was as if we were conducting a burial at sea! Once, in pouring rain, I led the procession to the grave-side. Our eyes met the unusual sight of the appearance, then disappearance, of a bucket, just above the rim of the grave. The grave-digger was unaware that the service was ended and we caught him in the act. On reflection, it was a foolish thing to do. No grave-digger should be six feet down in a grave without an assistant on hand – and especially so in foul, sleeting rain. It could easily have been a *double* interment.

At the other end of the spectrum we clergy are sometimes called upon to take the funeral of someone unknown, or someone completely bereft of mourners. My Vicar Kenneth performed such a service for a lady of whom nothing was known, save her Christian name "Hannah" which was written on a piece of paper and fixed to the coffin lid. These funerals were labelled in times past as "paupers' funerals". I had a number in Morecambe, though not all the deceased were penniless. Some were elderly folk, living in poverty and with little or no finance or family to organise a 'proper' funeral. Others, however, were young people, often victims of a drug overdose and abandoned by their friends for fear of police involvement. In all these circumstances and for some unknown reason the Co-op Funeral Service was always called upon to make the necessary arrangements. All such funerals had to be *burials* (in case of future exhumation?), preceded by a service in the stark, cold cemetery chapel by a minister of the Established Church. At every such service I asked the undertaker to be the congregation. I always gave the full Christian 'works', including a homily, and he and I ensured the 'pauper' received a rich dismissal.

These 'pauper funerals' are still rare but, by contrast, there is an emerging kind of funeral: the eco-friendly type. The 'green' epithet refers to the use of sustainable materials for coffins, caskets and urns. Rather than an oak or a mahogany-veneered coffin, or even one made out of chipboard, the latest fashion is to have a' chrysalis', made of bio-degradable materials. Today's line features a conventionally-shaped coffin of softwood around which are wrapped large leaves of water hyacinth and dried banana. My sole experience of a green funeral involved a cane, wicker-work chrysalis. It was of a torpedo shape but actually symmetrical, which confused the bearers as to which end went towards the west. Tradition has it that the head goes to that direction, so that at the Resurrection, in the last day, the dead will rise to face Jerusalem, where Christ rose from the dead. Conversely, priests are buried with their head to the east, in order that at the Resurrection they will rise to greet their flock. I haven't worked out yet what position my wife and I will adopt when we die! To add to the bearers' chagrin in this particular green funeral, the wicker basket, looking like a giant picnic hamper, had no handles. The wicker work allowed the bereaved family and friends to slot in single stems of flowers, so that the whole coffin was covered in foliage. It looked rather pretty but did nothing to help the undertaker's bewildered team in carrying and finally lowering the chrysalis into the earth. I suppose this episode related to an early prototype of green coffins. It is to be hoped that they have improved in design since then. But the chrysalis has an even more modern rival. One Yorkshire felt manufacturer has started producing coffins (and caskets) made from the wool of Dorset sheep. The corpse should be cosy!

The colour black continues to dominate funeral attire. Both for men and for women. It is a good thing that the lady can pull out her little black dress for the occasion and the man his dark suit and black tie. It shows some level of thought and respect for that which is to follow. Funeral directors – and there are about four thousand of them in the land – also dress accordingly, as do their assistants. And the hearse and limousines are in matching black too. The hearse driver often wears a black mackintosh and a peaked cap. The conductor himself is never without his black coat and jacket. Most often he wears pin-striped trousers and a shiny silk top hat. Such was the sartorial state of these gentlemen whom I accompanied to and from Preston Crematorium. The return journey to Chorley included a long stretch of motorway. There we were, seated in a line on the front bench-seat of a 3.5 litre Daimler hearse, emptied of its cargo: the peak-capped driver, the top-hatted funeral director and I in my cassock and surplice. "We've made it," whispered the undertaker, giving me a nudge. "Pardon?" "We've just made it. Look at the speedo!" We were doing a ton! 100 m.p.h. -just over, in fact. What a sight as we sailed past everything in the outside lane! Had we heard news of the Armageddon? Or were we just late for tea? It was wonderfully exhilarating, I can tell you!

Doing a 'ton' in a hearse reminds me that the basic, most minimal, church attendance used to be called 'four wheeler religion': going to church on the four wheels of a hearse for the despatching at a funeral; four wheels of a (stretch?) limousine for the matching at a wedding; and the four wheels of a pram for the hatching leading to Holy Baptism.

Prams and push-chairs

My first baptism was only half-performed by me. It was the all-important one of our baby daughter, Rebecca, who was baptised on the Ides of March 1970. I was only a deacon at the time and therefore unable, until my priesting, to absolve, bless or consecrate. Because I was taught correctly, only a priest could bless the water of Baptism and so Kenneth did the first bit of the rite and allowed me to perform the actual 'sprinkling', as it's technically called. It was a delightful service held in our very modern church of The Risen Christ. (People wanting a Baptism at this church would phone me, enquiring, "Hello, is that the Church of the Rising Sun?") Rebecca's Baptism was, as I say, delightful but had its quirky element. Our American curate also attended with his phalanx of little boys (!) whom, most oddly, he had equipped with Union Jacks. Most of the subsequent photographs of the event portray strange small boys waving our national flag!

A fair proportion of my house visits were connected with Baptism. At ordination we were charged "to search for [the Lord's] children in the wilderness of this world's temptations..." and with the task of baptising. The process usually began with the parents contacting the clergy about "a christening." The next stage often proved to be the first stumbling block: fixing the date. I always tried to stick to a strict schedule of baptisms, especially so when I had a multiplicity of parishes in my care.

"Baptisms at St Peter's," I'd say, "are on the first Sunday in the month at half-past nine."

"We were hoping you could do it on the 18th. We've booked the Coach and Horses for a 'do' afterwards."

"I'm sorry, but I've already got baptisms at St Ambrose's on that day." A stunned silence from the other end of the phone.

"Could it be *four* o'clock on the first Sunday, then?"

I would then have to undergo the whole rigmarole of explaining that we do baptisms at the *morning* Parish Eucharist. Why? Because those who are to be baptised should be seen to be among those people into whose fellowship they will belong by virtue of their baptism.

"Half past nine is a bit early," they complain, "Grandma's coming down from John O' Groats." A massive dilemma looms. Yes: half past nine is rather early but I've another service immediately following that one in the next parish."

"Could grandma come down the Saturday evening and stay the night?" I don't actually say this, since I must not interfere in someone else's domestic arrangements but, in all honesty, they should have consulted me about time and dates before booking the pub. It is a question of priorities: *in* the drink before *down* the drink! In my heart of hearts I know that a blank refusal will give the Church a bad name. Yet, as we *never* see the family in church, it must have a bad name to start with in the family's eyes. More often than not a compromise is made and I try, as best as I may, to accommodate their requests. The Church is good at compromises.

The visiting that follows the initial enquiry and confirmation of the date is then normally straightforward. 'Straightforward' in this context usually means battling with the television. Folk want to watch

Coronation Street and *Eastenders*, despite our mutually arranged date. Admittedly they are kind enough to turn off the sound but their glazed eyes, I can detect, are focused on 'The Rover's Return' rather than the Rector's requirements for Holy Baptism. They are probably splendid lip-readers, anyhow. As I became a more experienced (canny?) priest, however, I would position myself directly in front of the television, though this had the effect of screwing my audience's heads *around* me to keep up with the 'soap'. In my latter years I became even more canny: "Would you please turn the television off?" If it were not the television which the devil used to divert my pastoral visit, it would be the baby. It would, most unusually, require an extra bottle or its siblings were not settled and would keep jumping out of bed. But babies are wonderful and it's not their fault that their parents are sometimes quite feckless. So, in spite of Mum and Dad's lack of initiative, I remember Jesus saying "Suffer the little children to come unto me" and I baptise them.

My speediest Baptism visit took place in Morecambe. I knocked at the door to be greeted by the T-shirted father, who had the appearance of a heavyweight boxer. Attached to him on an equally hefty lead was a dog which immediately jumped up at me. My knee-jerk reaction was precisely that: I knee'd the dog, which I did not see, instinctively in the chest. My action totally surprised the creature which fell backwards with a thud. The man showed me into a tiny sitting-room, comprising a small sofa and another armchair and a gigantic plasma television screen. It was when I sat down in those cramped conditions that my eyes met my canine adversary. A very angry pit bull terrier. He was positioned between his master's legs, held on a very taut rein but making repeated efforts to attack me. Since I was only 18 inches away from an ever-advancing vicious array of sharp teeth and slavering mouth, I quickly checked the details on the baptism application form, said I looked forward to seeing them on Sunday and bade them a hasty good-bye. I hoped they wouldn't bring the dog on the day.

The longest Baptism visit came about through some routine pastoral work when I was a curate. I had called upon a pleasant young family who lived further up the road from where we lived. They had two sons, aged seven and nine, and a baby daughter. After a general chat the parents decided that the children ought 'to be done.' Thrilled at the prospect of five new additions in the congregations – I felt certain they would become regular members – I reported my success to the Vicar. He pointed out that the boys were too old for Infant Baptism and too young for Adult Baptism, which would be performed with Confirmation. They would have to wait until they were about eleven years old. The baby, of course, qualified but the lads would have to wait two and four years respectively. I had, therefore, to return to my 'converts' and explain the theology. It involved a series of calls to the house, a great amount of energy in allaying their disappointment and tempering their exasperation. It looked as if the curate did not know his job...he didn't. He was still learning. But he felt bad about the whole episode.

When, a few years later, I had my very first parish, I decided to adopt a strict Baptism policy. Simply put, this meant "no baptism unless the parents were willing to be committed to the Church – and to show that commitment by becoming regular members." The strange but marvellous thing was that the policy was a roaring success! Every child so baptised brought with it his parents. And the church grew! Of course, I was not unaware that parents might not ask for baptism because they knew my policy would make life difficult – though I *never* said I would refuse a baptism.

One evening I entered the village pub for a quiet drink. It was full of its regular village punters and those who had travelled in for the very good bar food. No sooner was I through the door than the landlady, who spotted me, addressed the entire gathering in a very loud and excitable voice. "There's the chap who won't christen my granddaughter!" The pub went eerily silent and all eyes turned on me. It was rather embarrassing but also exciting, since it is not every day that Christian doctrine features in a public house. Perhaps, like St Paul on the Areopagus, I should have turned the opportunity to my full advantage and expounded the Christian meaning of Holy Baptism. Except I am not St Paul. And it was Friday night at 'The Bull's Head.'

When it comes to names for the would-be baptised I have escaped the embarrassingly awkward offerings. My Vicar christened a baby with a most strange-sounding name, hyphenated to boot. "Where did you get that name from?" he asked the mother. "She's a fashion model in Vogue," she replied. "Name this child," a priest friend of mine said at a Baptism service. "Goo-ey" came the response.

"Goo-ey?" he repeated incredulously.

"Yes: Goo-ey" the parents affirmed.

"Can you spell it for me?"

"G, U, Y of course."

Another of my clergy friends would only baptise if the child was to possess a saint's name. Even at the font he refused to administer the sacrament because the child lacked a saint's name. The parents, equally stubborn, refused to add one small smidgen from hagiology. So they sat down around the font and thrashed it out. The baby finally received another name and was duly baptised. Most surprisingly the extra tag was the name of my friend the priest: which just goes to show that compromises can be obtained on the most delicate of occasions. I have to say that I do not approve of such a policy. However 'non-saintly' a name may be, its holder might eventually be beatified and canonised and thereby become a saint. Saint Goo-ey...?

Often the worst feature of a baptism service is the relatives and friends of the baptised who make up the 'congregation of the day'. Most have no idea what it is all about. When the collection comes round they offer pathetic excuses for not giving. "I've run out of small change," said one chap to my churchwarden, who was passing the plate. "What about a note, then?" he suggested. "I'll need that for the bar afterwards." Is this what is meant by thirsting after righteousness?

Afternoon baptisms at Chorley were frequently a nightmare. It was a large parish and we had an enormous number of christenings. We held them on a monthly basis but often it meant eight or nine children to be baptised. The nightmare was *not* the size of the building. The church was a Waterloo church and had a capacity of almost two thousand. The horror was the vomit the verger had to mop up after the service. And I am not referring to the sickliness of the babes in arms. It was that of the adults of the congregation, or more precisely the men folk. Not all of them by any means but a handful of men would have had too much to drink at the social gathering *before* the service and could not avoid spewing up at the back of the church as they tried to rush out of the main door. The downside of many an urban parish.

Meanwhile in the relative isolation of rural Craven a Baptism was truly a joy. One of my churches there was founded in the twelfth century and possessed some fabulous mediaeval artefacts. It also housed a plain but wide and deep font of the same age as the church. This Norman font must have witnessed thousands upon thousands of baptisms over its nine hundred years. The only problem was that latterly the small plug no longer fitted tightly. I first came to be aware of the problem during one particular baptism. I always favoured pouring into the font gallons of water. The sight and sound of the liquid splashing in somehow emphasised the 'drowning' element of the rite. I then blessed the contents of the font and proceeded with the rest of the rite, when I suddenly noticed the water level rapidly decreasing. It would not have been appropriate to interrupt the service and ask someone for a bung: there was nothing else to be done but race through the remainder of the words at great speed and trust there would be some water left in which to baptise the baby girl. As I reached the point when I received the child in my arms the water had all but disappeared. There was a damp film around the inside of the bowl and a few droplets which had collected by the outer rim of the font's plug-hole. Fortunately the parents and family could not see the all but empty font: it was too deep a bowl. Three times I gingerly, gently dipped my finger in the fluid ounce, touched her forehead and baptised her in the name of the Father, and of the Son and of the Holy Spirit. It was only a lick but it was water, blessed and holy.

The next day I took the font stopper and called in at the ironmonger-cum-DIY shop in our nearby town. "Have you got a Norman plug?" I asked impishly. "Would that be a 5 or a 13 amp?" enquired the manager. I explained I wanted a plug for a leaking twelfth century font. He had nothing that would fit: and if he had, plastic and the Norman era don't match. Instead he suggested Araldite to line the plug-hole. I bought some. I remembered Araldite's advertisement which for years featured above the words *Daily Telegraph* on the front page of that newspaper: '*a small deposit secures any article.*' Clever words. Prophetic words too, since in The Case of the Leaking Font a small deposit of water had secured a child for God!

Young folk

Dealing with baptism babes is a doddle compared to the pastoral care of their older siblings: those of primary and secondary school age. Most

Anglican parish clergy get involved with their local primary school, especially so if it is a Church School, of which he will be a Governor. School Assemblies can be a great opportunity for both teaching the Faith and for giving the child an experience of worship. But it is rarely either. In my experience, particularly in non-Church schools, I found my weekly 'turn' simply a chance for the Head teacher to be absent and to catch up with some paper work. I felt it was a pity that the God-slot did not have the endorsement of the teacher in charge. I reckon the children also had some opinion on it. More worrying than the absence of the Head was the fact that Assemblies seemed to be an excuse for the School Notices. The law states that an Assembly shall take place but it is open to a wide interpretation of what goes on.

One morning I had given (what I thought) a very good talk to the members of our primary school. It was about the artists the Dürer brothers: how the younger brother Franz sacrificed his own talents for the greater ones of his brother Albrecht. As a result of his brother's generosity and kindness, Albrecht painted "The Praying Hands". The whole assembly of children were 'right there', visibly moved by the story. I even had a transparency of the painting projected onto an overhead screen. At the end of the Talk I had anticipated a silent pause in which the message could be firmly planted into my audience's minds. No such luck! Immediately I finished, the Head strode forward and announced that the local policeman would be in school tomorrow to begin the Cycling Proficiency Tests. My young congregation naturally began to buzz with excitement and, in a stroke, the Dürer brothers were a distant memory. That kind of thing happened far too frequently in my opinion.

My perpetual fear of taking Assemblies was that I might 'dry up' during the leading of the prayers, especially The Lord's Prayer. If a clergyman forgets, for instance, what comes next after "Thy will be done," it doesn't look good! In 37 years I have, thank goodness, never stumbled over the Lord's Prayer. One dreadful day at Duke Street Primary School in Chorley I began a prayer in which the children repeated each line after me. It was a well-known prayer. We said it every week, as repetition is good for remembering. On this occasion, however, my mind went blank and I could not remember the next line. The kids, of course, would know it but because I had dried up, *they* dried up...and the prayer ground to a sudden halt. I admitted to staff and pupils that I'd forgotten my lines. There were smiles all round and we started the whole prayer again. This time I just went into full auto-pilot and completed the prayer without a hitch.

The best thing about Primary School Assemblies is that the children –and the staff – recognise you out and about in the parish. I recall one wise old parson telling me that all one really needs to do at these Assemblies is to smile. For a Christian minister a smile is paramount. Laughter is a world away from a smile because it is harder to control if spontaneous.

The curate in a neighbouring parish, a contemporary of mine, was leading an Assembly at his church school. I don't know the subject of his theme but it obviously entailed taking his clothes off. Within three items of his strip-tease the children were delirious, shrieking and yelling. They were beside themselves with uncontrollable laughter. Fortunately the Headmaster was at hand to interrupt proceedings before it became 'The Full Monty'. He quietened the children and the curate was excused Assembly duties forthwith.

The object of a talk I gave to my Children's Church one Sunday morning was for the youngsters to discover how we use our ears. Probably exploring young Samuel's hearing of God's call. I placed a young lad at the back of the church, blindfolded him and asked him to find me as I continued speaking from the front of the church. He stumbled around, bumping into the occasional pew or person, but eventually succeeded in arriving at my side. Taking his blindfold off, I asked him, looking triumphantly at the congregation, how he had found me. "By *smell*" he dimly replied.

Secondary School Assemblies are far more intimidating for the clergyman. For a start one is aware of an innate hostility bubbling away in the heart and mind of a teenager: not particularly targeted at the person but more to do with authority and status and the message which is both represented and articulated. Secondary School pupils are often extremely bright and clinically critical. The teenagers who came to my church told me that at their school all the visiting clergy were given scores for their performance. That in itself was quite daunting.

Sometimes I felt elated, sometimes dismayed at my 'performance' in front of two hundred or more young folk.

Once a year, at Christmas, St George's Chorley played host to all the Secondary Schools in the town. Our 'Waterloo Church', with a capacity nearing two thousand, could just about accommodate them all. Being the Vicar of the church, I stood at the door to welcome the boys and girls and members of staff as they arrived. One sixth form young man entered eating chips out of a bag. I refused him entry, pointing out that this was God's house, that we were about to conduct an act of worship, and some respect was in order. Behind the lad was a teacher who intervened: "Come on, Vicar" he implored, "the lad's got to have his lunch!" So much for a moral lead. The chips, however, were eaten *outside* the church.

Pastoral work with young people can also be very rewarding and great fun. Tremendous camaraderie amongst our large Youth Club in Wyken, where we published a couple of joke magazines to accompany the Parish Carnival. We organised three Good Friday Three Hours Projects, each involving four hundred children. We also ice-skated, ten pin bowled and barbecued. Football amongst the young lads had been a common thread throughout my ministry to young folk. Five-a-side Soccer Tournaments at Stratford upon Avon, where our team comprised of teenage boys from the more deprived parts of the town. I recall one member of the team being sick all over my new estate car *on its first outing,* as I drove us back from an evening soccer competition in Shipston on Stour.

St Nicholas' Sabden Choir team was perhaps the zenith of my managerial career in football! When our family arrived in Sabden in 1977 there were three or four boys in the small choir. My two elder sons joined these lads for a kick-around before Choir Practice every Tuesday night. This quickly developed into a dozen or so playing football. It did not take many brains to work out that these lads should only play football if they joined the choir. No one objected. The swelled ranks of trebles in the stalls became the Choir Team. It eventually increased to 22 young boys: enough for two teams.

With the help of our friendly village correspondent on the Clitheroe Advertiser, a challenge was thrown out for other church choirs or youth clubs to form a team and give us a game. An exciting, if unpredictable, fixture-list quickly materialised. Enthusiasm spread like wild fire – from players to their parents and grandparents. Our home matches prompted a number of the latter generation to provide a half-time quarter of an orange for each player and a hot coffee for all the spectators. Support was so keen that the printing of *The Spire*, St Nicholas' weekly news sheet, was postponed till Saturday evening when we knew the result of the Saturday's football match.

Proceeds from a Jumble Sale helped us to purchase ten team shirts from a local mill-shop. They were the blue and white hoops of Queens Park Rangers. We would, naturally, have preferred the claret and blue of Burnley, but the mill only produced this one strip. This was at a time when jerseys were not readily available for lads' teams. Beggars can't be choosers: and for every lad to wear the same colours was both rare and confidence boosting. It certainly produced an esprit de corps within our group of choirboys. Not that it particularly mattered but we won most of our matches. By the time we left the parish we had 22 boys in the choir. The Sunday singing might not have been King's College Cambridge but the zeal for Saturday's playing could not have been bettered.

Twenty five years later I was to return to the parish as Vicar once more. The choir was gone; the servers also. So had the young people. The football team merely a cherished memory. A 'Thursday Club' was formed and brought back some youngsters for the church but not sufficient for a football team... On the question of young people I cannot praise enough the work of the uniformed organisations. The dedication and drive of those involved in Scouting, Guiding, Church Lads Brigade and the rest deserve to be much more publicised. Their monthly Parade Sundays continue to provide a real opportunity for the parish priest to pass on the Good News. I hope I paraded God's standard not only in what I said but what I did.

Every now and then several clergy – chiefly Church of England – are able to have their pastoral horizons widened. They are asked to perform a duty extra-parochially. Mayor's chaplain, chaplain to a children's hospital or local maternity hospital; padre to a unit in the Armed Forces Reserves; chaplain to the County High Sherriff. I mention these positions because it has been my privilege to act in these capacities over the years of my ministry. There are many more extra-parochial tasks which we parsons are called upon to do. Every one of these gives the priest or minister a pastoral opportunity to tend the sheep, feed the lambs.

Parsons – and their wives! – are often invited to perform a single duty. The word 'parson' derives from 'person' which had the meaning of the most influential individual in the village community. Influential because, 150 years ago, he was likely to be the only one able to read and write. So the Person, or Parson, was the writer and reader of wills and other important documents in a family's life. Today, of course, almost everybody can read and write but the parson is still viewed as the Person: in reality, the sitting duck. He or his wife is the one to ask to open the Garden Party, choose the May Queen, crown the Rose Queen, present the prizes at school or Sunday School, judge children's works of art, welcome a VIP, and so on. It's a precarious path! And in the judging and choosing roles you cannot possibly win. The short Talk that precedes all these events is very much of a muchness. There is a definite limit to what can be said. I am not being cynical when I state that there exists a core pattern around which you sew some appropriate flannel. At Garden Parties the theme is to encourage the folk to spend up, around which something complimentary is said about the 'dramatis personae'.

I have a (very short) shortlist of jokes, the best one being about the mother who calls to see the Vicar because her little son has swallowed a coin. "You should see the doctor not me," says the Vicar. "My next-door neighbour told me to see you," she replies, "she says 'the Vicar can get the last penny out of anyone!'" Spend up! is my message. My wife Ann is especially adept at these occasions and does not have to resort to cheap humour.

The choosing of a May Queen is fraught with danger. The young girls walk around you, as embarrassed as you are, whilst you try to look an 'expert' of the catwalk. In selecting such a body there has to be some formula. Ours was a recipe based on age, effort, use of resources (especially if there were a lack of them) and sympathy. The same went for judging children's drawings and paintings.

Opening introductions to choirs or musical concerts were reasonably straightforward providing you did not over-egg the scene and leave the audience expecting the Halle or Opera North, when in reality it was local ladies' choir or an amateur quintet from the next town.

Giving the final Vote of Thanks was rather like a judge's summing -up after a very difficult case. Congratulate, commend; never condemn. As the concert progressed I used to look down the programme items and hone in on some theme. Songs of the countryside for example, would provide me with an effusive "...a brilliant badinage of bright, breezy bucolic ballads..." An orchestral concert with a selection of sea-faring tunes might evoke "...a melodic melange of magical music: mariners and mermaids and much more..." It is rather corny, I admit, and very much Sachs-esque from The Old Tyme Musical Hall. As a Vote of Thanks, however, it was always cheerfully received by performers and audience alike. And that's what matters.

Of limousines

"Is that the rector?" asked a voice on the telephone. I said it was. "I'm thinking of getting wed," she said. "Right," I replied, wanting to know more. "How do I go about it?" she asked. I explained the process to her. Weddings are another wonderful pastoral opportunity for clergy: if God is love and the prospective husband and wife are in love, as they ought to be, then there is every chance that we are talking about the same thing. The lady on the phone wished to get married in my parish church, though she resided in the neighbouring parish. Her fiancé, however, lived and farmed in my parish, so the venue was permissible. She would have to see her Vicar and request that the Banns of Marriage be called on three consecutive Sundays within three months of the wedding date. Her future husband would have to get his application for the banns from me, complete it and follow the identical rules. "What date had you in mind?" I asked. It had to fit in around the busy schedule of the farming calendar. But a date and a time was fixed for their nuptials.

A date for the Marriage Preparation, usually a few days before the Wedding, was also arranged. This was often mistaken for a rehearsal and unless I made it absolutely clear the couple would turn up with both sets of parents, bridesmaids and best man in tow. The Preparation was rather a chat and discussion about the real meaning of marriage, what the pair were actually entering into: it was the 'theology bit' of marriage, plus a 'run through', at close quarters, of the couple's movements – and in particular what they did with their hands at the chancel step! We don't need the backing group for that, though some are so apprehensive that a rehearsal with all the 'ancillaries' is the only way to calm them down.

"There's just one other thing, rector," said the lady on the phone anxiously, "do I have to wear one of those white fussy dresses?" I knew the bride-to-be. She was a large lady in every way. A large personality and a large physical frame which undoubtedly helped her become a champion sheep-shearer. "Of course not," I said. "That's good. I reckon I'll wear my jeans." A few months later the happy pair arrived at church for their Wedding. She in the largest, frilliest, flounciest dress I have ever seen. And what's more: their clinch and kiss over the registers on the vestry table was also of championship calibre.

The bride's dress is always something of a focus both for wedding-guests and friendly onlookers at the church lych-gate. Maximum amount of money for minimum amount of material is often the case. Brides are tough creatures. Many a winter wedding featured a bride with a strapless, off-the-shoulder creation. The wife of my churchwarden in one parish felt this style of couture was so inappropriate for the House of God that she specially knitted a white cardigan which she would thrust over the shoulders of the unsuspecting bride as she tottered up the church path. A bride's dress can be quite distracting for the officiating priest. He stands before the bride on the chancel step, a good nine inches higher than she. When the bride and her husband kneel, her low-cut dress and firmed-up bosom can produce a cleavage like the Grand Canyon. It's hard to know where to look! 'Top show' is so much concentrated on that her underwear too is often neglected. With strong bright sunlight streaming through the west door, many gowns become almost diaphanous. Brides beware!

On the subject of bridal wear the crowd of well-wishers admiring the bride were astounded to see me at one wedding grovelling on all fours around the ankles of the bride. Not some latest Rite of Welcome from Common Worship. Quite simply, one of her high heels had become wedged in the niche of the pavement. No amount of pulling her foot (and even her leg!) would extricate the shoe. I advised she took her foot out, balance on the other foot – not easy in three inch heels! –whilst I applied more force. It worked and the bride was able to continue her procession to the church door. The moral of these sartorial tales is for the bride to think less of "aisle, altar, hymn" and more of cleavage, underskirt and heels.

A few hours before the happy couple meet at the chancel step, the priest or minister has to complete the Marriage registers. Because the C of E is the Established Church of the land, the vicar is also the registrar. Care is the watchword when writing up the Church Registers. There are sixteen rectangles where accurate information is to be filled in, plus details of the place of marriage and the signature of the officiating minister. One lapse of concentration involves putting a straight line through the error, numbering it, initialling the number in the margin and inserting the correct data.

Our parish of Wyken was made up of thousands of car workers, many of whom were fitters on 'the track', the vast assembly lines of the Coventry factories. I made one error in the registers when completing the rectangle marked "Condition". This, of course, was asking if the groom were a bachelor or a widower. I wrote the word "fitter." The Registrar General was not interested in the groom's health!

The registers are copied from the banns form, with which it is almost identical. It is vital that the "away" party has his or her banns called and that the incumbent of the parish signs a short document stating that they have indeed been called and that "no impediment has been alleged." Without this slip of paper the marriage cannot go ahead – no such notice might mean that the intentions of the couple were queried or that there existed some illegality.

I had repeatedly requested this document from a chap whose wedding I was taking. He kept assuring me that the banns had been called and everything was in order. Yet no signed slip from his vicar appeared. The Friday evening before the wedding I laid the law down: produce the form or the wedding cannot take place. He feebly said that he had received it but couldn't deliver it to me because it was his 'stag night'. Instead, he'd leave it with his fiancée.

Two hours before the wedding, still no signed slip. I phoned the bride. Yes: she had just obtained it and would bring it up personally. She duly arrived at the vicarage, nails half-polished, hair in curlers. "He's a bloody nuisance!" she stormed, "He always has been!" A short time later she was smiling into his eyes and promising to "love, cherish and obey."

In former days the bridegroom's attire was a secondary consideration. He had to look smart and presentable, of course, but he and his 'team' of best man, grooms and ushers played a sartorial second fiddle to the ladies. That is now no more. At one wedding I took, the bride had a mere two bridesmaids. Her groom, on the other hand, was supported by *two* best men and a total of no less than *eleven* others. All top-hatted and tailed and encompassing the entire age-range.

Another young bridegroom was a bit of a rough diamond. At the Wedding Preparation in my study he asked me if, when he was at the chancel step awaiting his bride, he could turn round and see her coming up the aisle. "Of course," I told him, thinking that love conquers all. On the 'Day' we awaited his bride's entrance. He duly revolved, as requested, and watched her approach him. Then, in an extremely loud voice which filled the small village church, he exclaimed, "By hell, she's bloody marvellous!"

I officiated at a very smart wedding at St George's Chorley. Morning suits were de rigueur for just about every male guest. As the service progressed, I observed from my position at the chancel step that the best man's trousers were wet. A small puddle had collected by his left foot. During the (convenient) hymn I approached him and quietly asked if he were feeling all right. "Quite all right," he replied, somewhat puzzled, "why shouldn't I be?" I had assumed that he was nervous and consequently wet himself. I subtly pointed to the puddle by his foot. "Damn!" he reposted. "My water-pistol's leaked!" Why can't modern young men be content to throw confetti and rice, as we did in the old days?

The most colourful wedding I ever took involved a dazzling clash of both Eastern and Western culture and couture. English toppers and tails provided a splendid backdrop to the flowing silk saris of Indian lady guests. The wedding was also colourful in that it bordered on the crazy. The groom was a young man in his twenties; a bachelor of my parish and the ceremony was to take place on his 'home ground'. Despite his youth, he had the appearance of an elderly professor. He was a most intelligent man, a boffin in his sphere of biological science. His wife-to-be was of similar age but, unlike her groom she was girl-like, gentle and rather timid. She was British but had lived most of her life in the Indian sub-continent. Her relatives out there had inter-married with the indigenous population. Hence the number of dark skinned relatives which made up part of the congregation. For all sorts of reasons I sensed it might be a 'tricky' wedding, liturgically speaking, so I took the unusual step of insisting that the couple and their entourage attend a rehearsal. My feelings were not wrong. The rehearsal revealed that our groom was full of brains but empty of common sense. He simply could not get the hang of remaining at the altar step whilst I alone entered the sanctuary via the small gap in the altar rail. It took several practices to perfect this small act.

If the rehearsal was a calamity the actual wedding was chaotic. The groom arrived at church in good time. A good start. But he was in a great state of agitation which his best man dutifully attempted to allay, without success. I led the two men to their pew, the front one on the right, or south, side. I meted out some occupational therapy for the stressed groom: opening six hymn books at the right page for the first hymn, likewise with the order of service booklet. With the men in place we awaited the bridesmaids, though in fairness to the girls no ushers had yet graced the scene.

A flurry of commotion in the church porch announced the arrival of – the bride! She was at least a quarter of an hour *early*. Still no bridesmaids. Still no ushers. Guests were now arriving in increasing numbers. I took on the role of welcomer and usher, whilst a church member gave out the service books. "Bride or groom?" I enquired of each guest, though it was obvious to which side of the church I should lead those graceful ladies in saris.

With five minutes before the scheduled start of the wedding two breathless young chaps burst into the church. "We're the ushers!" exclaimed one. I hope I was not too impolite when I replied that most of their duties had been done. Then, at the time the bride should have arrived, the *bridesmaids* appeared. In the meanwhile the poor bride had been shivering in the draughty church porch, not wishing (nor daring) to enter church. (Would the organist, if he's spotted her at the door, have struck up the Bridal March?")

During all this confusing sequence the church choir had been steadily assembling in the nearby school hall. The bridal party having finally become complete – present though not correct of order – I was very relieved to start the proceedings. I arranged the bride and her father (she on his right arm) and the half-back line of bridesmaids. I signalled the church member, who signalled the organist, who immediately changed tack from a dainty pastoral piece of music to the punchy proclamation of Wagner's 'Lohengrin', alias the Bridal March or colloquially "Here comes the bride!" I led the procession down the aisle to the chancel step, where the bride and her father joined the waiting groom and best man. So far so good...except that I then noticed the empty choir stalls and remembered the choir still gathered in the school hall. I hoped they were still gathered! I whispered to the organist of my dilemma. He obliged by playing parts of Wagner most wedding congregations do not hear. Thankfully the choir, whose younger members were banking on the small choir fee, were still waiting. I speedily apologised, speedily said the Choir Prayer, and we trod down the church aisle as if that were our normal practice at every wedding.

The choir, with the deft skill of Red Arrows pilots, easily negotiated the seven people obstructing most of the aisle. The Introduction, opening prayers and readings were faultless. So, too, amazingly, were the Vows. I did play safe, however, and divided the text of the promises into bite-size chunks to avoid any slips. I wanted no repeat of Rowan Atkinson's marvellous but zany cameo in *Four Weddings and a Funeral*. However, I did observe that the groom's stance was rather odd. Throughout the service he leaned outwards at a considerable angle, as if he had served a full life on the high seas. It made the holding of hands and the exchanging of rings a task far more complex than it ought to have been.

The worst was still to come. During the hymn after the marriage – after, that is, I have pronounced the couple "husband and wife" – they are to follow me to the altar rail. Kenneth, my vicar when I was a curate, always told his bridal pair that the first walk they make as a married couple is to the altar of God. Once at the altar rail the pair continues to sing the hymn. After which they kneel. As our groom well knew – we had practised it repeatedly at the rehearsal – only I, and I alone, entered the sanctuary, the space behind the altar rail. Leading them thus to the altar step, I processed into the sanctuary and turned round to face the couple. Except the groom attempted to follow me. As I turned I bumped into him with some force. He fell backwards but luckily remained on his feet. Or more accurately his *foot*. His left shoe became entangled in his new wife's wedding dress. He then spent the remainder of the hymn vigorously shaking his left leg to free the offending foot from the lace of the gown. To no avail. Kneeling for the prayers presented a further physical contortion. However, by the time I had arrived at the final Blessing our wriggling, jiggling groom was free of his bride. "Those whom God has joined together" took on a new meaning at this nuptial. Happily the groom and his bride successfully manoeuvred down the aisle to the final fanfare of the organ.

"Funny wedding" confided the photographer as the be-ribboned limousine left the lych-gate in a shower of rice and confetti. "Oh?" I replied nonchalantly. "Aye," he went on, "I couldn't get them *organised* and the bridegroom kept *leaning* to one side. The photos will look a bit peculiar." Perhaps Rowan Atkinson could incorporate the whole episode into the film's sequel...?

By contrast the most *colourless* wedding I had the misfortune to take was in one of my urban parishes. I describe it as colourless because from the start to finish there existed no excitement, no anticipation, no vibrancy on the part of anyone involved with the impending marriage. Eight months previously a young woman approached me after the Parish Eucharist and asked if she could be married in my church. She lived in the town and in a street in my parish. There seemed to be no problem, though on further investigation it transpired she lived in the *next* parish. It sometimes happens that in big urban parishes two sides of a street can be in different ecclesiastical parishes. She resided in a street in which the parish boundary ran down the middle. Probably some historic hangover from a time when one side was built many years before the other, the first side being the border of its parish. So she was in the wrong parish. She insisted that she wished to be married in my church. I pointed out that there was a way to get through the bureaucracy. She had to attend the church in which she was to be married *habitually* (the official word) for six months. That meant attending the church's worship for that length of time, week in, week out. She readily agreed. I secretly considered that her coming to church for that length of time would be a good test of my preaching and teaching skills. Surely she would want to know more about the faith, perhaps be confirmed or become a regular church worshipper?

I would see her at church every Sunday and as her wedding date drew more closely I would ask her how things were progressing. Her initial positive responses gradually were replaced by doubts and anxieties. She and her boy friend still had nowhere to live. Her fiancé had promised to buy a flat in the city where they both worked but nothing had materialised. Yet she still felt everything would turn out well. With less than one month to go there was still no home on the horizon. Her doubts began to disintegrate into despair. She then learnt that he had arranged to play rugby for his team in the *afternoon* of the wedding.

At the pre-arranged Wedding Preparation at the Vicarage on the Tuesday evening I met the young man for the first time. He was a handsome and plausible young chap, who assured me that an apartment was in the pipe-line. On the Thursday evening her parents telephoned me: could I visit them the following morning? I went round to meet two very troubled people. They were utterly dumbstruck, sick with worry about their daughter and her imminent marriage. Could I try to dissuade her from getting married in twenty four hours? I tried. I did my utmost. Because I could see that her other half had done absolutely nothing to provide his new wife with *anything*. But she was resolute. The ceremony would definitely go on.

Come Saturday morning, the groom appeared in good spirits. The bride – typically for her – arrived right on time. And the service proceeded without a hitch. So, too, did the reception: smoothly, politely. Then, after the speeches, the bride left the banqueting room. She left the hotel. And she left her husband.

Revenge, it transpired, was her reason. She went right 'to the wire' because she wanted to cause her husband the greatest possible embarrassment to his family and friends. A kind of pay-off for all the abominable hurt he had caused over the past months. There was lots of hurt all round: her parents, in particular. I, too, felt some hurt. I had also been an unsuspecting party in the charade. I had been witness to their oaths before Almighty God; I had administered the Holy Sacrament of Marriage, blessed their rings, joined their hands and pronounced God's Blessing on them. I pondered hard about the validity of their marriage. Were they married despite the words they had uttered? Surely, for a marriage to be legal, certainly theologically legal, there has to be *true intention* in the minds of both parties. That was undoubtedly lacking in the mind of at least one of them. Without sounding unctuous or pompous, I felt God had been snubbed. I felt offended on God's behalf, though I knew full well he could take care of things himself.

I called on her parents the following week. They were devastated yet relieved. They had forgiven their daughter for her costly ploy and she continued to live with them. I never saw the girl again. Technically she lived outside the parish. To make matters worse my six months of leading weekly worship and preaching had not made the slightest impact!

Expressing weddings by colour might just include two 'black' ones. The first was the marriage of a young woman who liked to be labelled as a 'Goth': part of that contemporary culture which promoted punk, whose members dressed in deathly black and wore make-up to match. A neighbouring priest actually officiated but since it was in my parish I saw to all the details. True to form, the bride wore black, as did her bridesmaids. She requested that she came down the aisle to The Funeral March but my organist refused to play it, adding for safe measure that "Father Vaughan would not allow it". Quite right. I admit non-virginal brides still wear white, but black is the limit!

The other 'black' wedding referred to the time of day. A village marriage service set in the midst of winter. Since both bride and groom were from farming families they chose a time late in the day, in order that most of the farm work could be done, including the milking of the bride's father's large dairy herd. By law (in my day, at least) weddings in the Established Church could take place between the hours of 8am and 6pm. A generous choice, really.

They plumped for 5.30pm, when there would still be a little winter daylight in which to arrive at the church. But by 5.45pm the bride and her father had not arrived. The congregation began to fidget in their pews as they sensed the 'magic' six o'clock deadline looming. Word had got around that if we didn't start on the hour the wedding would have to be postponed. The groom, too, got himself into a bit of a frazzle. "Don't worry," I whispered to him, "we'll do the wedding whenever she arrives. We'll begin with a hymn or two just before six if she hasn't appeared. That will get round the legalities." "But where is she?" he agonised, "she only lives a mile away." The mile, however, was a narrow country lane with no passing-places for cars. Eventually the bride arrived, breathless and bothered but with five whole minutes to spare. "We couldn't pass the bloomin' thing!" she spluttered, "it had broken down in the middle of the lane!" She was referring to none other than the milk tanker on its way to her father's farm.

The service went perfectly, ending somewhat belatedly at almost seven o'clock. I vividly recall following the bridal party out of the church door to be met with a totally black canvas of darkness. It was most odd. The one and only time I had performed a wedding in the dark, so to speak. The photographer was obviously used to the situation. He had provided a brilliant arc-light to one side of the church porch, from where all the 'church photographs' would be shot for the Wedding Album. In black and white, I wonder?

Arc-lights and many more technical gadgetry have graced the Church scene in recent years. Most churches in our land have acquiesced to some form of technical aid, be it a mobile phone aerial from the spire or a waterless bio-loo in the tower. And what church today does not possess some type, however simple, of sound amplification? Most clergy, especially the younger, are used to wearing a radio-microphone. This small thimble of an object is clipped on to whatever bit of clerical garb conveniently protrudes. The 'mechanical' bit, plus battery, sits in your trouser pocket. Ripon Cathedral use a 'pseudo-pocket' – a sort of extra, hanging pocket on a string that goes diagonally from left shoulder to right thigh. From the pocket, whether real or artificial, the wire worms its way up your body to connect to the mike. There are only two things the wearer of such an aid needs to remember. Turn it to 'ON' when you are about to begin; and turn it to 'OFF' when you finish. There's even a red light to inform you that the machine is working, except you don't often see it because it's hidden in your pocket!

I normally remembered to switch the thing on but often forgot to complete the cycle. Conducting a wedding in a locum capacity at another church, I was equipped with the latest model of a sound system. It was so neat, so tiny, so lightweight that I forgot I was carrying it. After the final hymn the bride and groom, together with their parents and attendants, trooped into the very spacious vestry to sign the registers. For some inexplicable reason the whole party – some dozen adults

– stood solemnly and silently around the walls of this inner sanctum. I had seen jollier funeral cortèges. "For goodness' sake!" I loudly cajoled, addressing the awkward embarrassed assembly, "go round and give each other a kiss!" Whereupon the vestry door flew open and the churchwarden reminded me that I was still 'live', sonically speaking. The waiting congregation was highly amused by my faux pas.

Ann and I have often had the privilege of being invited to the wedding reception of those whom I have just married. They are almost all merry and joyous occasions. They are yet another opportunity for the parish priest to see his parishioners and family and friends enjoying themselves in special circumstances. And for *them* to see that he, too, can equally relish a good party. Sometimes, however, we find ourselves placed at a table for other reasons than simply "The Rector and Mrs Vaughan." Some diplomatic or political manoeuvring has been operated.

Once, after a country wedding in which we sang some of the hymns in Welsh – on the insistence of the groom's strong Welsh Baptist connections – we were allotted seats at a table, whose six other occupants were distant relatives of the groom. The diplomacy of the bride's parents who had arranged the seating-plan was all too obvious. Our six fellow-diners were ardently anti-English, illustrating their abhorrence of all that is Saxon by choosing to speak only in Welsh throughout the entire meal. I assume the bride's family thought that their new Celtic in-laws would be slightly less objectionable to a clergyman and his wife. The diplomacy miserably failed. It was a very long meal.

Another long meal was experienced in quite altogether differing circumstances. The best man was a lovely chap but suffered from a terrible stammer. He wisely kept his speech very short but regrettably spoiled himself by announcing that there were "t-t-t-wen t-t-ty ff-ff-ffive t-t-t-tele-gg-grams to r-r-read out!" Which he did ... painfully and slowly.

Very rarely I would receive an after-the-wedding invitation to attend the reception. Usually issued by the groom in the vestry once the registers were signed. Many couples who do not know the priest personally often feel self-conscious about including the clergy in their guest list. Yet, if the couple are thrilled that all has gone extraordinarily well, they might just ask the vicar along, as a genuine way of saying Thank You. "Are you free to come to the reception, vicar?" the groom invited. I normally politely decline but on this occasion I accepted. The bridal party and guests had all gone and I was left to complete the registers, cash up the collection and lock the church safe.

I always wear my cassock on pastoral occasions. This was one of them. I entered the hotel of the reception. "What will you have, vicar?" offered one of the ushers, "Buck's Fizz, sherry – or perhaps a pint?" It had been a hot day so I chose a beer. "Cheers!" he said. I acknowledged his phatic remark. I circulated amongst the guests, who either commented on how well the service had gone, or admired the display of the church flowers or extolled the beauty of the bride. It was only when I spotted the bride that I realised she was *not* the one who had stood before me some sixty minutes earlier. I had gone to the wrong reception.

I recollected that the groom had not told me of the venue. He would assume that I knew where it was. Since there were only two places in the town worthy of grand wedding banquets, I quickly downed the pint of Boddingtons and made for the other place, where, thankfully, I found myself among familiar faces. "What would you like to drink, vicar?" offered one of the ushers, "Buck's Fizz, sherry – or perhaps a pint?" It had been a hot day so I chose a beer...

Worship and worse

For a Christian priest pastoral care includes the leading of his people in worship. I have always laid great store by worship. I reckon an uplifting liturgy is more likely to lead people to God than a score of sermons. I was moved many years ago by the story of the Duke of Kiev who, in the tenth century wanted to adopt a new religion for his people. He sent ambassadors all over the known world to examine the worship of various faiths. It is said that the Duke himself favoured Islam, since he could then procure many wives. However, when his envoys returned, the ones who had visited the great church of Holy Wisdom, Aghia Sophia, in Constantinople reported that they "knew not whether they were in heaven or on earth," so moved were they by the Orthodox Liturgy. The Duke therefore adopted the Christian Orthodox Faith for him and his countrymen. And that's why Russia is Christian – and Orthodox – today.

That phrase about heaven and earth has been my ideal for liturgy and worship throughout my ministry. I am no fool and realise that the humble churches in which I have served have neither the wealth nor the expertise of that greatest church in Christendom. But we have done our best and I know that some people have been genuinely moved closer to God through the worship we performed and I had the privilege of leading.

Having said that, the seriousness of the holy sometimes produces the hilarious. Through human endeavour or error, we often accidentally reveal the funny side of life. I am sure the good Lord understands.

"Our vicar's grand," said Mrs Holt about me, "but he wants us in church every bloomin' day!" She attended (not every day!) one of my rural Warwickshire churches. The same one in which a strange flexible electric lamp sprang surprisingly out of the marble reredos set against the back of the altar. Its shell-shaped shade was fixed on the end of a coiled metal arm, stiff yet sufficiently manoeuvrable to be set at any permanent position. Its light bulb was the sort we used to have in chilly bathrooms or separate toilets, which emitted not only an uncomfortable brilliance but an appreciable amount of direct heat. It was for the latter reason that this ugly monstrosity had been affixed to the rear of the altar. My predecessor, an elderly incumbent, was completely bald and he insisted on keeping his pate warm, if not his feet, when taking the early morning Communion in winter. The lamp almost certainly blinded his parishioners as they knelt at the altar rail. However, the vicar's head was cosily warm and he was therefore able to engage his brain. The lamp's removal was the first thing I did. Besides, in those days I possessed a head of thick wavy hair.

Church heating has been, and always will be, a mighty problem. Congregations today have become too molly-coddled. They are all accustomed to their central heating and go about their homes in shirt sleeves or summer dresses. They expect church buildings to be as warm as their houses. Not so. We introduced some quartz-ray heaters into one of our village churches. It was a battle to convince the Diocesan Architect but in the end he relented and we fixed nine such heaters in the nine optimum parts of the building. They were extremely effective, though if you passed the church on the adjacent road at night, their brilliant red glow might easily lead you to call the Fire Brigade and report an internal blaze at the church. Each of the nine heaters had three filaments. Each heater and each filament could be operated individually from a central control panel in the vestry. One of my churchwardens, a part-time magician and known for his sense of fun, was responsible for the heaters.

Each and every Sunday our first worshipper – by a good ten minutes – was Mrs G. Mrs G's main aim in life was to quarrel with the parson. Having done this, she would then storm off to another parish, where in due time the process would repeat itself. Unlike most attenders, she did not have a special pew. She would sit wherever the mood took her. My magician churchwarden occasionally worked one of his spells on Mrs G. His trick was to get her to move seats without speaking to her. Mrs G would sit, say, in a corner at the back of the church. My warden would then impishly switch the appropriate quartz-ray heater on to full power. Mrs G, unable to withstand the heat, would move towards the front, near the lectern. The vestry control box would be addressed again and the heater focussed on that part of the church turned up to full power. Mrs G would move once more...and so it continued. She would make four or five moves in all before the service began. The warden, each time secretly spying on his subject's reaction, then diving back into the vestry to stifle his outrageous merriment.

By contrast, the church heating in Settle parish church was antique. Iron radiators they were. Huge Victorian artefacts, water-filled and fixed to the north and south walls. Lily was one of my Confirmation candidates. She was a 'character' in the town. It was difficult to gauge Lily's age; she was an extrovert not worried by what others thought of her, as she wandered around the market place in her faux leopard-skin coat, whatever the weather. That was the crux of it all: the weather. Lily's council flat had no central heating. When it was cold she sought warmth and refuge in the various establishments of the town, chiefly in the Settle Down Café during the week and the church of the Holy Ascension on Sundays. She would come early to church. The time of her arrival was directly proportional to the outside temperature. She would stand up against the hot radiators "to warm my bum," as she often explained. I did not mind at all. It was, somehow, part of the Gospel message

(Gospel *massage?*) But my lady churchwarden objected. Most strongly. She gave Lily a thorough telling-off. "I'm only getting' mi'self warm!" Lily rightly responded. "Well, you can't do it here," the warden ordered, "and, besides, you're not *facing east!*" It is these totally unnecessary authoritarian attitudes like that which give the Church a (deservedly) bad name.

At the other end of the scale, the heating system in our very modern Church of the Risen Christ in Wyken had pews, in which electrical elements were installed into the seats. Worshippers were able to feel a gentle, comfortable warmth all around them. One wag did suggest that if the congregation did not stand for the Creed, we could turn up the current and they would quickly be on their feet! In Settle, Lily happily ignored her censure and continued in the vein of Psalm 39, "my heart grew hot within me...while I mused, the fire blazed."

Facing east, of course, is to look towards Jerusalem, the geographical point of Christ's Resurrection and the hope of eternal life. Altars are generally situated at the east end of churches, to which all eyes focus as the chief service of the Church is celebrated. During my second stint at Sabden we held services in 'The Institute' whilst St Nicholas' was being re-roofed.

The Institute had been the home of the parish snooker team in the years before and just after the Second World War. The building boasted a full-sized table by the world-renowned Riley's of Accrington. The table, sadly, had been removed and sold just prior to the commencement of the roofing work. Where once the snooker table stood there was now the small lady-chapel altar. One of the large rectangular light shades which had previously highlighted the 'D' and lower pockets of the green baize now shone directly under the altar! It gave a rather hushed and expectant feel to the proceedings as we celebrated the Holy Communion. It was as if we were at Sheffield's 'Crucible'. Perhaps we should have re-named the service 'The Snookarist"! Several years before, the Blackburn Diocese would hold its triennial Clergy Conference at Butlin's Metropole Hotel on Blackpool's windy promenade. Some of us would often abscond from the lectures and make our way to the hotel's basement, where the 'green altars' stood. Green altars? The snooker tables, of course!

What went on around the altar and in the sanctuary was very important to me. I always offered my Confirmation candidates the chance to be altar-servers once they had been confirmed. Happily – especially in the village churches – many did. Boys in particular need some raison d'etre to continue in their church-going. Lads need to be *active*. Serving at the altar was a good way to keep their interest – and, at the same time teach them something more about the faith. There's nothing quite like being involved at close quarters as an aid to learning. "Let a boy hold a candle and the candle will hold the boy," is sound advice. Once a server is trained in the correct way he or she can serve anywhere. Carolyne eventually served at York Minster when she progressed to the College there.

We only used incense in my churches on special high days. The servers, naturally, delighted in 'playing with fire'. Getting the charcoal really glowing before adding the incense grains is the secret. You can't rush these things. Extra time was required for this duty but, like most things, young folk become quickly adept. By the time the congregation started to arrive there was invariably a dense fog of smoke in the North corner of the church. The sweet smell of incense lasted for several days, even a week or two, after the event, if we were lucky. At College I always wore a 'hairy' tweed jacket, as the incense somehow 'stuck' to the material much longer than it would to a 'smooth' one. The residual scent was always a glad reminder of the Feast recently celebrated. Not everyone, however, appreciated this lingering smell. "He's been using that stuff again!" snorted one lady from a sister parish of the group, "It makes me feel *ill*."

Incense is a wonderful visual – and nasal – aid. I liked to demonstrate its meaning at School Assemblies, especially at Epiphanytide when we recalled the gifts of the Wise Men. It was always tricky. Incense is burned in a thurible, which is a metal container at the end of three long chains. A fourth chain operates a lid, full of holes, which can be manoeuvred to sit firmly on the container. Once the grains begin to smoulder on the hot coals, the lid is closed and the whole apparatus swung from the server's side in a forward/backward action. The 'holy smoke' pours or puffs out of the holes and leaves a trail, a cloud, of awe-full (or awful, depending on your tastes!) aromatic smoke.

For the school demo I had to arrive much earlier in order to ignite the charcoal in the container. Members of the kitchen staff were warned that it was *not* the school dinner burning. A staff member was also detailed to man the fire alarm, since it normally triggered off the system. These Assemblies always went well. The children were enthralled. It's not every day that someone comes into the school hall with his 'handbag on fire'!

The real problem, particularly when I had travelled in by car, arose when the Assembly was over and the children had filed out to their forms. What should I do with a terrifically hot cauldron of burning coals and incense which continued to spew and spill copious amounts of smoke? I would hang around school for a while, attempting to damp down my visual aid but it was an impossible task on school premises. The only alternative was to carefully position the thurible in the car's well of the passenger seat in an upright, stable state and drive *very slowly* back home. I recall one episode in my Warwickshire parishes when I had to stop the car because of the fog: not outside but *inside* my vehicle!

Incense is also used at Festal Evensong, sadly a rare act of public worship today, before and after the Magnificat. I arranged such a service once in my capacity of Deanery Worship Group leader. It took place in the glorious surroundings of Giggleswick School chapel. Here, the vestries were in the basement, which is where we prepared the charcoal and incense. With two minutes to go we were all 'fired up' and ready for the off. Unfortunately one of the visiting clergy tripped up over the thurible and its red-hot coals were tipped out all over the handsome wooden floor. Almost at once there were several sizzling spots of burning wood. My servers frantically stamped on these mini-firebrands whilst I attempted to scoop up the spitting grains with the incense-boat spoon. We were late starting but no one upstairs was the wiser of our mishap. Admittedly the School chaplain might have questioned the presence of black scorch marks on the vestry floor...

I would, no doubt, have got another kind of black mark from the then Archdeacon of Coventry. I invited him to preach at Evensong at St Edith's Monks Kirby. It was a gigantic church, impossible to heat. It was also so very damp that each week after the Sunday service I took home the altar books and large lectern Bible. The latter was not missed until the Venerable preacher strode solemnly to our brass eagle of a lectern to read the First Lesson. No Bible! He looked around and about him but to no avail. He enquired of me: I, too, could not lay my hands on a copy. I'm not sure what he did but it was not one of my best moments. Rather like a pub without beer.

It was at the same church, St Edith's, that our united parish of eight villages held a joint service. All of my ten churchwardens were present, nine of whom were farmers. The tenth was Mike, the Royal Navy Commander and he assumed responsibility for the others' duties. I came across his written instructions to them some days after the event. The list of duties included welcoming worshippers, handing out prayers books and hymnals. At the end of the service they were all to "proceed to rear and square off." Was this a reference to the stacking of the books or to the wardens performing 'a right turn' after the final hymn?

Another liturgical mishap occurred during my first curacy at Wyken. Our small terraced house, like all our neighbours', was on the receiving end of abandoned beer bottles and, worse, smashed milk bottles. Gangs of youths would think it exhilarating sport to throw empty milk bottles, filched from our doorsteps, across the road. We dutifully wrapped up the broken shards in newspaper and put them in the dustbin.

In a number of churches the Blessed Sacrament is reserved for the sick and the dying. Normally the bread consecrated at Communion is intincted with wine and kept in a small wall-safe, or aumbry, within the sanctuary. To indicate that our Lord's Presence is there in the Sacrament a light is fixed over the aumbry door. Because of safety, an increasing number of such lights are electric: a tiny electrical 'flame' darts sporadically from some artificial candle. Sometimes a seven-day candle does the job; and decreasingly so, oiled-filled receptacles with a floating burning wick. Our Holy Cross church had the latter. Every so often the glass container would become blackened by the burning oil and the naked flame. "Would you take it home?" asked Kenneth my Vicar, "and give it a good clean?" I took it home and placed it on the top of the kitchen cupboard, awaiting a thorough 'de-coke'. Then forgot all about it.

Several days later the absence of the familiar sanctuary lamp in the lady-chapel reminded me that I ought to clean it. I asked Ann where it was. "The sanctuary lamp?" she queried incredulously. "I thought it was some dirty old glass beaker someone had left outside the house!" Needless to say, the lamp had been wrapped in newspaper and deposited in the dustbin along with the other 'recreational' items of glass. I ran to the bin to retrieve it. Too late. Typically, the bins had been emptied the day before. There was nothing else to do but own up to 'the Boss' and offer in its stead one of our clear glass coffee cups – the half-spherical ones without handle which fitted into a plastic outer case. It was a good swap. Kenneth smiled at our embarrassment at having 'rubbished' a holy article. "He'll never be a bishop now," he jokingly told Ann. He was right, of course.

The European movement really got under way in the early 1960s. The Common Market, the Treaty of Rome, the 'ecu' which ultimately became the euro, all pointed to a wider brotherhood of people. It spawned scores of new names: 'euroland', 'eurozone', 'Eurostar', 'Eurovision' and 'eurosceptic'. It was also at this very time that it became fashionable for the Church of England to 'go Greek' and refer to the Holy Communion as the 'Eucharist'. This change of title was perhaps prompted by the development of a new liturgical order, based on recently discovered early worship texts. Coming on the heels of all this Europeanization, one lady remarked to her parish priest, "Vicar, I'm beginning to like this new Euro-Christ."

Another thing that is new is the Passing of the Peace. Of course, the Pax, or Kiss of Peace to give it its correct title, is liturgically as old as the hills. Well, as old as Christianity – and even older, since its roots lie in Jewish ceremonial. But in its communal form it had disappeared, in the English liturgy at least, many centuries ago. Today it is all the rage in our churches, though a very formal shaking of hands has replaced the ancient and original kiss. After all, we're British.

We once found ourselves seated next to a retired Royal Navy Admiral in the Anglican cathedral in Valletta, Malta. At the point of the Peace I turned to my side to proffer my hand in Christian love and greeting to the Admiral. To my surprise he was kneeling – crouching would be a better description – in the lowest possible position. He explained afterwards that he hated the "hail-fellow-well-met bit" and found the only possible way to avoid it was to fall to one's knees in an attitude of deep prayer.

He went on to tell us of a "ghastly" experience he had in London's St Paul's Cathedral. The celebrant (whom I knew very well) was a most gregarious and effusive priest. So much so that at the Peace he greeted almost every member of the huge congregation as he made his way to the back of the cathedral. So carried away was he with his liturgical embrace that he forgot he was *presiding* at the Eucharist and was not seen again at the service! "I reckon he must have gone home" concluded the Admiral.

When I introduced this practice at St George's in Chorley, I decided to preach about it the week before. A sort of advance warning. I was aware of the views of an elderly regular worshipper, who was suspicious of all new innovations. He threatened to stop attending church. Fortunately he was present the following Sunday and I deliberately asked my wife to sit next to the old man. When it came to the Peace, she immediately grasped his hand, shook it most warmly and said "How are your chrysanthemums doing?" Pumping Ann's hand up and down he continued at great length to inform her of all his horticultural activity. It worked a treat. And it wasn't long before he was making all the initiatives at this juncture in the worship!

Some of the laity can be awkward cusses. I suppose we clergy can be too. One of my parishioners would insist in coming up to the altar rail for communion loudly singing the accompanying hymn. I became quite paranoid about it and reckoned he did it simply to annoy me. Perhaps he did. I mentioned this irritation to a priest friend of mine. "Treat it like the sign of the cross," he advised, "it's his way of crossing himself." Sound advice which banished my paranoia. Besides, he did have a fine Welsh tenor's voice.

I heard another voice on another occasion in another church. It was the morning of Ascension Day at St Ambrose's Grindleton. I had gone into church to say Mattins. Some re-plastering and repainting work had been carried out recently on the chancel ceiling. I therefore thought nothing of the ladder propped up at the chancel step. "Good morning, Trevor!" said the voice way up on high. We had a very large crucifix hanging from the roof above the chancel arch. I called to mind Guareschi's priest, Dom Camillo, and his conversations with the Crucified Lord in *his* church in the small village in the River Po valley. Was it the Crucified

Lord speaking to me? "Good morning, Trevor!" repeated the voice...and there, way up, above the crucifix was Jeff, our engineer sidesman, who was making an early start on cleaning our Lord of the spillages of plaster and paint.

* * * * *

An integral part of Christian worship are the Intercessions, the prayers of the people for the Church, the world, our families and the community in which we live, for the sick and the departed. Intercessions in the wrong hands can be lethal. Lay people – and some clergy! –need to be trained in conducting Intercessions, for they are an art form. They must not be too short or hurried, which can give the impression of complacency. Neither must they be too lengthy, when concentration ebbs away and sleep overcomes the people. And the language of these prayers must be a happy medium between formality and informality.

There are several traditional phrases which still carry the numinous. One of my Lay Readers always referred to the departed as those "on another shore" – delightful. On the other hand we hear such trite tripe. One lady intercessor always began "You know, Lord, it's the Thirteenth after Trinity today..." The Intercessions can often sound as uninspiring as a shopping list. All too frequently these intercessors forget they are addressing God and start, instead, to *inform* the congregation. Kenneth, normally meticulous in these things, once included in his prayers: "And we pray for Mary Jones who has a 50/50 chance..." I wonder what odds the Lord was giving on her recovery! There is a delightful story of some bright spark who asked his rector to pray for Dolly Gray. She wasn't ill...she was running in the 3.30 race at Newmarket.

Praying for the dying is always tricky. It's always best not to mention the word 'dying' because God knows best. I was once asked to pray for the mother of one of my parishioners. The old lady was at the point of death and fervent prayers were requested. I obliged...and her name remained on my Intercessions list for two years! In the meanwhile the old lady's family had sold her home and shared out her possessions. She recovered sufficiently to complain that her death had been somewhat "exaggerated".

When praying for the departed it might sound obvious to state that one should ascertain that the deceased really is departed. Just before the morning Eucharist at Sabden a lady called in at the outside vestry door to say that a village church stalwart, Lizzie Wood, had died. Much to my chagrin, I had not even heard that the lady was ill and therefore had not visited her. When my informant had left, my churchwarden corrected the name of the deceased. "They still call folk by their *maiden name,*" he explained. I was relieved in so much that I had certainly visited *this* Lizzie on numerous occasions – and taken the Blessed Sacrament to her also. Subsequently I prayed for her soul in the Church's Prayers at the Eucharist. Many of the older regulars knew Lizzie well and were naturally distressed to hear the news via the Intercessions – never the best method!

After church many of these good people called at Lizzie's house to offer their condolences to her son Colin. And there, sitting up in her bed, very much alive, was the 'departed' lady. By midday the news reached me. Apparently my informant, on her way to church, had seen Lizzie's neighbour calling at the house with a pile of freshly laundered sheets, which she took to be *winding-sheets* for burial. It transpired that the kind neighbour had done some washing for Colin! I went down to the house to apologise to both mother and son. They, too, understood and saw the funny side of the affair. However, Lizzie was not well and I took the opportunity to pray with her and for her. She died in the early evening of that day.

We Christians can – and should – pray for the dead because Christ has died and by His death He put death to death. The Resurrection is the central focus of our faith and Easter, its Festival, is the chief of all the holy days. The Church, through its liturgy and worship, attempts to highlight the Easter message. Our churches are deliberately bereft of flowers and decoration during Lent in order to emphasise the contrast between 'wilderness' struggle and the eventual Easter victory. Holy Week even more so: crucifixes and crosses are covered and after the Maundy Thursday re-enactment of the Last Supper, altars and everything else are stripped of their furnishings.

My first Holy Week in one parish met with confrontation. The lady who 'did' the altar and sanctuary flowers told me she would be decorating the church on the Friday as she usually did. "I'm afraid you cannot," I said, "It's Good Friday. The church is to be left bare to symbolise our Lord's death on the cross." She insisted that she always decorated on Good Friday, since she went to the point-to-point races on 'Easter Saturday.' I dug my clerical heels in. No flowers would grace the church building until the communal village effort on the Saturday, when carpets would be vacuumed, furniture polished, linen laundered and vessels buffed: ready for the 'big day'. "Damn!" she snorted, as she saw I would not give way. As usual, of course, a compromise was reached. She could make up the floral arrangements on the Friday but would leave them hidden in the vestry. The 'Saturday team' would then carefully transport them into the sanctuary. 'Easter Saturday', by the way, is *not* the day after Good Friday. That day is Holy Saturday, or Easter Eve. The day in question arrives six days after Easter Day.

The Orthodox Easter greeting, "Christ is risen!" with its response "He is risen indeed!" has always been an important element of my Eastertide liturgy. Imitating our Orthodox friends I have tried to use the greeting, though usually with a confused or even adverse reply. I telephoned a priest friend of mine during Easter week. He picked up the receiver. "Christ is risen!" I proclaimed. "I'm very sorry to hear that," he answered. Somewhat astonished I explained. "Keith," I said, "it's Trevor. I was giving you the Easter greeting, 'Christ is risen!'"

"Oh, I'm terribly sorry," he said, "I thought you said "A crisis has arisen." There was no answer to that.

"Christ is risen, Mary!" I exclaimed to the wife of my churchwarden at the church door after the Easter Day Communion. "I don't like your shoes, they don't match your frock," was her Paschal reply.

There were more than frocks at one gathering I attended. One of the north's leading church furnishers was holding a sale of unwanted stock. Advertised in all the church newspapers, the sale was to include all manner of ecclesiastical items at knock-down prices. The sale was on a first come first served basis. I arrived early at the factory shop. Not early enough! The place was packed, seething with dog-collared gentlemen and a handful of monks and nuns in their habits. The prices may have been knock-down but there wasn't room for knocked down people. Think of a crowded dance floor for the Last Waltz of the evening. Then think of each dancer armed to the teeth with churchy items: I had bought two albs for my servers, a dashing modern Italian cope in emerald green and a nine feet high processional crucifix. I shuffled almost blindly around the shelves and stands, weighty clothing over one arm, whilst the other arm strained to keep the processional cross in an upright position. In this soft-shoe shuffle I patiently steered a somewhat serpentine swathe through the sacred scrimmage to the exit. It was exacting work but great fun – and the discounts, like a clergyman's ultimate pension, were out of this world!

Still on the subject of the sartorial, there were a few liturgical occasions when I did not wear even the most basic of my clerical garb, my cassock. These were when I was invited to preach at a non-Conformist chapel, usually during the Week of Prayer for Christian Unity in January. One particular year I was to be the guest preacher at our local Methodist Church's afternoon worship.

The previous evening Ann and I had travelled out of the village to one of the many excellent Ribble Valley restaurants for dinner. We always enjoyed dressing up for the occasion: Ann in a lovely dress and I in my best suit. We thoroughly enjoyed our 'date'. We returned late in the evening to an empty rectory, as all our four offspring were old enough to be 'doing their own thing'. We stoked up the fire with logs and in the light and warmth of their flames continued indoors our romantic night out. One thing led to another and before too long items of underwear joined trousers and dress somewhere on the living room floor...

Much, much later, we gathered our things and staggered sleepily upstairs to bed. I put my suit jacket on to make it easier to transport my belongings up to the bedroom.

A busy Sunday morning of two Communion services followed: the usual fare. I always wore an easy clerical shirt, with 'tunnel' collar, through which a short strip of white plastic could be slipped. And a pair of corduroy trousers, which withstood the wear on the knees with all the genuflecting! In any case, over these items I put on my alb, a large white cassock-type robe, which hid a multitude of sartorial sins.

Come the afternoon and my part in the ecumenical service at the chapel, I decided that I ought to wear my 'Sunday best': a waistcoat-like vest-stock with garrottingly tight dog-collar, back collar-stud pressing painfully into one of the neck vertebrae and the front stud poking into my Adam's apple. Polished black shoes and best suit ensured that I did not let the C of E down.

No part was allotted to me in the worship that followed, save the sermon. I was able therefore to relax in the worshipful atmosphere until my appointed duty. A few moments and a hymn before I was to mount the pulpit, the young chapel minister welcomed me. Most eyes, I suppose, turned on me at this mention of my name. I hope to goodness those eyes were quickly directed elsewhere, as I felt I was going to cough. I reached for my handkerchief in my jacket pocket and quickly stifled the cough. My immediate thought was that the hanky was rather big. I looked down at my hand and to my horror discovered that I had pulled out my underpants from the night before! I think I got away with it. No one mentioned the episode after the service. But then they wouldn't. It would be too embarrassing, especially in the chapel...

The Songs of Zion

Organists come in all shapes and sizes. Each with their idiosyncrasies. A retired priest sometimes acted as locum organist for me at Settle. I think he preferred the pedals to the prayers, the stops to the sermon.John always took his shoes off when he approached the organ. Holy ground, perhaps, but he played better in his stockinged feet, he said. That way he could *feel* the pedals.

Arthur was the organist in my first parish. He led an enthusiastic choir of three men, four ladies and five children. He possessed a droll Warwickshire humour. Bill and Wilma, brother and sister, had clocked up well over a hundred and twenty years of service to Wolvey choir between them. Though Bill was married, he always kept a brotherly eye on his unmarried sibling. When, half-way through one Christmas Midnight Mass, Wilma had to go out to answer a call of nature, she was aware of Bill's anxiety. So as she made her (very) conspicuous exit, she stopped at every other row of pews and informed the occupants, "Tell our Bill I'm all right!" She returned well before the need to "Tell our Bill," having made use of a corner in the Vicarage garden.

Arthur our organist was firm but always most considerate. He was also a very large man. His frame was so wide that his reserved seat in the grandstand at Nuneaton Borough Football Club was actually *two*. The club had removed the seats' intervening arm. I went with him to a few matches. He set his stop-watch as the referee's whistle blew for the start of the game. From then on he assiduously watched the referee's timing. Just as a good musician would. Arthur loved his football almost as much as his music. When my team Burnley was knocked out of the F A Cup by Wimbledon – then a non-League side – the following morning, as I entered church, he played "Hills of the North rejoice!" Just his sense of humour. He transcribed a setting of Merbecke for celebrant and the Wolvey choir and, memorably, organised an outing to the Rectory of the Revd Teddy Boston, whose miniature-gauge steam engine puffed and pulled passengers on a track around the perimeter of his rectory garden.

We had two Harrys in my next parish, Sabden. One Harry was a local man who had a regular Friday night spot at The Pendle Witch's piano, where he was very popular. A great witness to his Christian faith. This Harry was an ardent fan of the jazz musician Louis Armstrong and would often play at the end of Communion an organ voluntary, suitably arranged, from Satchmo's repertoire. The other Harry was a retired Midland Bank manager. (He once told me that the telephone number of the Bank's Hasting Branch was 'Hastings 1066'). This Harry had much more of an interest in classical music. When he arrived in the village I went to welcome him and his wife Connie. Within a short while he came to see me to ask if he might be allowed to play the church organ recreationally. He had suffered a nervous breakdown which had left him with hands that trembled and shook. The therapy worked wondrously. His hands became steady and Harry became our assistant church organist.

Mrs Wild was a sweet and elderly lady, a retired teacher, who had provided the music at Grindleton for a very long time. Sadly she had become quite forgetful and at one morning service she broke down, weeping uncontrollably in the middle of a hymn. The hymn, naturally, ground to a halt, as she explained through her tears – and the organ curtain – that she could no longer play the hymn. In the awkward pause that followed Dr Forster offered to play. "I think I know this one" he said diplomatically and took up the seat at the organ, whilst Mrs Wild retired to a corner of the church, attended by a couple of caring ladies from the congregation.

Later that week I received a letter from a recovered Mrs Wild, tendering her resignation and adding that Dr Forster was a much more competent organist than she. I accepted her resignation and the Church thanked her for her many long years of devoted service.

Dr Forster took up the reins. His kind remark during the episode in church was a huge understatement. He was a Doctor of Music and some time organist at St George's Windsor. He used to give a Talk to various village groups on his experiences at Windsor, describing, among other stories, the delightful account of his playing the piano for the pantomime which featured two small princesses called Elizabeth and Margaret. Dr John and his wife Mollie suddenly left the Ribble Valley for Harrogate. The *rain* in the North West proved too much for them Twenty years later, when we moved to Ripon, we understood their decision: it is far drier on the east side of the Pennines. Remarkably, I came across Mollie over twenty years later, now widowed, comfortably ensconced in a Ripon Nursing Home and well into her nineties.

Another John succeeded Dr Forster. He was also the churchwarden as well as the 'unofficial' church photographer, since most bridal pairs chose him to do the Wedding album. It meant, of course, that when John was behind his camera he could not be behind the keyboard. We were fortunate to be able to call on a number of locums. Mischievously, John would often play relevant music before the Sunday morning service. After a good night out at The Buck or Duke of York, he invariably played "Blow the Wind Southerly". He made a rendition of "My Very Good Friend the Milkman" the day after our farmer-milkman's daughter's wedding.

Anthony was the usual locum organist when John was on his assignments and became my organist at The Holy Ascension, Settle. He had a breadth of musical experience, being a cradle Roman Catholic. Consequently our small choir sang some wonderful settings. In 'civvy street' Anthony was a driver of Ribble buses. Settle's three-manual organ was placed 'round the corner' in the north aisle, obliterating any view of chancel and sanctuary. To help matters he fixed an enormous external bus mirror to the organ console. It certainly made him feel much more at home!

Church Choirs, too, come in various shapes and sizes. In my ministry I have been very fortunate to have some very faithful and committed groups of singers. Stratford upon Avon's choir was the finest of my 'lot': they regularly produced records and in Mr John Strickson had a professional musician. To have this choir at your wedding would cost you double fees because of copyright. Of the remainder of 'my' choirs, all had top marks for loyalty, endeavour and fun. They were amateurs in the fullest sense of the word: lovers. Lovers of singing and making "a joyful noise to God." It is strange how the word 'noise' assumes a pejorative meaning. I once thanked the choir for "their glad noise to God" after their Evensong anthem at St Barnabas' Morecambe. In the vestry afterwards I was assailed by their complaints. They were affronted by my use of the word 'noise'. "Was it *that* bad?" they protested. No. It was good. Very good. 'Noise' means 'sound' and I was trying to say that their voices were obeying the instruction of Psalm 66 – "Make a joyful noise to God!" I don't think they were convinced.

Choirs, also, provide a splendid Christian ministry. At a funeral, when distressed mourners find it difficult to sing the hymns, the choir performs vicariously, sustaining the momentum of the funeral rite. The Wolvey choir was tremendous that dark Epiphany evening when churchwarden Henry was dying in the church porch. They sang the whole stock of Christmas and Epiphany hymns until the ambulance came.

The choir at St Nicholas' Sabden grew and grew, thanks mainly to our choir football team. Twenty two lads eventually filled the choir stalls – or sanctuary as servers. Jack Britcliffe was our enthusiastic choirmaster. He and his wife, Dorothy, had no children, so the youngsters in the choir became very much his 'children'. At every Tuesday evening choir practice the lads would play some prank on him. He would laugh and laugh, loving every minute of it. He organised a Sponsored Hymn Sing, arranging everything in finest detail, right down to each chorister's five minute drink and 'loo' break. The Two Harrys supplied the music as we succeeded in singing every item of One Hundred Hymns for Today.

The people around Pendle Hill and the Ribble Valley were naturally good singers. The same damp climate that helped cotton weaving to flourish also lubricated and tuned the indigenous vocal chords. Sabden had a unique tradition as far as hymns were concerned. Special tunes to certain hymns, which always surprised the visitor: "While shepherds watched," for example, was rendered to the tune 'Lyngham', better known for its setting to "O For a Thousand Tongues to Sing," with all its repeated lines and complex men's parts at the end of each verse. It had been customary, since I don't know when, to sing a couple of verses of this old carol (to Lyngham, of course) at the opening of 'The Christmas Tree', the church's Christmas Fair. Not many Bazaars, Fairs or Sales of Work start their proceedings with a hymn! 'Rimington' was the tune to which Sabdeners sang "Jesus Shall Reign". Its composer, Francis Duckworth, hailed from a small village which bore the tune's title, a mere handful of miles around Pendle Hill. The choir had nicknames for certain other hymns. For example, "the plumbers' anthem" for "All Hail the Power of Jesu's Name" which contains the line "who fixed *this floating ball*"; "the Darts Club song" for "Lord of our life and God of our salvation" which sings of our 'envenomed' foes hurling their darts. And so on.

I often attended choir practice at St Nicholas'. One Tuesday night we decided to change one of Sunday's hymns. I called up to Harry, at the organ way up high in the far west gallery to inform him of the substituted hymn. Harry was rather hard of hearing. I had to shout the message to him half a dozen times and he still did not receive it loud and clear. So he began to make the long trek down the stone staircase to the nave door. "What's the new hymn?" he asked. "O Thou who camest from above," I replied. We all saw the funny side of it and from that day on would knowingly smile to each other whenever we were about to sing it. Jack would spend some time explaining difficult theological words which cropped up in the hymns. Punctuation, too, was important. "Jesus lives no longer now" without the correct punctuation is the very denial of our Easter faith!

The choir at St Ambrose's Grindleton also 'did the ton' of One Hundred Hymns for Today. The actual one hundred hymns were a convenient number to sing over one Saturday afternoon. Equally accommodating was the fact that sponsorship money per hymn was easily calculated when multiplied by the full complement, which was accomplished. Dr Forster led the event. "Don't worry about John," his wife advised me, "he won't need a short break. He has a bladder of iron."

When I returned to St Nicholas' Sabden some 26 years later for my second stint as incumbent, there was no choir football team, no choir, no organ. In fact there was *no church*. As I mentioned earlier, the Sunday morning congregation assembled, instead, in The Institute. Music for the hymns came via a C D player. The parish had purchased a complete set of hymn tunes on ten disks. Whilst the set offered about 200 hymns, most were unsuitable. Dubious tunes and unfamiliar words: 'Wrong & Unknown' rather than 'Ancient and Modern.'

One Sunday I chose my five usual hymns. I furnished Kevin with the appropriate disk and track numbers. We all stood up to sing the hymn but only a handful sang. I signalled to Kevin to stop the machine. "I thought you would know that hymn," I remarked to the people. "Hands up those who know it." Three hands belonging to three teachers were raised. "It's all right for them," shouted an ex-choir lady, "they've been to *other churches*!" That was the downside to living in a relatively isolated village up Pendle Hill. Yet Sabden had a fine musical tradition. When I first went to Sabden in 1977 I was told the following wonderful tale. No one today seems able to confirm or deny its veracity. I just hope it is true.

There were four churches in the village, each with a full and eager choir. The Baptist Chapel choir decided to sing Handel's "Messiah" for Christmas and began rehearsals in the autumn. Someone suggested that the other church choristers be invited to share in the production. Which they willingly did. The massed choir was a great improvement for the oratorio but not for the venue. With so many singers there was little room in the chapel for the audience. Most members of the choir were cotton weavers and one of them thought that Mr Stuttard might be able to help out.

James Stuttard was the owner of Union Mill. It was a known fact that the upper floor of the mill was completely void of looms and stores. It would be an ideal and spacious location for both singers and listeners. Mr Stuttard was approached and gladly offered his mill for the concert.

Meanwhile organist, conductor and choir continued their rehearsals in the Baptist chapel with increasing anticipation and excitement. It was strange that it took so long for the problem of *music t*o emerge. There was obviously no possibility of transporting the chapel organ, pipe by pipe, down to the mill. That went for the instruments of the other places of worship. The Committee told Mr Stuttard of their plight. "I have a friend," he said, "who has a band. It might be that they could play. Would that do?" Anything was better than nothing and the Committee was grateful for their sponsor's care and concern. "They'll require a few wagons to meet them at Padiham station," he added, "For their instruments." It was agreed: a couple of horse-drawn wagons would be there to meet the six o'clock train.

The Concert Day arrived. I'm told a few local farmers drove their wagons down to the space alongside the platform to await their guests. The train pulled in. The players appeared on the platform and gathered around the luggage-van at the rear of the train. Its door then swung open to reveal the name of the band...The Hallé Orchestra from Manchester! It goes without saying that the "band" was everything – and more – that the chapel organ could offer. The Hallé inspired the conductor, who animated the choir, who captivated the large audience. Was there ever a village 'Messiah' to rival this one?

Sabden St Nicholas possesses a fine organ. It was constructed in 1879-80 by John Laycock of Glusburn near Cross Hills in the old West Riding of Yorkshire. Whilst it underwent total restoration in 1995 neither the organ's tonal nor mechanical aspects were altered. What the church possesses now is exactly the same instrument as built by Laycock one and a quarter centuries ago.

Once the worship had resumed in St Nicholas', after a two year and a £160,000 roof repair, I appointed Roger Britnell as organist. Roger was – and is –an enthusiastic musician. He even played the organ at his own Wedding! He is also an accomplished organist. In order to maintain the Laycock organ, for it is something of a 'celebrity' now, Roger planned quarterly musical concerts. These always featured one or two noted instrumentalists or singers from the wider locality, or perhaps a choir. Interspersed with these splendid performances was Roger's own brilliance, either at the Laycock or on his own electronic organ, which, along with all the electronic gadgetry, he transported in his custom-built trailer. The evening's performances would be punctuated by his own comments about the piece to be played or about the soloist.

On one occasion he asked my wife to turn the pages for him whilst he played some extraordinarily frenetic piece. Ann unobtrusively left the audience to go aloft while Roger was describing the music we were about to hear. "There is the love of my life!" he suddenly exclaimed, pointing towards the gallery, which Ann had just reached. He was, naturally, referring to 'old Laycock' not my wife! In keeping with Sabden's historical love of music we got good attendances at all the concerts. And 'old Laycock', despite its years, enjoyed increasingly good health.

A Gentle Pulpiter?

"Go and preach the Gospel" St Francis ordered his brothers, "and use *words* if necessary." Words have always had a fascination for me. I enjoy crosswords and other word games. The early Christians used symbols made up of, or around, words. They had to use such devices since discovery meant persecution or death. A Christian house or secret place of worship might carry a small fish sign. The Greek word for fish is IXTHUS, which is an acronym for "Jesus Christ Son of God, Saviour." A tile found in Reading in Roman Britain had a word square scratched upon it.

S A T O R

A R E P O

T E N E T

O P E R A

R O T A S

As you can see the message can be read from top to bottom or left to right. It's quite clever: the words mean "Arepo the sower guides the wheel slowly". Perhaps a harmless Harvest message though it is much more likely to be a secret code for prayer – the Lord's Prayer. Take all the 25 letters and remove the two As and two of the Os, which stand for Jesus, the Alpha and Omega, the beginning and the end. The remaining 21 letters spell out PATERNOSTER ("Our Father") in a cross-shape, N being the central, pivotal letter.

Words can be powerful. The written word more mighty than the sword. Words issued from the pulpit, too, can and should be equally mighty. We clergy are privileged to be able to stand each week and address our congregations. Preaching is deadly serious business. St Paul in his letter to the small church in Rome wrote: "How are they to believe in him of whom they have never heard? How are they to hear without a preacher?" The Greek word for 'messenger' is our English word 'angel' which appears in the middle of the word 'evangelisation'. Preachers are evangelists are messengers. I have always worked very hard on my sermon preparation but, rather like the meals you have eaten in your life, the vast majority are quickly forgotten. Without our meals, of course, we would not be here. And that goes for the sermon too. Without the staple diet of the weekly homily, Christian souls also would wither and perish.

The old adage for sermons no longer applies, if it ever did: "Tell 'em what you're going to tell 'em; tell 'em; then tell 'em what you've told 'em!" No wonder sermons were so interminably long-winded. When a clergyman sets out on his preaching ministry he tends to prolong the exercise. It is natural: he feels he must tell his congregation *all* that he knows about the subject – for fear of leaving something vital out.

I recall one embarrassing moment in the pulpit during my first curacy. When I arrived at the sermon's *sixth* page (!) I realised that it was not there. It was completely missing. Pages 7 and 8 were there but no page 6. I waffled on hopelessly trying to continue the thread of my argument. The more I waffled, the deeper the hole I dug for myself. Suddenly from the pulpit – 'six feet above contradiction'- I spotted the offending page. It lay on the desk of the clergy stall immediately in front of the Vicar. Deciding to abandon my prattle, I called down to my Vicar and asked him to pass up my missing sheet. No reply. Awkwardly I asked again. Still no reply. He was fast asleep!

The great C19th Baptist preacher, the Revd Charles Haddon Spurgeon, is reported to have advised his student preachers: "When you speak of heaven let your face light up and let it be irradiated by a heavenly gleam; let your eyes shine with reflected glory. But when you speak of hell – your ordinary face will do."

The homily, particularly, should have a challenging end, a clearly thought-out middle and an arresting opening. If a preacher can produce a good beginning and by it deter his listeners from unwrapping their sweets, then he is winning. Sometimes the sharp opener might have a surprise response. "Any Harvest thanksgiving in the twentieth century should take into consideration the role of technology," I once began a sermon. Before I could proceed an elderly lady, of notorious eccentricity, called out in a high-pitched voice, "I don't agree!"

At a Regimental service I began with a rhetorical question: "What football team is mentioned in the Bible?" I was going to speak about King Solomon's wisdom and thought it good ploy to begin with the visit of the Queen of Sheba, referred by St Matthew in his Gospel as The Queen of the South (Scottish First Division). Again, before I could continue a local trooper from the assembled ranks shouted, "Wigan, sir!"

At another Regimental 'do' in St Lawrence's, Chorley, I reminded the soldiers of their Annual Camp the previous summer. They wanted to find a 'MacDonald's' in the area of the exercise. I ventured to suggest they needed a 'grid(dle) reference'. St Lawrence was said to have been martyred on a grid-iron in the C3rd.

My opening sentence "Nobody loves a fairy when she's forty" caused much interest – and a few eyebrows – to be raised on Ash Wednesday, when I taught about the biblical number forty.

Visual aids in pulpits are often ineffective. Especially written ones, for no matter how large the writing is there will always be some at the back who cannot see and some at the front who have cricked their necks looking up. Other aids, however, can be a powerful tool in getting the message across. The Old Testament prophets used them dramatically.

Preaching in Skipton Parish Church to my old school, Ermysted's, on Founders' Day, the purpose of my homily was to encourage the boys to aim high in life, to imitate the lives of saints etc, etc. I compared the saints' halo to winning a 'cap' at sport, illustrating my point by displaying – and donning! – the old school cap, sadly abolished some 30 years ago. The very visual image of a fifty year old parson in cassock, surplice *and school cap* hopefully hit the target.

I don't hold any regional, national or world records but I am rather proud of the fact that I am (probably) the only person to preach at my school's Annual Founders' Day service in 1989, then, five years later, to officiate at the service, owing to my dear friend Canon Donald Aldred's sudden death, and finally to be Guest Speaker at the Old Boys' Dinner in 1998. It's the only hat-trick I've scored!

People *do* listen to sermons. Preaching at the Midnight Mass at Settle on the theme of 'no room', I threw in the remark that our tiny and ancient vicarage cooker left 'no room' for the turkey. At the end of the Mass, the landlady from the 'Royal Oak' had graciously offered to cook it for us.

I believe that humour is a necessary element in preaching, though it should not be an end in itself, or contrived. A joke must always be relevant to the teaching aim. Exegesis, exhortation, discourse, dissemination: all facets of the preached word and as equally pastoral as all that I have written about before. The preacher is carrying out the Lord's command to "feed my sheep".

There are also many other modes of evangelisation. I have been privileged to share in some quite distinctive enterprises.

J Arthur Rank, the great film maker, was a devout Christian and in his day set up the Home Film Fellowship. It was based at the Centre, which bears his name, at the Royal Agricultural Showground at Stoneleigh in Warwickshire. The Fellowship lent parishes a 16mm projector on which its own produced films could be shown. Each month a parish representative – in our case, me – would receive a large aluminium can containing the month's spool of film.

One such film which left a deep impression on most of our parish viewers, was the story of Bishop Leonard Wilson. How his imprisonment in Changi Jail at the hands of the Japanese during the Second World War led to the (incredible) conversion of his torturer and his eventual Confirmation by the Bishop years later. After two showings of the film in my parish I would post it off to the next recipient on the list and await the succeeding celluloid missive. For the folk in my villages the project was rather like going to the cinema, albeit it in the church hall, but with the added bonus that some evangelisation was on the menu. We had appreciative audiences who came in good numbers.

Rather less sophisticated than Mr Rank's films were my own slide-shows. Our son Philip, a photographer, produced a brilliant set of 35mm slides of Orthodox ikons to accompany my Talk. This I would present at any group desperate to ask for it: church societies, chiefly, but sometimes a secular gathering like the local Rotarians who welcomed 'a small dose of religion' at their evening meetings.

The Illustrated Talk on ikons that I gave to the Gisburn branch of the Mothers' Union will stay with me for ever. I agreed to 'appear' before them at their very large Village Hall. "Is there anything we can provide for you," asked the M U Secretary down the phone. "Not really," I replied, "I shall bring my own screen and projector. I just need a plug socket – and curtains, of course." The 'Mothers' met monthly in the afternoons. It naturally precluded any would-be young mothers who most probably were working, but the Gisburn Branch members were not alone in preferring the daylight sessions, in order that its elderly members could get home before dark.

It was a February afternoon: no point in presenting an Illustrated Slideshow at the height of midsummer, since most venues did not go in for thick, lined curtains or blinds. That particular February afternoon was gloriously bright. As I clambered up the Village Hall steps, screen in one hand, weighty projector in the other, I elbowed open the double doors. A tiny notice, sellotaped to the door's window pane caught my eye. "Owing to the repairs all meetings will take place in the main hall." It was signed by the Village Hall Committee. It was to be taken seriously. The much smaller, more informal room, where we intended to meet, was obviously hors de combat.

Armed with my paraphernalia I burst into the large hall-cum-badminton-court, the clatter of my entry interrupting the ladies' business meeting, which, as was its wont, preceded the guest speaker's 'turn', thus getting the 'business side' of things over before the main item on the agenda. As the 'main item', I quietly deposited my equipment and tip-toed around the base-lines and tram-lines searching for a socket. It was then that I saw the windows. Not just ordinary windows but *chapel* windows, tall and wide and deep. The problem, however, was not their size but that they were *curtain-less!* I sensed then that it was 'curtains' for my Talk. And it went without saying that the only electric plug points were adjacent to the windows.

After the Lady Chairman's Introduction I tactfully suggested that it would very difficult to *actually* see the slides; and without the slides my *Illustrated* Talk would not be illustrated and therefore, rather pointless. I tried my very best to get out of the predictable disaster, promising I would come again another day (or after dark!). But the ladies of Gisburn M.U. are made of sterner stuff. They would not hear of it. Not for nothing the Mothers' Union hymn determinedly begins "We have a purpose to fulfil"!

Consequently a team of ladies followed me about the vast area of the hall, testing various locations. I carried the cumbersome screen, now fully extended, whilst a retinue of four carefully transported the table with the projector, followed by the 'chief bridesmaid' holding the cable. After a series of trials the optimum location was to be found by erecting the screen deep into the stage. The projector meanwhile was precariously balanced on a towering pile of hymnals and M.U magazines on the table, pointing awkwardly and at an image-blurring angle towards the shiny silver surface.

It was utterly useless. "In this ikon Our Lady's face is heart-shaped, her eyes are like almonds and her lips fine and small: the Eastern symbol of beauty." I explained desperately. "If you look very intently, you might be able to make it out," I lied. Loyal, purposeful, motherly Gisburnians peered blinkingly into the glassy sea of a blank white canvas. I groaned inwardly. It was totally hopeless. The end could not come quickly enough. And true to form, the Chairperson thanked me most warmly for an interesting Talk, from which, she said, they had all learned something. What that something was, I'd never know. Unless it was the thought that "without blinds at the windows its curtains for slideshows".

Yet another ploy I used in my preaching and teaching the Gospel was the recurring theme of the doings of the Dogsbody family. They were a fictitious family with whose exploits, I hoped, my congregation would identify, as I strove to get over some particular aspect of faith and theology. For example, in my attempt to teach about Our Lord's Ascension, I invented the story that young Harry Dogsbody, at the start of a new school year, went *up* a class but went *down*stairs to it. It was actually what happened at the Church School in Barnoldswick. The Dogsbodys seemed quite popular with my church folk. At our Farewell Dance at Wolvey I even received a Good Luck Telegram from "Alloysius, Hilda and all the Dogsbodys."

"Father Dogsbody" was an extension of this original idea and he became, when I moved to Sabden, a cartoon character which featured in the monthly Blackburn Diocesan magazine. A comical slant on getting some teaching aim across. Jokily signing myself 'tREV', I began drawing large cartoons on a flip-chart for children's sermons. My counterpart at

Sabden's Roman Catholic church, Fr Leon Morris, used a ventriloquist's dummy for the same purpose as my cartoons. Fr Morris was a short, jolly chap with a good head of sandy red hair. His doll sported a bright orange mop of hair (not too dissimilar from his manipulator) and was kitted out in cassock and dog-collar.

News of our 'evangelism' reached the BBC's 'Look North' television studios and we were both invited to be interviewed on Tuesday 21st March 1978 in the half-hourly regional programme after the main six o'clock News. A taxi called for us. Its three clerical passengers – one with orange hair! – caused many a head to turn in our direction as the vehicle threaded its way through the busy rush hour of Manchester's streets. Both Leon and I must have been very much at ease in front of the cameras, as there was no need to do any re-takes. As we left studio N, we were told we would be 'on air' at about 6.50pm that evening. There was no possibility of our reaching home before then, so we persuaded our taxi driver to stop at a pub before the appointed time of our appearance.

A hostelry was spotted and we dashed in, ordered a pint each – and one for the driver – and asked if we could watch BBC television. The barman obliged and turned on the set. The small band of pub regulars was bemused at this sudden entrance of two clerics. Even more so when they saw our 'doubles' on the TV screen. I had been handed a cheque from the BBC for £14.42 – "To the Reverend Trevor Vaughan – For talking to Alistair Macdonald about his cartoons". The experience, for us, was priceless.

Spreading the word of God through the medium of newspapers is legitimate and can be a valuable method. In some of my parishes the weekly local paper operated a 'Thought for the Day' column. In this, local priests and ministers (and the local imam) took it in turns to write a relevant article. It wasn't everyone's cup of tea and some declined. But it was a good opportunity to reach a wider audience, though I must confess there was very little feedback from the public. Even one's own parishioners rarely commented!

The very last article I wrote in this medium achieved the best response I ever had. *The Clitheroe Advertiser* had run a lengthy debate on the Borough Council's decision to introduce wheelie-bins. Every householder was going to be given three bins, differently coloured to identify the waste material. It was at this time that many overtly Christian customs and characteristics were being 'dumbed down' and debarred by bureaucratic authorities hell-bent on political correctness. My feature was a tongue-in-cheek 'prophecy' on our being supplied with further wheelie-bins in the foreseeable future. These would include a purple receptacle for unused parish magazines, the 1662 Book of Common Prayer and old hymnals; and a gold one for the day when we must discard crucifixes, palm crosses, altar candles and the like!

Some clergymen are adept at composing just the right sort of 'Letter to the Editor', who then publishes their contribution. Often these are an admirable apologia for our Faith. It never worked for me: two such missives to the *Daily Telegraph* failed to render publication.

My only other salvo to a newspaper was one to the *Church Times* a couple of weeks before the big General Synod debate on the ordination of women to the priesthood in November 1992. The paper had run a month-long discussion on the topic, which they claimed was impartial and gave to both sides an equal share of column space. Having just completed my degree in linguistics, I was very keen to analyse these articles. I found that by inference and by the superior number of columns given over to the 'pro' party there was an incredibly large imbalance, weighted something like eight times as much in favour of the proponents. I wrote to the editor, hoping to see my letter in print. No such luck. Instead, however, I received a *hand-written* reply from the editor denying any such impartiality. There was simply no need for a busy editor to pen a reply, unless he knew, of course, that I had a point. If the cap fits, wear it.

I stopped buying the *Church Times* after that. Until then I was a regular reader and looked forward to its delivery every Friday. At one busy period before Christmas, my copy had not arrived. I phoned Lambert's the newsagents in Settle. "I haven't got this week's *Church Times*" I explained to the lady. She told me to "hold on". "Elsie!" I heard her shout in the shop, "have the comics come in?" That says it all.

All these different approaches are legitimate means of proclaiming the Gospel. The world is your pulpit. From it and in it the parson must preach.

In Shakespeare's *As You Like It* Celia speaks at length of love, to which Rosalind makes the comment "O most gentle pulpiter! What tedious homily of love have you wearied your parishioners withal..." I trust *this* pulpiter did not weary *his* too much.

In the play's previous scene Touchstone, the court jester, has assumed the life of a shepherd. How does he like it? asks Corin the shepherd. "Truly, shepherd," Touchstone replies, "in respect of itself, it is a good life; but in respect that it is a shepherd's life, it is naught."

Is the 'shepherding' of a parish priest simply "naught"?

Is it nowt? A ministry of nothing?

CHAPTER SEVEN

Clowning about: about clowning

A shepherd's life: "it is naught" says Touchstone. The court jester-turned-country bumpkin becomes a shepherd but his good-natured jollity and jesting are never absent. Shakespeare uses Touchstone's fooling as a commentary on the present situation – both in the play and in real life. Touchstone is a clown; yet a wise clown. Unafraid to laugh generously and kindly at others; unashamed to ridicule himself.

Has all that I have recounted been of naught? Has all the fun been merely flimflam? The serious side a sham? The counsel given, the blessings bestowed, the defence of what I thought was right and just and true: has it all been a delusion?

"Of course not," you might say, "think of the authority which bestowed this ministry upon you." *Apostolic* authority, no less. The authority upon which I have based my entire ministerial action. Yet, if I am now pronounced a disloyal Anglican – and a priest, at that – does not that make all I have done and said worthless and meaningless and nonsense? Does it not simply confirm and compound Pope Leo's damning dictum that a ministry such as mine has been 'utterly invalid', 'altogether void'? An invalid ministry which has now been consigned to an even greater invalidity by my own Church's decree? A shepherding worth naught? A Ministry of nothing?

"What do you want to be when you grow up?" We know what the young J H Briggs wanted to be: 'Nowt!'

As a boy I always wanted to be a circus clown. I was never smitten with the dream of driving an express train or drawn to the noisy clang of the dashing fire-engine. I was never mesmerised by the military uniform or even attracted to work in the town's aero-engine industry.

I still vividly recall our summer holidays in the immediate aftermath of the Second World War. How my parents took us to the west coast of Lancashire for our summer break. Usually to Blackpool and Southport. It was those baggy-trousered, wide-mouthed, red-nosed gentlemen of the circus ring at Blackpool's Tower Circus who captivated me. The laughter they brought was pure gold. I wanted – all my boyhood – to be a circus clown. To bring mirth and merriment. At Blackpool Tower in the late 1940s and early 50s there performed the best clowns in the business. Chiefly Charlie Cairoli and Paul. At the ring-side I was fairly indifferent to the acrobats and trapeze artists, quickly lost interest in the lions and tigers and found such items as pram-pushing poodles an utter embarrassment.

To me the whole evening's entertainment was set alight by the sheer magic of the clowns. I would look down the programme to discover how many times they were due to appear. Not that the programme ever informed me, for clowns are excellent fillers-in. They perform for brief moments between acts. But what a delight! One clown would be chasing a glittery paper butterfly attached – just out of arm's reach – to his bowler hat. Another would be throwing freezing cold water down his colleague's wide trousers. And a third would be for ever tripping up over his giant outsize boots. This was the aperitif. The whetting of the appetite before the main course, which was the long spot given over to the antics of those vivid, comic characters.

Clowns come in all shapes and sizes. 6 feet 13 inches, the under 4 feet midget and the ten feet tall man on stilts. All wear outrageous clothes to exaggerate their stature, as they constantly poke fun at themselves. Fat clowns, thin clowns, jolly, full of fun. Armed with custard pies, jelly and blancmange (food for a party!) which eventually find their way into somebody's face or down someone's pants. Pulling chairs from under each other, daubing wallpaper paste everywhere bar the wallpaper –

and the inevitable buckets of cold water soaking every clown in turn. Then a clown will involve the audience by throwing a bucketful over them. Except, this time, it's paper confetti, not water.

Yet for all the excitement and laughter, one clown could say something, do something, which would spell-bind the spectators. He could make the crowd roar. He could render them silent. The clown is a fool. A mirth maker. But he can also be a figure of pathos. He manipulates his audience in a flash. His clever use of exaggerated grease-paint can bring a child to tears and sadness; many an adult, too. The frivolous, the ridiculous, the impossible, the sad, the pathetic and bathetic – all are there at the clown's disposal. Human nature is the source and province of his action. And I wanted to be part – no, an *instigator* – of all that comedy and clowning.

It is not surprising that kings of the Middle Ages employed their own personal clowns in their palaces. The jester was an integral part of the Court at that time. The jester's humour and capers saw the funny side of the most serious affair, offering a proper perspective to the dourest of political situations.

Peter Berger, the American sociologist and Lutheran theologian, examined the role of the ordained minister in his treatise *Letter on the Parish Ministry*. In it he endorses the widely held criticism that such a ministry is irrelevant, ineffective and generally absurd. The 'foolishness' of the ordained ministry, he suggests, stems from the sheer 'impossibility' of the Gospel. The Virgin Birth, the Resurrection, the Ascension are all in themselves 'absurd' to the world. And he argues that the priest has to work within this sphere of the absurd. The Christian Gospel is foolish as perceived by our world. And this foolishness only makes any sense in the light of the greatest absurdity of all – that God became man and 'dwelt among us full of grace and truth.' Peter Berger is saying that by virtue of the context in which the priest or minister functions, the very essence of his work must also be foolish and implausible.

It is not difficult to appreciate the parallel between minister and clown.

Look at the clown. His antics are not merely ludicrous; they are full of meaning about life. The clown chases the eternally-elusive butterfly attached to his hat. He will never catch it and he knows he won't. But he still goes on chasing. The clown is telling the truth about us humans: our constant search for the bright and beautiful, always just beyond our grasp, always unattainable. The clown is continually giving of himself. Rising to every occasion for his audience, irrespective of his own feelings. He is skilled in drawing his people into the event. They are no longer spectators but involved participants in the act, which is life itself.

The clown confronts individuals, challenges crowds. The clown evokes response, both physical and emotional. He dances and fools throughout the world. His movements are often misunderstood. Deep-down, however, he is aware of the situation. He gives it its true perspective. The clown turns tears into laughter, joy into sadness, the ridiculous into the serious, Hosanna! Into Crucify! And Crucifixion into Resurrection. The Greeks called it 'metanoia', which is an about-turn, a turning upside-down or inside-out. What we would call a conversion.

The clown contradicts the assumptions of the world. He teaches that our priorities are often wrong. He knocks down our false and petty gods. His actions throughout are unusual. He behaves like a fool but he *liberates* human beings from their mental and physical imprisonments. He gives a glimpse of what we might become, what we really can be. His act is utterly, completely, for others throughout.

The Orthodox Church in its great wisdom had an important place for the holy fool, or 'the fool in Christ'. Here is a person, so filled with the Holy Spirit, that he has undergone a metanoia and proceeds to perform this about-turn to its very limits. More radical than anyone else, he turns the world's values on their head by his actions. He is a living witness to the truth that Christ's Kingdom is not of this world. By his 'fooling' he validates the possibility of the impossible. The holy fool of the Byzantine and, later, the Russian Church, is a nobody. He is a nothing and exercises a 'ministry of nothing'. All that he does appears to serve no useful purpose. Yet one startling word or action from him can shake us from our complacency. Like the clown his exploits are both audacious and humble. As Bishop Kallistos Ware wrote, because he has renounced everything the fool in Christ is truly free. He cites the holy fool Nicolas of Pskov, who dared to place in the hand of Tsar Ivan the Terrible a piece of meat dripping with blood. His 'foolishness' allowed him to censure this dangerously wicked tsar, who, instead of meting out punishment, treated him with conspicuous deference.

The priest or minister, to no lesser degree, is called to do and to be the same. The Church's beliefs, her worship, her ethics, seem ridiculous to the world. The priest, like the clown and the holy fool, plays out these aspects despite his own feelings. The good news of God confronts individuals, challenges crowds. No one should be able to sit on the fence (or circus ring!) and not be drawn in. We are all bidden to respond.

Again, as does the clown, the priest gives a true perspective to life. "Come unto me all that travail and are heavy laden and I will refresh you"; "Whoever seeks his life will lose it and whoever loses his life will gain it." St Paul reiterates Christ's sayings: those early apostles were "poor yet making many rich...treated as impostors yet true...reviled but a blessing...sorrowful but always rejoicing." Contradictory, crazy, absurd: straight from the clown's repertoire. But the key to life.

In the footsteps of his Lord, the minister or priest is the 'man for others'. The solemnity of death, the joy of birth, the compassion for the sick, the gaiety of the Sunday School party: all moods, all feelings packaged up in vicarious fooling. A man for others. Be it clown or minister, the work is the same. The clown and the minister are one. Both are doing for others and perform in this framework of foolishness. The clown ministers and the minister clowns. The secret of both is man's salvation.

Dietrich Bonhoeffer, the modern German martyr, felt compelled to be part of a group of people who plotted to assassinate Adolf Hitler. For a Lutheran pastor this was no easy option. From the very beginning he was opposed to the Nazi movement, as a result of which he was forbidden to teach and, in 1936, was dismissed from his lectureship. The Nazis also banned him from Berlin The assassination plot, however, failed and Bonhoeffer was imprisoned by the Gestapo in 1943. Whilst in prison he managed to write several papers and letters to his friends, revealing his own distinctive theology. He also wrote about being 'a fool for Christ's sake', a state which he called 'hilaritas'. This Latin word, he explained, would translate as 'a confidence in one's work, a certain boldness and defiance of the world and of popular opinion, a steadfast certainty that what one is doing will benefit the world, even though it does not approve.' Not a million miles from the motives of the clown and holy fool!

Bonhoeffer himself expressed this hilaritas in his own life. In 1939 he was on a lecture tour in the USA when war broke out but he felt it his duty to return to his native Germany. His friends realised the danger he would be in by returning. They desperately tried to dissuade him. But to no avail. Because of his defiant opposition to Hitler he was arrested and subsequently spent two years in prison. He was hanged in Flossenburg concentration camp on April 9th 1945 shortly before the end of the war. Bonhoeffer displayed that foolishness, that hilaritas which contradicted and transcended worldly wisdom and bore such incredible witness to the risen Lord.

* * * * *

Almost forty years ago I preached a sermon on this topic. It was one of my first sermons, given under the supervision of my College tutor. I still possess the full text which I delivered at St George's Church, Swallowbeck near Lincoln a mere twelve weeks before my ordination. Whilst I now cringe at the style of the sermon, its truths are still valid. In the sermon I maintained that the laity, also called to be fools for Christ's sake, might – and often do – abrogate their vocation. The minister or priest, however, cannot. "The priest is expected" (I preached) "to fulfil a ministry vicariously, that is, on behalf of and for the sake of the laity." The priest, therefore, is the public embodiment of the absurdity of the Gospel.

So the clown ministers and the minister clowns.

At the outset, my family thought my ministry to be 'nowt'. At the end, my own Church's charge of 'disloyalty' certainly seems to me as if the ministry I performed in all the intervening years was similarly worthless, foolish and nothing. Just before retirement I was crossing a busy street in Clitheroe. A man, about my age, was crossing in the opposite direction. Shaking his fist in a truly aggressive manner, he yelled at me: "Why don't you get a *proper* job?" He obviously meant it.

Have I been a fool in Christ? Or simply a fool? I have ministered and clowned. But in the absurdity of the Gospel? That which is 'nowt' to the world.

Has it, then, been a ministry of nothing? In the right sense, yes. Perhaps my boyhood ambition wasn't too wide of the mark. Nor, perhaps, my labours of the past forty years.